JOURNAL FOR THE STUDY OF THE NEW TESTAMENT SUPPLEMENT SERIES
190

Executive Editor
Stanley E. Porter

Editorial Board
David Catchpole, R. Alan Culpepper, James D.G. Dunn,
Craig A. Evans, Stephen Fowl, Robert Fowler, George H. Guthrie,
Robert Jewett, Elizabeth Struthers Malbon, Robert W. Wall

Sheffield Academic Press

The Book of Revelation and the Johannine Apocalyptic Tradition

John M. Court

Journal for the Study of the New Testament
Supplement Series 190

Copyright © 2000 Sheffield Academic Press

Published by Sheffield Academic Press Ltd
Mansion House
19 Kingfield Road
Sheffield S11 9AS
England

Typeset by Sheffield Academic Press
and
Printed on acid-free paper in Great Britain
by Bookcraft Ltd
Midsomer Norton, Bath

British Library Cataloguing in Publication Data

A catalogue record for this book is available
from the British Library

ISBN 1-84127-073-3

CONTENTS

Chapter 1

INTRODUCTION: THE BOOK OF REVELATION AND THE
JOHANNINE APOCALYPTIC TRADITION

It is important to see the book of Revelation in the particular historical
context of the believing community which created it, because Christianity and its documents and doctrines relate to specific moments of history. But it is also important to see the book as a visionary interpretation of the church and its future; here we need to give full weight to the
ideas and images contained in the visions. The complementarity of different approaches, historical, literary and psychological is vital for a
modern understanding of the text (as I tried to demonstrate in my study
guide on Revelation).[1]

We do not need to take Revelation literally, but we should take it
seriously. It shows a relationship between pain, martyrdom and Christian belief. And it clearly depicts a continuity between past, present and
future for the church and the individual believer, from which the disil-
lusioned churches of today can learn. The text and tradition may also
speak directly to the current doctrinal discussions in Christian circles
about the reality of a vision of hell.

The book of Revelation has been seriously neglected by academic
biblical scholarship until comparatively recently. This helps to explain,
as consequences, two sets of phenomena: it has long provided a happy
hunting ground for proof texts in Christian extreme-evangelical and
fundamentalist groups; and most recently it has appeared as a polemical
text for political use, furnishing material in Liberation Theology for
example.[2] The present work seeks to restore the equilibrium and to

1. John M. Court, *Revelation* (New Testament Guides; Sheffield: JSOT Press,
1994).
2. See, e.g., John M. Court, 'The Book of Revelation', in R.J. Coggins and J.L.
Houlden (eds.), *A Dictionary of Biblical Interpretation* (London: SCM Press, 1990),
pp. 593-95.

provide in several ways a more balanced, both academic and inclusive, approach to the book.

In relation to other books of the Bible scholars have been particularly careful to explore questions of sources, textual traditions and derivative works (for example the study of Paul's letters and the deutero-Pauline writings). With the book of Revelation this process has been one-sided and truncated: commentators such as R.H. Charles[3] were very concerned about the source materials; and the nature of John's Greek has been variously examined (e.g. by G. Mussies[4]). But the immediate possibilities of derivative apocalypses and related traditions remain largely unexplored. In fact until now there has been no recent edition of either the secondary Apocalypse of John or of the later work, an apocryphal Greek apocalypse 'fathered' upon St John Chrysostom.

The present book has four parts, by means of which it is hoped to present for publication a more adequate and comprehensive account of the Johannine apocalyptic tradition: this volume contains the Greek texts of three apocryphal apocalypses, each with an introduction, an English translation and critical notes; I also reproduce an English version of a further apocryphal apocalypse existing only in a Coptic text. I seek to assess the general nature of the relationship of these texts to the canonical book of Revelation. In this way it should be possible to identify any definitive characteristics there may be of the Johannine apocalyptic tradition overall.

I have a further dream, not fulfilled in this present volume. For the book of Revelation it seems to me highly desirable to represent not only the canonical book itself, together with those identifiable characteristics of the derivative traditions in the Johannine apocalypses, but also to reflect the influence of the book of Revelation upon many generations of Christian artists even up to the present day. It is necessary to concentrate on the potent symbols and significant themes of the book, as they were applied for example in illuminated manuscripts and in medieval 'doom' paintings. A catalogue of the art forms and examples would itself fill volumes; what would be intended in my dream is a selective presentation of the variety of applications of a number of key themes. The object would be to produce an essentially visual 'reading' of the

---

3.   R.H. Charles, *A Critical and Exegetical Commentary on the Revelation of St John* (International Critical Commentary; 2 vols.; Edinburgh: T. & T. Clark, 1920).

4.   Gerard Mussies, *The Morphology of Koine Greek as used in the Apocalypse of St John: A Study in Bilingualism* (Leiden: E.J. Brill, 1971).

text, to demonstrate to what extent our modern view of this book has to be based on such a heritage of interpretations. Only then can it speak of modern politics, as one millennium ends and a new one begins. But, unlike Professor Caritat in Stephen Lukes's allegorical novel,[5] we should not be 'obsessed with the study of past ideas about the future to the exclusion of a close interest in the present'.

It is highly unlikely that the four 'Johannine' apocalypses included here have ever been studied together, before this present volume. The individual texts are not normally found even in the much more comprehensive collections of apocryphal and pseudepigraphical texts which serve the modern (sometimes gnostic) interest in 'alternative' texts of Gospels, acts and apocalypses. But even more strangely one cannot even find mention of all four together in the introductory notes in such collections under the heading of 'later apocalypses'. This makes the present opportunity to see the texts together and evaluate them of special importance.

As editor of the revised version of M.R. James's classic work *The Apocryphal New Testament*,[6] J.K. Elliott treats of *Other Apocryphal Apocalypses* towards the end of the book, from p. 682. It is in the form of notes, without any text, that he lists on p. 684 the Johannine apocalypses as follows:

4. Apocryphal Apocalypses of John
1. (Tischendorf) based on several manuscripts, while text itself is considerably older, possibly 5th Century; 'typical question and answer account of the other world'; English version—Walker 1870 Edinburgh (ANCL)
2. Another Greek apocalypse, attributed to John Chrysostom, published by F. Nau in 1914; the text is 6–8th Century
3. 11th Century Coptic manuscript, published by E.A.Wallis Budge in *Coptic Apocalypses in the Dialect of Upper Egypt* , London 1913; pages 59-74 are the text and pages 241-57 the English translation

There is a similar, if more annotated, listing in Wilhelm Schneemelcher's *New Testament Apocrypha. II. Writings relating to the Apostles; Apocalypses and Related Subjects*.[7]

5.   Stephen Lukes, *The Curious Enlightenment of Professor Caritat* (London: Verso, 1995).
6.   J.K. Elliott, *The Apocryphal New Testament* (Oxford: Clarendon Press, 1993).
7.   W. Schneemelcher, *New Testament Apocrypha*, II (Rev. edn; Tübingen:

Most surprisingly, there is not a more complete listing even in literary studies of the apocalyptic genre, such as those in the special issue of *Semeia* 14 (1979) *Apocalypse: The Morphology of a Genre*. The relevant article in this volume on 'The Early Christian Apocalypses' was written by Adela Yarbro Collins. She describes how 24 Early Christian texts fit the definition of Apocalypse:

> 'Apocalypse' is a genre of revelatory literature with a narrative framework in which a revelation is mediated by an otherworldy being to a human recipient, disclosing a transcendent reality which is both temporal, insofar as it envisages eschatological salvation, and spatial, insofar as it involves another, supernatural world (p. 62).

These Early Christian apocalypses are of two basic types: Type 1 offers primary revelation through vision or audition; type 2 offers primary revelation through an otherworldly journey.

Of the examples of Type 1, 'the [canonical] Book of Revelation is the only one of this group of Christian apocalypses with...a clear interest in the politics of their times'. This is in contrast to Jewish examples.[8] Pseudonymity is not essential in the Early Christian corpus, although it is, of course, frequently found. Not least because the seer of the canonical book of Revelation apparently uses his own name, it is concluded that pseudonymity is not an essential part of the definition for the genre of apocalyptic.

The following are the Johannine examples of the genre listed and discussed by Adela Yarbro Collins, with a summary of her main comments:

1.   The canonical apocalypse, the book of Revelation, in which the external epistolary form is subordinated to the essentially revelatory character of the book. The focus is on exhortation, which stresses the importance of standing firm in faith and love and enduring tribulation. The exhortation is reinforced by eschatological threats and promises. This work is classified as an apocalypse of type 1b: 'Apocalypses of Cosmic and/or Political Eschatology with Neither Historical Review Nor Otherworldly Journey'. Such a definition, disputing historical points

---

J.C.B. Mohr [Paul Siebeck], 1989; ET R.McL.Wilson; Cambridge: James Clarke, 1992).
    8.   Yarbro Collins, 'The Early Christian Apocalypses', p. 64.

of reference, is clearly related to Adela Yarbro Collins's interpretation of chs. 6–22 as a recapitulatory series of eschatological visions corresponding to a common pattern.[9]

2.   The Apocalypse of St John the Theologian (or the Questions
      of John) edited by Tischendorf. This work is dated sometime
      after 100 CE; its actual dependence upon the book of Revela-
      tion is noted, as is the fascination with Antichrist, in chs. 6–8,
      including the physical description to be found in ch. 7. This
      text is also classified, like the canonical apocalypse, as type 1b.

3.   The Apocalypse of John the Theologian, attributed to John
      Chrysostom (c. 347–407 CE). The text was edited by Nau
      (1914) and is otherwise known as the Second Greek apocry-
      phal Apocalypse of St John. In form it is actually a simple
      dialogue between 'John' and 'the Lord'. The proposed range
      of possible dates is sixth to eighth century CE. Although there
      is in the work both an eschatological expectation of a personal
      afterlife and an interest in the heavenly world, in the context of
      mystical experience (both aspects which relate very positively
      to the canonical apocalypse) Adela Yarbro Collins concludes
      that Questions of John the Theologian (as she renames it)
      'should not be categorized as an apocalypse because it lacks
      the characteristic of mediated heavenly revelation'.[10]

4.   Mysteries of St John the Apostle and Holy Virgin (Coptic
      Apocalypse). The work is extant only in Coptic, in a manu-
      script published by Budge (1913). It is an account of the rev-
      elation which John the beloved disciple received in the course
      of a heavenly journey. A distinctive feature of the work is its
      extensive adaptation of Egyptian mythology, associating the
      activity of heavenly beings with the fertility of the earth.
      Despite the range of aetiological references to human experi-
      ence in general, and the cosmic nature of the conflict between
      Michael and the angel of wrath, Adela Yarbro Collins classi-
      fies this work as an apocalypse of type 2c: 'Apocalypses with
      an Otherworldly Journey and Only Personal Eschatology'.

9.   A.Y. Collins, *The Combat Myth in the Book of Revelation* (HDR, 9; Mis-
soula, MT: Scholars Press, 1976).
10.   'The Early Christian Apocalypses', p. 103.

Adela Yarbro Collins does not mention the Third Apocalypse of John in her survey. There may be some very distant relationship to the Apocalypse of James, which she notes as a Coptic text published by Budge in 1913. But the text I include here is Greek, not Coptic; and although it involves James as participant in the dialogue, its most striking feature is that the revealer figure is John (in a most interesting reversal of roles).

Given the incompleteness of these collections and surveys, their uncertain and disputed aspects, and the lack of supporting evidence from the texts themselves, there is abundant reason to present together for the first time in this volume the whole range of Johannine apocalyptic material.

Generalizations exist about the way in which the Christian apocalyptic traditions have evolved. Recently Ronald L. Farmer observed:

> It is noteworthy that the first function—that of providing an alternative world vision and interpreting present persecution—is characteristic of the earlier Christian apocalyptic texts, whereas the second function—that of controlling the behavior of Christians by vivid descriptions of eschatological punishment—is characteristic of the later Christian apocalypses.[11]

He quotes from Elizabeth Schüssler Fiorenza's comment about the changing socio-political situation of the Christian communities:

> It signals a shift from an alternative vision of the world and political power to the rejection of the world for the sake of the afterlife, from a countercultural Christian movement to a church adapted and integrated into its culture and society, from a sociopolitical, religious ethos to an individualized and privatized ethics. [This shift in function] engenders a shift in apocalyptic language and form, from evocative-mythopoetic symbols and political language to allegorical descriptions of eternal punishments and moralistic injunctions against the sins of the individual.[12]

The present study will afford an opportunity to evaluate such an essentially sociological account of the contrasts, with respect to the Johan-

---

11. Ronald L. Farmer *Beyond the Impasse: The Promise of a Process Hermeneutic* (Studies in American Biblical Hermeneutics, 13; Macon GA: Mercer University Press, 1997), p. 145.

12. Elisabeth Schüssler Fiorenza, 'The Phenomenon of Early Christian Apocalyptic', in D. Hellholm (ed.), *Apocalypticism in the Mediterranean World and the Near East* (Tübingen: J.C.B. Mohr, 1983), pp. 313-14.

nine tradition. Towards this end, the next chapter introduces a discussion of the role of visions of hell and the afterlife within the Christian tradition.

Figure 1. *Woodcut Heaven and Earth* (Mary Evans Picture Library)

Figure 2. *The End of the World is Nigh Again...* © 1996 Steven Appleby. Reproduced by permission

Chapter 2

VISIONS OF HELL

> In our day, fear of the wrath of God has been largely replaced by fear of global warming and the declining sperm count.[1]

Alphonse Daudet wrote a short story, 'Le curé de Cucugnan' in which the eponymous hero, the Abbé Martin decides to pay a visit to Heaven to see how his former parishioners are faring. To his sorrow he could not discover any of them there. Nor were there any in Purgatory, for they were all roasting in Hell. With singed feet the priest returns to his flock, to urge them to behave better in order to avoid a similar fate.

Jerome K. Jerome, actor, schoolmaster and journalist, best known for his comic classic *Three Men in a Boat* (1889), died some 70 years ago. In his autobiographical essays *My Life and Times* (1926) he challenged churchmen to make up their minds about the significance of Hell and make the results public. His own childhood experiences had been traumatic:

> I was brought up to believe in a personal God who loved you if you were good; but, if you were wicked, sent you, after you were dead, to a place called Hell, where you were burnt alive for ever and ever. My mother had the idea that it was not really for ever and ever; because God was so full of loving-kindness He would not want to hurt any creature more than He could help; and that, when they had been punished sufficiently and had repented, He would forgive them. But that was only her fancy; and perhaps it was wrong of her to think so...
>
> Even as it was, not all mankind were to be saved, but only those who 'believed'. If you didn't believe the story you were still to be damned. As a child, my difficulty was that I was never quite sure whether I

---

1. David Marquand, 'Moralists and Hedonists', in David Marquand and Anthony Seldon (eds.), *The Ideas that Shaped Post-War Britain* (London: Harper Collins, 1996).

believed or not. That I made every effort in my power to believe it, goes without saying. My not believing would break my mother's heart: that I knew. Added to which, it meant going to Hell. From many a fiery pulpit, I had heard vivid and detailed descriptions of Hell. The haunting horror of it was ever present to my mind. Face downwards on my pillow, I would repeat 'I do believe', over and over again: ending by screaming it out aloud, sometimes, in case God had not heard my smothered whisperings. For periods, I would be confident that I had conquered—that I really did believe: there could be no doubt about it. And then the fear would come to me that, after all, I was only pretending to believe; and that God saw through me and knew I didn't.[2]

Other more recent novelists have conjured contrasting descriptions of Hell, or of what it might mean to talk about the context of eternal damnation. Here are four distinctive examples, to illustrate the point:

It was very silent in the wasteland, very cold and dark. I thought how strange it was that hell should be conventionally depicted as hot and noisy, an inferno of leaping flames and screaming souls welded together in a ceaseless roaring activity. I also thought how strange it was that the Modernists could attempt to slough off hell by defining it as an antiquated concept which could have no meaning for twentieth-century man. Hell was dereliction in the wasteland—the wasteland in which the soul was imprisoned when God was absent, the wasteland where there was no convenient exit marked 'Salvation' and no convenient signpost directing one to the spiritual presence of Christ.[3]

In the sermon he gave on graduating from the theological college, Thorvald took Hell as his subject. He spoke before the bishop and several professors of theology who had come, drawn by the rumours of this young graduate who preached with all the remorselessness of a Jesuit. His sermon made a powerful impression on those who heard it. It caused distant church bells to peal and the organ pipes to sigh darkly and the inside of the church to smell of red-hot iron filings and singed linen. None of those in attendance would ever forget the way in which Thorvald Bak had, at one stage, worked his way up on to the edge of the pulpit, where he had then hunkered down, hovering like a big bird of prey, and said, quite softly, 'Hell shall be the coals under the boilers of faith!'[4]

2. Jerome K. Jerome, *My Life and Times* (London: Hodder & Stoughton, 1926; reissued Folio Society, 1992), pp. 206, 210.

3. Susan Howatch, *Ultimate Prizes* (Glasgow: William Collins/Fontana, 1990), p. 205.

4. Peter Hoeg, *The History of Danish Dreams* (London: The Harvill Press 1996), p. 57.

Then suddenly he [Amos] leaped from his seat and thundered at the top of his voice:

'Ye're all damned!'

... Amos's voice now took on a deceptively mild and conversational note. His protruding eyes ranged slowly over his audience.

'Ye know, doan't ye, what it feels like when ye burn yer hand in takin' a cake out of the oven or wi' a match when ye're lightin' one of they godless cigarettes? Ay. It stings wi' a fearful pain, doan't it? And ye run away to clap a bit o' butter on it to take the pain away. Ah, but' (an impressive pause) *'there'll be no butter in hell!* Yer whoal body will be burnin' and stingin' wi' that unbearable pain, and yer blackened tongues will be stickin' out of yer mouth, and yer cracked lips will try to scream out for a drop of water, but no sound woan't come because yer throat is drier nor the sandy desert and yer eyes will be beatin' like great red hot balls against yer shrivelled eyelids...'[5]

'This is what you want: infinite worlds!'

'Surely you will allow me at least more than one. Otherwise where would God have set Hell? Not in the bowels of the earth.'

'Why not in the bowels of the earth?'

'Because'—and here Roberto was repeating in a very approximate fashion an argument he had heard in Paris, nor could he guarantee the precision of his calculations—'the diameter of the center of the earth measures two hundred Italian miles, and if we cube that, we have eight million miles. Considering that one Italian mile contains two hundred and forty thousand English feet, and since the Lord must have allowed each of the damned at least six feet, Hell could contain only forty million damned, which seems few to me, considering all the sinners who have lived in this world of ours from Adam until now.'

'That would be true,' Caspar replied, not even deigning to go over the calculation, ' if the damned were inside their bodies. But this is only after the Resurrection of the Flesh and the Last Judgement! And then there will no longer be either earth or planets, but other heavens and other earths!'

'Agreed, if the damned are only spirits, there will be a thousand million even on the head of a pin.' [6]

A report of the Church of England's Doctrine Commission, entitled *The Mystery of Salvation*, was published in 1995. Immediate interest and

5.   Stella Gibbons, *Cold Comfort Farm* (Harmondsworth: Penguin Books, 1977), p. 85.
6.   Umberto Eco, *The Island of the Day Before* (London: Minerva/Mandarin, 1996), pp. 315-16.

debate in the media focused on its views about being damned (rather than being saved), for the report had been highly critical of the traditional religious images of hellfire and damnation, and recommended that Hell should be seen as effectively annihilation and nothingness. It is said that Hell is the final and irrevocable 'choosing of that which is opposed to God so completely and so absolutely that the only end is total non-being'. Such a view would be closest to that of 'dereliction in the wasteland' in the first example quoted above, drawn from Susan Howatch's novel.

The report was discussed at the the July 1996 meeting of the Church of England General Synod in York. A Vicar from the West Midlands strongly criticized the contention that Hell was nothingness, saying this did not fit with the teaching of Jesus who spoke of the 'worthless servant thrown into the darkness, where there will be weeping and gnashing of teeth.'

> Many people think it unacceptable that the Church was teaching that the likes of Hitler, Stalin and Pol Pot were just snuffed out, therefore bracketing them with everyone else not in Heaven. If judgment is simply nothing stronger than annihilation or non-being, why did Jesus mention these matters at all? Jesus warned of something more than spiritual extinction. We are not free simply to filter off the currently unpalatable and unfashionable. We must not settle simply for annihilation because that is more comfortable for the modern mind. The Church is called upon to 'graft back' on to Christian teaching what has been lost in recent years: that is some element of the fear of God, to say clearly that ungodly living and evil will have ungodly consequences in the next life.[7]

A theological college teacher argued that the concept of the 'wrath of God' must not be rejected, even though it had been misused in the past: 'It has been used simply as a threat to hang over individuals, to warn them of something dreadful to come, unless they pull themselves together. God's wrath is not just a threat to individuals. It signifies His hatred of evil.'[8]

The Right Reverend Alec Graham, Bishop of Newcastle, who had chaired the working party that produced the report, in responding to the debate, said:

7. The Revd Andrew Dow, vicar of St John the Baptist at Knowle, West Midlands, as reported in *The Times*, 15 July 1996.
8. The Revd William Challis, Vice-Principal of Wycliffe Hall, Oxford, as reported in *The Times*, 15 July 1996.

We are convinced of the reality of choice which God has given to us, and convinced too that God did not bring this universe into being, nor millions of people within it, in order to damn them or to condemn them to futility. We are not being dogmatic about annihilation. But the working party wanted to remove any 'crudely sadistic notion' from the understanding of Hell. The working party had examined the New Testament closely. There is indeed torment, there is destruction and there is exclusion. Clearly these are not to be understood literally. If they were, they would be contradictory. There is something both irrevocable and terrible about the judgment of God. There is a problem about how to speak of God's judgment in such a way as to enable people to realise it is awful, but not in such a way as to make God a monster.[9]

There is no doubt as to the historical significance of Christian, and indeed pre-Christian, traditions about Hell. What is at issue is the significance of such ideas in the modern world; if they are indeed relevant, how should they be applied and interpreted in contemporary circumstances? Earlier generations may well have been tormented by a paralyzing fear of eternal punishment. Some groups today will still believe that a conscious punishment for all eternity is the destiny of all unbelievers. But can such teaching be compatible with belief in a loving God? And is there any element of justice in a concept of eternal punishment which excludes the possibility of any change of heart by those who are so condemned? Such questions relate to an agenda for Christian evangelism, as expressed by Dr John Hapgood (the previous Archbishop of York):

Do present-day Christians really believe, as many of our forebears undoubtedly did, that all unevangelised souls go straight to Hell? Or is it more true to say that goodness forced on people under threat of torture is not goodness at all? That the motive for evangelism must be love not fear?[10]

There is a special point in asking such questions of modern relevance in the context of the present examination of Johannine apocalyptic texts. Although the fundamentalist 'Biblical Christians' simply cite Bible texts in defence of a doctrine of Hell, almost everything depends on how those texts are interpreted. These traditional pictures of Hell owe more to a cumulative impression, developed in an ongoing creative exegesis and imaginative apocalypticism, especially notable in the Mid-

9.   As reported in *The Times*, Monday 15 July, 1996, p. 5.
10.   Article 'This Is Not Hell' in *The Independent*, July 1991.

dle Ages and in the poetry of Dante and Milton, than ever they do to the original texts of Scripture, or even the teaching of the earliest Christians. No small distortion to the image is achieved by failing to acknowledge the nature of the original context in the Bible, to notice the difference between physical description and imaginative imagery, and even to allow for the possibility of mistranslation or misunderstanding. If the tradition uses the language categories of a dramatic dualism, the desire to preach salvation almost inevitably entails the contrasted and minatory depiction of damnation.

The modern relevance of the idea of Hell does not depend on the strict category of physical realism. If we were to say that ideas of Hell are self-created, in an imaginative way, this would not entail their being 'all in the mind' and hence insignificant. There may well be ethical problems in any perception of what Hell means; but to raise such criticisms is not identical with suggesting that Hell should be irrelevant on ethical grounds. To quote John Hapgood again, this

> is not in any way to abandon the belief that actions can have eternal consequences. In fact Hell is a profound symbol of the seriousness of moral choices, and of the irreducible character of human freedom... [Hell] is not an objective reality, not a place or state created by God as a means of executing his justice, but is the way we experience self-absorption, despair and unwillingness to open ourselves to His love. Heaven, by contrast, is not self-created but is the God-given fulfilment of all His intentions for us. There is therefore a real lostness from which we need to be rescued. But it is not a lostness imposed upon us by God as a punishment, and therefore raises no question about God's moral goodness or His love towards us.[11]

There is an interesting comparison with the modern tendency to produce a psychological version (and frequently an explanation—an explaining away) of eschatological language. This is nicely represented in Steven Appleby's cartoon in the series *Small Birds Singing* (see figure 2).[12] In contrast the ancient dualist cosmologies appear (at least superficially) to press toward a kind of scientific realism, describable in a kind of astronomical/astrological form appropriate for their era. To illustrate this, see the following description:

11. See n. 9 above.
12. *The Times Magazine*, 9 November, 1996.

Sky Phenomena, According to an Astronomical Poem by Aratus

> Aratus says that there are in the sky revolving, that is gyrating, stars, because from east to west, and west to east, they journey perpetually, (and) in an orbicular figure. And he says that there revolves towards 'The Bears' themselves, like some stream of a river, an enormous and prodigious monster, (the) Serpent; and that this is what the devil says in the book of Job to the Deity, when (Satan) uses these words: 'I have traversed earth under heaven, and have gone around (it)' [Job 1.7], that is that I have been turned around and thereby have been able to survey the worlds. For they suppose that towards the North Pole is situated the Dragon, the Serpent, from the highest pole looking upon all (the objects), and gazing on all the works of creation, in order that nothing of the things that are being made may escape his notice. For, though all the stars in the firmament set, the pole of this (luminary) alone never sets, but careering high above the horizon, surveys and beholds all things, and none of the works of creation, he says, can escape his notice (Hippolytus, *Refutation of All Heresies* 4.47).

When, however, John Hapgood writes of the contemporary significance of Hell, he does not treat of pure psychology or of scientific realism. Instead he employs the conventions of modern theology and operates with the language of symbol. Broadly speaking, this is the same method employed by the New Testament writers, when they used the actualities of Gehenna, the Jerusalem rubbish dump in the Hinnom valley, with lurid descriptions of its burning fires and undying worms, to depict a place of punishment that was separated by a great gulf from the presence of God. This had a physical starting-point, but the language was not to be taken literally; yet to say it is not meant literally in no way denies its potency. There is an ambiguity and elusiveness in symbol, but it treats of theological truths. As Brian Horne expresses it, we need images and stories, so as to 'begin to approach the coexistence of evil and the God of love'.[13]

These are some of the perspectives from which we consider concepts of Hell and damnation in our modern world. We need to bear them in mind as we move to investigate the Johannine apocalyptic texts, and their visions of Hell and the world beyond, that are the main subject of this volume.

13. Brian Horne, *Imagining Evil* (London: Darton Longman & Todd, 1996).

Chapter 3

THE SECOND APOCALYPSE OF JOHN

Introduction

The Second Apocalypse imitates the canonical book of Revelation in many respects. As Heinrich Weinel stated, it seems to have been written as a completion of the earlier work ('wesentlich als Ergänzung zu ihr geschrieben zu sein scheint')[1]. The principal respects in which it performs such a supplementary function are in describing the physical characteristics of the Beast/Antichrist figure, and in dealing with a whole sequence of practical or merely curious questions about conditions of life in the future. It should be remembered that John, in the canonical Apocalypse, does not display such curiosity, seeking to know more and more, compared for example with other contemporary apocalypses (e.g. *4 Esdras* 4.35-52).

The Antichrist is described in *2 Apoc. Jn* 7, in nightmarish terms that are more familiar to us from horror films; the picture here belongs to the same tradition as is found in the Apocalypse of Esdras:[2] τὸ εἶδος τοῦ προσώπου αὐτοῦ ὡσεὶ ἀγροῦ· ὁ ὀφθαλμὸς αὐτοῦ ὁ δεξιὸς ὡς ἀστὴρ τὸ πρωῒ ἀνατέλλων, καὶ ὁ ἕτερος ἀσάλευτος· τὸ στόμα αὐτοῦ πῆχυς μία· οἱ ὀδόντες αὐτοῦ σπιθαμιαῖοι· οἱ δάκτυλοι αὐτοῦ ὡς δρέπανα· τὸ ἴχνος τῶν ποδῶν αὐτοῦ σπιθαμῶν δύο· καὶ εἰς τὸ μέτωπον αὐτοῦ γραφή· ἀντίχριστος.

There is, however, in *2 Apoc. Jn* some variation in the constituents:

> His face appears dark as Hell, the hairs of his head sharp as arrows, his brows wild like a field; his right eye is like the star which rises early, his other eye as a lion's; his mouth measures half a yard, and his teeth a span; his fingers resemble sickles; his footprint measures a foot and a half; and on his forehead the name Antichrist is engraved.

---

1. 'Die spätere christliche Apocalyptik', in H. Schmidt (ed.), *EYXAΡΙΣTHION (Gunkel Festschrift)* (Göttingen: Vandenhoeck & Ruprecht, 1923), p. 149.

2. See Tischendorf (1866), p. 29.

This kind of character sketch is reminiscent, in the most general way, of the description of the apostle Paul, in the late second century *Acts of Paul*:

> He saw Paul coming, a man small of stature, with a bald head and crooked legs, in a good state of body, with eyebrows meeting and a nose somewhat hooked, full of friendliness; for now he appeared like a man, and now he had the face of an angel' (3.3).[3]

Opinions now vary as to whether such a description of Paul is idealized or unfavourable. But few would go as far as E. Preuschen in suggesting that such traits were designed to identify Paul as the Antichrist.[4] There are no grounds that I can see for regarding the description in *2 Apoc. Jn* as anti-Pauline.

The concern for the future, and particularly the details of the Last Judgment and the resurrection life, can be illustrated by one unusual extract from ch. 11 (where the apparently rural character of this work's language is at its most striking):

> Just as the bees do not differ one from another, but are all of the same appearance and size, so every human-being will be at the resurrection. Not fair-skinned, nor red-skin, nor black, not Ethiopian nor different facial features, but all will rise with the same appearance and size. The whole human species will rise bodiless.

It is more than tempting to compare this whole text's use of rural imagery with the creation language of the meditations by the seventeenth-century mystic from the Welsh Marches, Thomas Traherne. One of his best known texts is the following:

> The Corn was Orient and Immortal Wheat, which never should be reaped, nor was ever sown. I thought it had stood from Everlasting to Everlasting. The Dust and Stones of the Street were as precious as Gold. The Gates were at first the End of the World, the Green Trees when I saw them first through one of the Gates transported and ravished me; their Sweetness and unusual Beauty made my Heart to leap, and almost mad with Extasie, they were such strange and Wonderfull Things; The Men! O what venerable and Reverend Creatures did the Aged seem! Immortal Cherubims! And yong men Glittering Sparkling Angels and Maids strange Seraphick Pieces of Life and Beauty! Boys and Girles Tumbling in the Street, and Playing, were moving Jewels. I knew not

3.   *New Testament Apocrypha*, II (ed. W. Schneemelcher; Cambridge: James Clarke, 1992), p. 239.

4.   *ZNTW* 2 (1901), pp. 169-201.

that they were Born or should Die. But all things abided Eternaly as they
were in their Proper Places. Eternity was Manifest in the Light of Day,
and som thing infinit Behind evry thing appeared; which talked with my
Expectation and moved my Desire. The Citie seemed to stand in Eden,
or to be built in Heaven. The Streets were mine, the Temple was mine,
the People were mine, their Clothes and Gold and Silver was mine, as
much as their Sparkling Eys fair skins and ruddy faces (*Centuries of
Meditations* 3.3).

The antiquity of this Apocalypse is difficult to establish, because
of the scarcity of references to anything that is historically datable.
Wilhelm Bousset supposed that the work must be dependent upon the
'Questions and Answers' of Ephraem the Syrian (c. 306–373), in order
to explain the remarkable interrogatory pattern that persists throughout
the book. Ephraem was a biblical exegete and dogmatic writer from Nisibis who later lived in Edessa, producing a range of work both polemical and didactic. A favourite subject of his was the last judgment which
he described in terrifying colours. Although he wrote in Syriac, his
works were early translated into Aramaic and Greek. If this dependency
upon Ephraem can be established, then the Apocalypse would be dated
after 400 CE, or at the earliest the very end of the fourth century.

Heinrich Weinel concluded that such a date was likely on other, more
speculative, grounds. The way the Bible is quoted could be indicative
of an identifiable tradition of exegesis, with a literal basis but a quest
for the underlying 'deeper' meanings. These quotations are specific and
formally introduced, in a way that is quite distinct from the book of
Revelation, which almost never uses formal quotations (see, however,
the Trishagion from Isa. 6.3 in Rev. 4.8, cf. *2 Apoc. Jn* 17) but clearly
makes great use of the Old Testament nonetheless, by allusion. We
should notice that *2 Apoc. Jn* does not quote Revelation among these
biblical proof-texts introduced by a set formula (although the text of
Revelation is a direct influence, as seen especially in the wording of
chs. 18 [Rev. 5] and 27 [Rev. 21]); there are several formula quotations
from the Gospels (particularly Matthew) and Paul, but the vast majority
of the texts are from the Old Testament, especially in the Psalms, texts
which are regarded as prophecies. This attitude to the Psalmist (David)
as prophet is found quite frequently in Patristic writing: see, for the
early fifth century, the *Conferences* of John Cassian 10.11: 'The good
man will sing [the Psalms] no longer as verses composed by a prophet,
but as born of his own prayers'. For further specific details on the selection of quotations, and a comparison with the other deutero-canonical

Figure 3. *St Helena (rt. hand figure)* (Barber Institute)

Johannine apocalypses, see the tabulated evidence in the conclusion of this study.

As we have already noticed, there is in this Apocalypse a religious curiosity about individuals and their survival (e.g. the form of the resurrected body). This individualistic attitude could be contrasted with the older apocalyptic concern with the future hope, expressed in more collective imagery such as the kingdom of God. It may be related to a monastic individualism.

There is one reference (*2 Apoc. Jn* 13) which may provide a specific historical point of contact: 'Then I will give orders for the lifting up of the great and venerated cross on which I stretched out my hands, and all the ranks of my angels will prostrate themselves before it'.

This may well reflect the tradition of the Empress Helena's discovery of the True Cross in 326 CE, during that visit to the Holy Land, when she founded basilicas on the Mount of Olives and at Bethlehem. This tradition is documented by Sulpicius Severus, Ambrose and Rufinus, all of whom were writing at the end of the fourth century. The discovery is mentioned several times by Cyril of Jerusalem, who also refers to a vision of the cross in the heavens:

> For in the days of Constantine your father, most dear to God and of blessed memory, there was discovered the wood of the cross fraught with salvation, because the divine grace that gave piety to the pious seeker vouchsafed the finding of the buried holy places. But in your time, your Majesty, most religious of Emperors, victorious through a piety towards

God greater even than that which you inherited, are seen wonderful
works, not from the earth any more, but from the heavens. The trophy of
the victory over death of our Lord and Saviour Jesus Christ, the only-
begotten Son of God, I mean the blessed cross, has been seen at Jerusalem blazing with refulgent light!' (*Letter to Emperor Constantius* 3).

The theological tone of Cyril's reference (dated 351 CE) to the heavenly cross seems very close to this theme of *2 Apoc. Jn*. The symbolic
cross is specifically the 'True Cross'; a comparison with the apocryphal
Gospel of Peter 10 shows how different earlier references had been to
the symbolism of the cross. The 'fact' of Helena's discovery has been
enhanced with an inner meaning, perhaps developed within pious expectation of the Parousia; the images and symbols, and all the people by
virtue of their piety, are caught up to heaven together. *2 Apoc. Jn* 13
itself is explicit in quoting the ideas about the Parousia, from 1 Thess.
4.16-17, with reference to this complete rapture.

Other indications in the text may illuminate the context, but are
harder to pin down. In chs. 21 and 22 the category of 'Greeks' includes
heretical thinkers, while the classification of 'Hebrews' shows that anti-
Semitic traditions (cf. 1 Thess. 2.15) are certainly retained. The 'Greeks'
are distanced, so this writer clearly does not identify with them. This is
a context where Old Testament terms (e.g. high priests, levites) are still
being used within the Christian tradition. The natural comparison is
with the Didache, which also shares an essentially rural background for
its language. Alternatively, the writings of Cyprian show how later
Christians returned to Jewish themes, making use of Old Testament
language with special reference to priesthood.

In *2 Apoc. Jn* one feels a proximity to certain traditions of Judaism,
alongside the language of anti-Semitism. Given the rivalries among
Jewish groups and between Jews and Jewish-Christians, seen in the
New Testament period and exemplified in Matthew's Gospel, the con-
junction of Jewish and anti-Semitic attitudes is less surprising. The clues
provided by comparisons with Matthew, the Didache and Ephraem
Syrus, all come together to suggest the strong possibility of a Syriac-
Christian context (more likely than a North African provenance) for
2 Apoc. Jn. Here is a pious, apocalyptic community which stresses the
biblical continuity, while insisting on significant differences in interpretation and practice.

The nature of this community can be further clarified against the
background of the enormous growth in the monastic movement in the

fourth century CE. In contrast to the Egyptian (Pachomian) traditions, Syrian monasticism was less orderly and marked by an emphasis on individualism. While Jerome is fiercely critical of these Remoboth, ('from the caves which serve us for cells we monks of the desert condemn the world. Rolling in sack-cloth and ashes, we pass sentence on bishops' [*Ep.* 17.2]), for John Chrysostom in Antioch 'the Syrian monks coming in from the desert were heavenly visitants at church festivals'.[5] The Syrian traditions might be said to have their antecedents in the learned asceticism of the Qumran community, and more directly among the Christian circles of Encratites in the Syriac-speaking East.

The *Second Apocalypse of John* 27 describes, in the language of Revelation and Jn 10.16, a heavenly life-style, a community (flock) of 'human beings made like angels because of their virtuous way of life'. The author's ideal is the best combination of emphases on individualism and community, in the Syrian manner. But this can be taken further with reference to the issues of doctrine and heresy raised in ch. 21: 'heretics who defiled the faith by not believing in the holy Resurrection; those who did not confess Father, Son and Holy Spirit'. It is quite possible that this text is strongly anti-Origenist.[6] Such a view derives general support from the literal way that the text uses Revelation as a basis, in a manner that would be offensive to a follower of Origen.

On the specific allegations of heresy, Origen was widely thought to have denied the resurrection; and because he seemed to propound subordinationism within the Trinity he was regarded as an 'Arian before Arius'. The substance of a charge of Origenism (or the range of heretical teaching associated with Origen) is illustrated by Jerome's account of the eight questions raised by Epiphanius of Salamis against John of Jerusalem:[7]

> The questions relate to the passages in Origen's work, *On First Principles*. The first is this: 'for as it is unfitting to say that the Son can see the Father, so neither is it fitting to think that the Holy Spirit can see the

5.   Stuart G. Hall, *Doctrine and Practice in the Early Church* (London: SPCK, 1991), p. 178.

6.   Stuart Hall has suggested this to me in correspondence, and I am much indebted to him for his assistance in this area, although any misrepresentations of course are mine.

7.   J. Stevenson, *Creeds, Councils and Controversies* (rev. W.H.C. Frend; London: SPCK, 1989), p. 192.

Son.'... Fifthly, he most openly denies the resurrection of the flesh...
Sixthly, he so allegorizes Paradise as to destroy historical truth.

These are the relevant allegations, of Arianism, denial of the resurrection, and avoidance of literal exegesis. They are not necessarily what Origen himself believed.

Nautin analyses acutely the way Jerome distorted Origen's views on resurrection.[8] Crouzel is clearly convinced that Origen both believed in the resurrection and also was a better trinitarian than most. But this was not how many perceived the situation in the fourth century, particularly Greeks who read Epiphanius and Latins who read Jerome. And Origenism proved to be a cause of intense division among the monks of Jerome's day; it brought about the quarrel between Jerome and his former friend Rufinus; it also recurred in Egypt in the 390s, leading to the destruction of Evagrius's monastic school. Much later, after further conflicts in the sixth century, it resulted in the imperial condemnation of Origen and Evagrius. There is a strong probability that *2 Apoc. Jn* allows us to see this controversy from a Syrian monastic perspective at the end of the fourth century.

A Note on the Second Apocalypse of John and the Apocryphon of John

The *Apocryphon of John* is a Gnostic work in Coptic from the Nag Hammadi Library. It seems likely that an original text in Greek of at least the first part of this work existed before 180 CE, because this appears to be the source used by Irenaeus (*Adv. Haer.* 1.27) for his account of the Barbelo-Gnostics. The relation of its thought to a Sethian type of Gnosticism, such as that of the Audians, would explain the mention by the Nestorian Theodore bar Konai in section XI of his Book of Scholia in Syriac. Theodore actually calls it the Apocalypse of John. This sets a kind of precedent for the modern scholar J. Doresse, who seems to have confused the *Apocryphon of John* with *2 Apoc. Jn* in its relationship with the mediaeval *Interrogatio Iohannis* of the Bogomils and Cathars, when he wrote: 'The Audians were to modify the Book of John a little further, and perhaps in their turn hand it on, in its mediaeval form of the *Interrogatio Iohannis*, to the different Manichean groups of the Balkans and the West.'

It is true that the *Apocryphon of John* does adopt the form of a

8.   P. Nautin, *Origène I* (Paris: Beauchesne, 1977), Chapter 8.

dialogue between John and the Revealer in its later chapters. But it starts with the visionary narrative followed by doctrinal exposition in monologue that are typical forms of the classic Gnostic gospel. W. Schneemelcher describes it as a 'gnostic revelation document which has been only secondarily transformed into a conversation between Jesus and John'.[9] And in its emphases the *Apocryphon of John* belongs to Sethian Gnosticism, with its doctrine depending upon the exegesis of the opening chapters of Genesis, while the subject matter of the dialogue, between John and the voice, in *2 Apoc. Jn* does not correspond to this in either respect.

The Text of the Second Apocalypse of John

The earliest attestation of this work which can be dated with any precision—and that to the ninth century CE—is found in the scholia to the grammar of Dionysius of Thrace. Immediately after ascribing the apocalypse of Paul to Paul of Samosata, there is mention of a pseudo-Johannine apocalypse:

> καὶ ἑτέρα ἀποκάλυψις ἡ λεγομένη τοῦ θεολόγου. οὐ λέγομεν δὲ τὴν ἐν Πάτμῳ τῇ νήσῳ, μὴ γένοιτο· αὕτη γὰρ ἀληθεστάτη ἐστίν· ἀλλὰ τὴν ψευδώνυμον καὶ ἀλλότριον.

> there is another called the Apocalypse of the Theologian. We are not speaking of the one in the island of Patmos, God forbid, for that one is supremely true; but of a pseudonymous and spurious one.

Joseph Simonius Assemani (1687–1786) records that he found the book in Arabic in three manuscripts: 'apocalypsim Iohannis apostoli aliam ab ea quam ecclesia catholica suscipit'.[10]

The first edition of this text was by Andreas Birch in 1804: he collated manuscripts from the Vatican (Palatino-Vaticani 346) and Vienna (Lambecio V. Bk.8, Nesselio 119). Constantine Tischendorf used five additional manuscripts for his edition of *Apocalypses Apocryphae* in 1866, on which the present study depends. Of these five manuscripts, two came from Paris (Paris 947 of 1523 CE; Paris 1034 of fifteenth century) and three from Venice (Venice Marc.class.XI codex XX; Venice

---

9. W. Schneemelcher, *New Testament Apocrypha*, I (James Clarke, 1991), p. 387.

10. *Bibliotheca Orientalis* (4 vols.; 1719–28; recording manuscripts collected in the East for Pope Clement XI, Vatican Library), III, part 1, p. 282.

Marc. class.II codex XLII; Venice Marc. class.II codex XC—these are from fifteenth and sixteenth centuries and the first named is the oldest). Tischendorf remarked on the extremely wide variations in manuscript readings. There is evidence for a continuing tradition of textual elaboration appropriate for later ages. There is much to be said therefore for concentrating initially on the least elaborated text, while noting where the principal additions occur. The text of these additions can be found in the critical apparatus of Tischendorf's 1866 edition.

Ἀποκάλυψις τοῦ ἁγίου Ἰωάννου τοῦ θεολόγου

1. Μετὰ τὴν ἀνάληψιν τοῦ κυρίου ἡμῶν Ἰησοῦ Χριστοῦ παρε-
γενόμην ἐγὼ Ἰωάννης μόνος ἐπὶ τὸ ὄρος τὸ Θαβώρ, ἔνθα καὶ τὴν
ἄχραντον αὐτοῦ θεότητα ὑπέδειξεν ἡμῖν, καὶ μὴ δυνηθέντος μου στῆναι
ἔπεσα ἐπὶ τὴν γῆν καὶ ηὐξάμην πρὸς κύριον καὶ εἶπον· κύριε ὁ θεός
μου, ὁ καταξιώσας με δοῦλόν σου γενέσθαι, ἄκουσον τῆς φωνῆς μου
καὶ δίδαξόν με περὶ τῆς ἐλεύσεώς σου· ὅταν μέλλῃς ἔρχεσθαι ἐπὶ τῆς
γῆς, τί μέλλει γενέσθαι; ὁ οὐρανὸς καὶ ἡ γῆ καὶ ὁ ἥλιος καὶ ἡ σελήνη
τί μέλλουσι γενέσθαι ἐν τοῖς καιροῖς ἐκείνοις; ἀποκάλυψόν μοι πάντα.
θαρρῶ γὰρ ὅτι ὑπακούεις τῷ δούλῳ σου.
2. Καὶ ἐποίησα ἡμέρας ἑπτὰ προσευχόμενος, καὶ μετὰ ταῦτα
νεφέλη φωτεινὴ ἥρπασέν με ἀπὸ τοῦ ὄρους καὶ ἔστησέ με πρὸ προσώπου τοῦ οὐρανοῦ, καὶ ἤκουσα φωνῆς λεγούσης μοι· ἀνάβλεψον, δοῦλε
τοῦ θεοῦ Ἰωάννη, καὶ γνῶθι. καὶ ἀναβλέψας εἶδον ἀνεῳγότα τὸν
οὐρανόν, καὶ ἐξήρχετο ἀπὸ τῶν ἔνδοθεν τοῦ οὐρανοῦ ὀσμὴ ἀρωμάτων
εὐωδίας πολλῆς, καὶ εἶδον φωτοχυσίαν πολλὴν σφόδρα παρὰ τὸν
ἥλιον φωτεινοτέραν. 3. καὶ πάλιν ἤκουσα φωνῆς λεγούσης μοι· θεώρησον, δίκαιε Ἰωάννη. καὶ ἀνέτεινα τὸ ὄμμα, καὶ εἶδον βιβλίον κείμε-
νον, ὡς νομίζειν με, ἑπτὰ ὀρέων τὸ πάχος αὐτοῦ· τὸ δὲ μῆκος αὐτοῦ
νοῦς ἀνθρώπων οὐ δύναται καταλαβεῖν, ἔχοντα σφραγίδας ἑπτά. καὶ
εἶπον· κύριε ὁ θεός μου, ἀποκάλυψόν μοι τί ἐστιν γεγραμμένον ἐν τῷ
βιβλίῳ τούτῳ. 4. καὶ ἤκουσα φωνῆς λεγούσης μοι· ἄκουσον, δίκαιε
Ἰωάννη· τοῦτο τὸ βιβλίον ὃ ἑώρακας, γεγραμμένα εἰσὶν τὰ ἐν τῷ
οὐρανῷ καὶ τὰ ἐν τῇ γῇ καὶ τὰ ἐν τῇ ἀβύσσῳ, καὶ πάσης φύσεως
ἀνθρωπίνης κρίματα καὶ δικαιοσύνη. 5. καὶ εἶπον· κύριε, πότε μέλλουσιν ταῦτα γενέσθαι, καὶ τί διαφέρουσιν οἱ καιροὶ ἐκεῖνοι; καὶ
ἤκουσα φωνῆς λεγούσης μοι· ἄκουσον, δίκαιε Ἰωάννη· μέλλει τῷ
καιρῷ ἐκείνῳ γενέσθαι πλησμονὴ σίτου καὶ οἴνου, οἵα οὐ γέγονεν ἐπὶ
τῆς γῆς οὐδ' οὐ μὴ γένηται ἕως οὗ ἔλθωσιν οἱ καιροὶ ἐκεῖνοι. τότε ὁ
στάχυς τοῦ σίτου ἐκφυεῖ ἡμιχοίνικον, καὶ ὁ ἀγκὼν τοῦ κλήματος ἐκφυεῖ
χιλίους βότρυας, καὶ ὁ βότρυς ἐκφυεῖ ἡμίσταμνον οἴνου· καὶ τοῦ
ἐπερχομένου ἔτους οὐ μὴ εὑρεθῇ ἐπὶ προσώπου πάσης τῆς γῆς
ἡμιχοίνικον σίτου οὐδὲ ἡμίσταμνος οἴνου.

APOCALYPSE OF SAINT JOHN THE THEOLOGIAN

Italicized terms are explained in the notes at the end of this section.

1. After the ascension of our Lord Jesus Christ, I John found myself alone on *Mt Tabor*. There he showed us the *undefiled fulness* of his divinity. I was *unable to stand* but fell on the earth and prayed to the Lord: 'O Lord, my God, you who count me worthy to be your servant, hear my voice and teach me about your coming. What will happen when you are to come on earth? How will heaven and earth, sun and moon be affected at that time? Reveal everything to me—I speak confidently because you hear your servant'.

2. I was praying for *seven days*, and then a *cloud* of divine brightness took me from the mountain and set me in sight of heaven, and I heard a *voice* say to me: 'Look up, God's servant John, and have knowledge'. Looking up, I saw heaven opened, and from within heaven came a fragrant *incense* as of a great sacrifice; and I saw a great outpouring of light, much brighter than the sun. 3. Again I heard a voice saying to me: 'Observe, *righteous John*'. I strained my eyes and I saw a book there, as I thought, the size of seven mountains. The human mind cannot grasp its length, and it had *seven seals*. I said: 'Lord, my God, reveal to me what is written in this book'. 4. I heard a voice: 'Listen, righteous John, what is written in this book which you have seen concerns heaven, earth and the *abyss*, and verdicts on the whole of human nature and *righteousness*'. 5. I said: 'Lord, when will this happen, and what will make those times appear different?' I heard a voice: 'Listen, *righteous John*, at that time there will be corn and wine to meet all needs, such as has not happened on the earth, nor will happen, until those times come. Then an ear of *corn* yields a pint of grain, the branch of a vine a thousand bunches of grapes, and a bunch of grapes half a jar of *wine*. *In the following year* there will not be found anywhere on the whole earth either a man's daily ration of grain or a half-jar of wine'.

6. Καὶ πάλιν εἶπον· κύριε, ἀπὸ τότε τί μέλλεις ποιεῖν; καὶ ἤκουσα φωνῆς λεγούσης μοι· ἄκουσον, δίκαιε Ἰωάννη· τότε φανήσεται ὁ ἀρνητὴς καὶ ἐξορισμένος ἐν τῇ σκοτίᾳ, ὁ λεγόμενος ἀντίχριστος. καὶ πάλιν εἶπον· κύριε, ἀποκάλυψόν μοι ποταπός ἐστιν.

7. καὶ ἤκουσα φωνῆς λεγούσης μοι· τὸ εἶδος τοῦ προσώπου αὐτοῦ ζοφῶδες, αἱ τρίχες τῆς κεφαλῆς αὐτοῦ ὀξεῖαι ὡς βέλη, οἱ ὄφρυες αὐτοῦ ὡσεὶ ἀγροῦ, ὁ ὀφθαλμὸς αὐτοῦ ὁ δεξιὸς ὡς ὁ ἀστὴρ ὁ πρωῒ ἀνατέλλων, καὶ ὁ ἕτερος ὡς λέοντος, τὸ στόμα αὐτοῦ ὡς πῆχυν μίαν, οἱ ὀδόντες αὐτοῦ σπιθαμιαῖοι, οἱ δάκτυλοι αὐτοῦ ὡς δρέπανα, τὸ ἴχνος τῶν ποδῶν αὐτοῦ σπιθαμῶν δύο, καὶ εἰς τὸ μέτωπον αὐτοῦ γραφὴ ἀντίχριστος· ἕως τοῦ οὐρανοῦ ὑψωθήσεται καὶ ἕως τοῦ ᾅδου καταβήσεται, ποιῶν ψευδοφαντασίας. καὶ τότε ποιήσω τὸν οὐρανὸν χαλκοῦν, ἵνα μὴ δώσει ἐπὶ τὴν γῆν δρόσον· καὶ κρύψω τὰς νεφέλας ἐν ἀποκρύφοις τόποις, ἵνα μὴ ἐπάγωσι δρόσον ἐπὶ τὴν γῆν· καὶ καταστείλω τοῖς κέρασιν τῶν ἀνέμων, ἵνα μὴ πνεύσει ὁ ἄνεμος ἐπὶ τῆς γῆς.

8. Καὶ πάλιν εἶπον· κύριε, καὶ πόσα ἔτη μέλλει ποιεῖν οὗτος ἐπὶ τῆς γῆς; καὶ ἤκουσα φωνῆς λεγούσης μοι· ἄκουσον, δίκαιε Ἰωάννη· τρία ἔτη ἔσονται οἱ καιροὶ ἐκεῖνοι, καὶ ποιήσω τὰ τρία ἔτη ὡς τρεῖς μῆνας, καὶ τοὺς τρεῖς μῆνας ὡς τρεῖς ἑβδομάδας, καὶ τὰς τρεῖς ἑβδομάδας ὡς τρεῖς ἡμέρας, καὶ τὰς τρεῖς ἡμέρας ὡς τρεῖς ὥρας, καὶ τὰς τρεῖς ὥρας ὡς τρεῖς στιγμάς, καθὼς εἶπεν ὁ προφήτης Δαυίδ· τὸν θρόνον αὐτοῦ εἰς τὴν γῆν κατέρραξας, ἐσμίκρυνας τὰς ἡμέρας τοῦ χρόνου αὐτοῦ, κατέχεας αὐτῷ αἰσχύνην. καὶ τότε ἀποστελῶ Ἐνὼχ καὶ Ἡλίαν πρὸς ἔλεγχον αὐτοῦ, καὶ ἀποδείξωσιν αὐτὸν ψεύστην καὶ πλάνον, καὶ ἀνελεῖ αὐτοὺς ἐπὶ τὸ θυσιαστήριον, καθὼς εἶπεν ὁ προφήτης· τότε ἀνοίσωσιν ἐπὶ τὸ θυσιαστήριόν σου μόσχους.

9. Καὶ πάλιν εἶπον· κύριε, καὶ ἀπὸ τότε τί μέλλει γενέσθαι; καὶ ἤκουσα φωνῆς λεγούσης μοι· ἄκουσον, δίκαιε Ἰωάννη· τότε τελευτήσει πᾶσα φύσις ἀνθρωπίνη, καὶ οὐκ ἔστιν ἄνθρωπος ζῶν ἐπὶ πᾶσαν τὴν γῆν. καὶ πάλιν εἶπον· κύριε, ἀπὸ τότε τί μέλλεις ποιεῖν; καὶ ἤκουσα φωνῆς λεγούσης μοι· ἄκουσον, δίκαιε Ἰωάννη· τότε ἀποστελῶ ἀγγέλους μου, καὶ ἀροῦσιν τὰ κέρη τοῦ κριοῦ τὰ κείμενα ἐπὶ τὴν νεφέλην, καὶ ἐξέλθωσιν ἔξω τοῦ οὐρανοῦ καὶ σαλπίσουσιν Μιχαὴλ καὶ Γαβριὴλ μετὰ τῶν κεράτων ἐκείνων, καθὼς προεῖπεν ὁ προφήτης Δαυίδ, ἐν φωνῇ σάλπιγγος κερατίνης· καὶ ἀκουτισθήσεται ἡ φωνὴ τῆς σάλπιγγος ἀπὸ περάτων ἕως περάτων τῆς οἰκουμένης· καὶ ἀπὸ τῆς φωνῆς ἐκείνης τῆς σάλπιγγος σαλευθήσεται πᾶσα ἡ γῆ, καθὼς προεῖπεν ὁ προφήτης, καὶ ὑπὸ τὴν φωνὴν τοῦ στρουθίου ἀναστήσεται πᾶσα

6. Again I spoke: 'Lord, *what do you intend* to do next?' I heard a voice which said to me: 'Listen, righteous John; next will appear the *Denier*, who is banished in the darkness, the one called Antichrist'. I said: 'Lord, reveal to me his nature'.

7. And the voice I heard told me this: 'His face appears dark as Hell, the hairs of his head sharp as arrows, his brows wild like a field; his right eye is like the star which rises early, his other eye as a lion's; his mouth measures half a yard, and his teeth a span; his fingers resemble sickles; his footprint measures a foot and a half; and *on his forehead* the name Antichrist is engraved. He will be exalted to heaven and will descend to Hades, as he creates misleading *manifestations*. Then I will turn the sky *brazen*, so it will not moisten the earth; I will hide the clouds in secret places, so that they will not bring moisture on the earth; I will calm the powers of the winds, so that the *wind will not blow* on the earth'.

8. Again I asked: 'Lord, for how many years is the Antichrist to operate on the earth?' The voice said to me: 'Listen, righteous John, the time will be *three years*. But I will make three years to be like three months, three months like three weeks, three weeks like three days, three days like three hours, and three hours like three moments, just as David prophesied ('You have cast his throne to the ground. You have cut short the days of his life; you have covered him with shame' [Ps. 89.44-45]). Then I will send *Enoch and Elijah* to convict him; they will expose him as a liar and deceiver. But he will destroy them at the altar, just as the *prophet* said ('Then bulls will be offered on your altar' [Ps. 51.19]).

9. Again I said: 'Lord, what will happen after that?' And I heard a voice which told me: 'Listen, righteous John, then the whole human species will die; no *human being is alive* on the whole earth'. I said: 'Lord, what do you intend to do after that?' The voice I heard said: 'Listen, righteous John, I will send my angels; they will take the *ram's horns* from their place on the cloud. *Michael and Gabriel* will go out of heaven and sound those horns, just as David foretold ("with the sound of a trumpet of horn" [Ps. 98.6 LXX]). The sound of the trumpet will be audible from one end of the world to the other, and the whole earth will be shaken at that trumpet's sound, just as the prophet foretold ("at the

βοτάνη, τουτέστιν ὑπὸ τὴν φωνὴν ἀρχαγγέλου ἀναστήσεται πᾶσα
φύσις ἀνθρωπίνη.

10. Καὶ πάλιν εἶπον· κύριε, οἱ ἀποθανόντες ἀπὸ τοῦ ᾽Αδὰμ μέχρι
τὴν σήμερον, καὶ οἱ κατοικοῦντες ἐν τῷ ᾅδῃ ἀπὸ τοῦ αἰῶνος καὶ οἱ
ἀποθανόντες ἐπ᾽ ἐσχάτων τῶν αἰώνων ποταποὶ ἀναστήσονται; καὶ
ἤκουσα φωνῆς λεγούσης μοι· ἄκουσον, δίκαιε ᾽Ιωάννη· πᾶσα φύσις
ἀνθρωπίνη τριακονταετὴς ἀναστήσεται.

11. Καὶ πάλιν εἶπον· κύριε, ἄρσεν καὶ θῆλυ τελευτῶσιν, καὶ ἄλλοι
γηραλέοι, καὶ ἄλλοι νεώτεροι, καὶ ἄλλοι βρέφη· ἐν τῇ ἀναστάσει
ποταποὶ ἀναστήσονται; καὶ ἤκουσα φωνῆς λεγούσης μοι· ἄκουσον,
δίκαιε ᾽Ιωάννη· ὥσπερ γάρ εἰσιν αἱ μέλισσαι καὶ οὐ διαφέπουσι μία
τῆς μιᾶς, ἀλλ᾽ εἰσι πᾶσαι μιᾶς εἰδέας καὶ μιᾶς ἡλικίας, οὕτως καὶ
ἐν τῇ ἀναστάσει ἔσονται πᾶς ἄνθρωπος· οὐκ ἔστιν οὔτε ξανθὸς οὔτε
πύρρος οὔτε μέλας, ἀλλ᾽ οὔτε αἰθιοψ ἢ διάφορα πρόσωπα· ἀλλὰ
πάντες ἀναστήσονται μιᾶς εἰδέας καὶ μιᾶς ἡλικίας· πᾶσα φύσις
ἀνθρωπίνη ἀσώματοι ἀναστήσονται, καθὼς εἶπον ὑμῖν ὅτι ἐν τῇ ἀναστάσει οὔτε γαμοῦσιν οὔτε ἐγγαμίζονται, ἀλλ᾽ ἢ εἰσὶν ὡς ἄγγελοι τοῦ
θεοῦ.

12. Καὶ πάλιν εἶπον· κύριε, ἔστιν ἐν τῷ κόσμῳ ἐκείνῳ γνωρίσαι
ἀλλήλους, ἀδελφὸς ἀδελφόν, ἢ φίλος τόν φίλον, ἢ πατὴρ τὰ ἴδια
τέκνα, ἢ τὰ τέκνα τοὺς ἰδίους γονεῖς; καὶ ἤκουσα φωνῆς λεγούσης μοι·
ἄκουσον ᾽Ιωάννη· τοῖς μὲν δικαίοις γνωρισμὸς γίνεται, τοῖς δὲ
ἁμαρτωλοῖς οὐδαμῶς, οὔτε ἐν τῇ ἀναστάσει δύνανται γνωρίσαι
ἀλλήλους. καὶ πάλιν εἶπον ἐγὼ ᾽Ιωάννης· κύριε, ἔστιν ἐκεῖ ἐνθύμησις
τῶν ὧδε ἢ ἀγρῶν ἢ ἀμπελώνων ἢ ἄλλων τῶν ἐνθάδε; καὶ ἤκουσα
φωνῆς λεγούσης μοι· ἄκουσον, δίκαιε ᾽Ιωάννη· ὁ προφήτης Δαυὶδ
φάσκει λέγων· ἐμνήσθην ὅτι χοῦς ἐσμέν· ἄνθρωπος ὡσεὶ χόρτος αἱ
ἡμέραι αὐτοῦ· ὡσεὶ ἄνθος τοῦ ἀγροῦ, οὕτως ἐξανθήσει, ὅτι πνεῦμα
διῆλθεν ἐν αὐτῷ καὶ οὐχ ὑπάρξει, καὶ οὐκ ἐπιγνώσεται ἔτι τὸν τόπον
αὐτοῦ. καὶ πάλιν ὁ αὐτὸς εἶπεν· ἐξελεύσεται τὸ πνεῦμα αὐτοῦ καὶ
ἐπιστρέφει εἰς τὴν γῆν αὐτοῦ· ἐν ἐκείνῃ τῇ ἡμέρᾳ ἀπολοῦνται πάντες
οἱ διαλογισμοὶ αὐτοῦ.

13. Καὶ πάλιν εἶπον· κύριε, καὶ ἀπὸ τότε τί μέλλεις ποιεῖν; καὶ
ἤκουσα φωνῆς λεγούσης μοι· ἄκουσον, δίκαιε ᾽Ιωάννη· τότε ἀποστελῶ
τοὺς ἀγγέλους μου ἐπὶ προσώπου πάσης τῆς γῆς, καὶ ἀροῦσιν ἀπὸ
τῆς γῆς πᾶν ἔνδοξον καὶ πᾶν τίμιον, καὶ τὰς σεπτὰς καὶ ἁγίας
εἰκόνας, καὶ τοὺς ἐνδόξους καὶ τιμίους σταυρούς, καὶ τὰ ἱερὰ τῶν
ἐκκλησιῶν, καὶ τὰς θείας καὶ ἱερὰς βίβλους· καὶ τὰ τίμια καὶ ἅγια
πάντα ἀρθήσονται ὑπὸ νεφελῶν ἐν τῷ ἀέρι. καὶ τότε κελεύσω ἀρθῆναι

voice of a bird" every plant "will rise up" [Eccl. 12.4])—which means
that the whole human species will rise up at the voice of the archangel'.

10. Again I said: 'Lord, about the dead—from Adam until today, and
all those who inhabit Hades from the earliest times, and those who die
at the end of time—in what form will they rise?' I heard a voice which
said: 'Listen, righteous John, the whole human species will rise as
thirty-year-olds'.

11. I asked again: 'Lord, they are male and female when they die,
some elderly, some young, and some babies; *at the resurrection* in what
form will they rise?' The voice I heard said to me: 'Listen, righteous
John, for just as the bees do not differ one from another, but are all of
the same appearance and size, so every human-being will be at the
resurrection. Not fair-skinned, nor red-skin, nor black, not Ethiopian
nor different facial features, but all will rise with the same appearance
and size. The whole human species will rise bodiless, just as I told you
that "in the resurrection they neither marry nor are given in marriage,
but are like angels of God" [Mt. 22.30]'.

12. I spoke again: 'Lord, is it going to be possible in that world to
recognize one another—a brother his brother, a friend his friend, a
father his own children, or the children their own parents?' The voice
which I heard said: 'Listen, John, for the righteous there is *recognition*,
but definitely not for sinners: they are unable to recognize each other at
the resurrection'. Again I (John) spoke: 'Lord, is there *recollection* in
that world of the things here—fields or vineyards or other things here?'
I heard a voice which said: 'Listen, righteous John, David the prophet
states: "I remembered that we are dust. As for man, his days are like
grass; he flourishes like a flower of the field; for the wind passed over
it, and it will not exist, and it will know its place no more" (Ps. 103.14-
16 LXX). And David also said: 'His breath will depart and he returns to
his earth; on that day all his plans will perish' (Ps. 146.4 LXX)'.

13. I said again: 'Lord, what do you intend to do after that?' The
voice I heard said to me: 'Listen, righteous John, then I will send my
angels over all the earth's surface; they will take up from the earth all
that is wonderful and valuable, the revered and holy images, the glorious and precious crosses, the *churches' holy things*, and the divine and
sacred books; everything valuable and holy will be taken up with clouds
in the air. Then I will give orders for the lifting up of the great and

τὸ μέγα καὶ σεβάσμιον σκῆπτρον, ἐν ᾧ τὰς χεῖράς μου ἥπλωσα ἐν αὐτῷ, καὶ προσκυνήσουσιν αὐτῷ πάντα τὰ τάγματα τῶν ἀγγέλων μου. καὶ τότε ἀρθήσεται πᾶσα φύσις ἀνθρώπων ἐπὶ νεφελῶν, καθὼς προεῖπεν ὁ ἀπόστολος Παῦλος· ἅμα σύν αὐτοῖς ἁρπαγησόμεθα ἐν νεφέλαις εἰς ἀπάντησιν τοῦ κυρίου εἰς ἀέρα. καὶ τότε ἐξέλθῃ πᾶν πνεῦμα πονηρόν, τὰ ἐν τῇ γῇ, τὰ ἐν τῇ ἀβύσσῳ, ὅπου ἐάν εἰσιν ἐπὶ προσώπου πάσης τῆς γῆς ἀπο ἀνατολῶν ἡλίου μέχρι δυσμῶν, καὶ κολληθήσονται πρὸς τὸν ὑπηρετούμενον παρὰ τοῦ διαβόλου ἥτοι τὸν ἀντίχριστον, καὶ ἀρθήσονται ἐπὶ τῶν νεφελῶν.

14. Καὶ πάλιν εἶπον· κύριε, καὶ ἀπὸ τότε τί μέλλεις ποιεῖν; καὶ ἤκουσα φωνῆς λεγούσης μοι· ἄκουσον, δίκαιε Ἰωάννη· τότε ἀποστελῶ τοὺς ἀγγέλους μου ἐπὶ προσώπου πάσης τῆς γῆς, καὶ κατακαύσουσιν τὴν γῆν πήχας ὀκτακισχιλίας πεντακοσίας, καὶ κατακαήσονται τὰ ὄρη τὰ μεγάλα, καὶ αἱ πέτραι πᾶσαι χωνευθήσονται καὶ γενήσονται ὡσεὶ κονιορτός, καὶ κατακαήσονται πᾶν δένδρον καὶ πᾶν κτῆνος καὶ πᾶν ἑρπετὸν ἕρπον ἐπὶ τῆς γῆς καὶ πᾶν συρόμενον ἐπὶ προσώπου τῆς γῆς, καὶ πᾶν πετεινὸν πετόμενον ἐπὶ τὸν ἀέρα, καὶ οὐκέτι ἔσται ἐπὶ προσώπου πάσης τῆς γῆς σαλευόμενον τι, καὶ ἔσται ἡ γῆ ἀκίνητος.

15. Καὶ πάλιν εἶπον· κύριε, καὶ ἀπὸ τότε τί μέλλεις ποιεῖν; καὶ ἤκουσα φωνῆς λεγούσης μοι· ἄκουσον, δίκαιε Ἰωάννη· τότε ἀποσκεπάσω τὰ τέσσαρα μέρη τῆς ἀνατολῆς, καὶ ἐξέλθωσιν τέσσαρες ἄνεμοι μεγάλοι καὶ ἐκλικμήσουσιν πᾶν τὸ πρόσωπον τῆς γῆς ἀπὸ περάτων ἕως περάτων τῆς γῆς· καὶ ἐκλικμήσει κύριος τὴν ἁμαρτίαν ἀπὸ τῆς γῆς, καὶ λευκανθήσεται ἡ γῆ ὥσπερ χιών, καὶ γενήσεται ὡς χαρτίον, μὴ ἔχουσα σπήλαιον ἢ ὄρος ἢ βουνὸν ἢ πέτραν, ἀλλ' ἔσται τὸ πρόσωπον τῆς γῆς ἀπὸ ἀνατολῶν μέχρι δυσμῶν ὡς ἡ τράπεζα καὶ λευκὸν ὡσεὶ χιών· καὶ πυρωθήσονται οἱ νεφροὶ τῆς γῆς, καὶ βοήσει πρός με λέγουσα· παρθένος εἰμὶ ἐνώπιόν σου, κύριε, καὶ οὐκ ἔστιν ἐν ἐμοὶ ἁμαρτία. καθὼς προεῖπεν ὁ προφήτης Δαυίδ· ῥαντιεῖς με ὑσσώπῳ καὶ καθαρισθήσομαι, πλυνεῖς με καὶ ὑπὲρ χιόνα λευκανθήσομαι. καὶ πάλιν εἶπεν· πᾶσα φάραγξ πληρωθήσεται, καὶ πᾶν ὄρος καὶ βουνὸς ταπεινωθήσεται, καὶ ἔσονται τὰ σκολιὰ εἰς εὐθεῖαν καὶ αἱ τραχεῖαι εἰς ὁδοὺς λείας, καὶ ὄψεται πᾶσα σὰρξ τὸ σωτήριον τοῦ θεοῦ.

16. Καὶ πάλιν εἶπον· κύριε, καὶ ἀπὸ τότε τί μέλλεις ποιεῖν; καὶ ἤκουσα φωνῆς λεγούσης μοι· ἄκουσον, δίκαιε Ἰωάννη· τότε καθαρισθήσεται ἡ γῆ ἀπὸ τῆς ἁμαρτίας, καὶ πληρωθήσεται πᾶσα ἡ γῆ εὐωδίας διὰ τὸ μέλλειν με κατέρχεσθαι ἐπὶ τὴν γῆν· καὶ τότε ἐξέλθῃ τὸ μέγα καὶ σεβάσμιον σκῆπτρον μετὰ χιλιάδων ἀγγέλων θρησκεύοντες αὐτό, καθὼς προεῖπον· καὶ τότε φανήσεται τὸ σημεῖον τοῦ

venerated sceptre (cross) on which I stretched out my hands, and all the ranks of my angels will prostrate themselves before it. Then all mankind will be lifted up on clouds, just as the apostle Paul foretold ('together with them we shall be caught up in the clouds to *meet the Lord in the air*'—1 Thess. 4.17). Then every evil spirit will come out— those in the earth, those in the abyss, wherever they may be over all the earth's surface, from east to west—and they will be united with the devil's servant, that is Antichrist, and will be raised on the clouds'.

14. I spoke again: 'Lord, what do you intend to do then?' I heard a voice saying to me: 'Listen, righteous John, then I will send my angels over all the earth's surface. They will burn up the earth to a *depth of 4250* metres; the great mountains will be burnt up; all the rocks will be melted down and turn to dust. Every tree will be burnt up, and *all livestock* and reptiles on the earth, everything swarming on the earth's surface, and everything flying in the air; there will no longer be anything on the earth's surface that depends on it. The earth will be motionless'.

15. Again I said: 'Lord, what do you intend to do after this?' I heard a voice which said: 'Listen, righteous John, then I will uncover the four regions of the east, and *four great winds* will erupt and winnow the earth's surface from end to end. The Lord will *scatter* sin from the earth *like chaff*; the earth will be made white as snow. It will resemble a papyrus document. Without cave, mountain, hill or rock, the surface of the earth from east to west will be flat as a table and *white as snow*. The inward being of the earth will be set on fire, and a voice will call to me : 'Lord, I am a *sinless virgin* in your presence'. (Just as David prophesied: "Purge me with hyssop and I shall be clean; wash me and I shall be whiter than snow" [Ps. 51.7]. And on another occasion he said: "*Every valley* shall be filled up, and every mountain and hill be made low; the twisted places shall become straight, and the rough places level roads. And all flesh shall see God's salvation" [Isa. 40.4-5])'.

16. Again I said : 'Lord, what do you intend to do after this?' The voice I heard told me: 'Listen, righteous John, then the earth will be cleansed from sin; all the earth will be filled with fragrance, because I am about to descend to the earth. Next the great and venerated *sceptre* appears, with thousands of angels worshipping it. Then, *as I have said previously*, 'the *sign of the Son of Man*' will appear from heaven "with

υἱοῦ τοῦ ἀνθρώπου ἀπὸ τοῦ οὐρανοῦ μετὰ δυνάμεως καὶ δόξης πολλῆς. καὶ τότε θεωρήσει αὐτὸ ὁ τῆς ἀδικίας ἐργάτης μετὰ τῶν ὑπηρετῶν αὐτοῦ καὶ βρύξει μεγάλα, καὶ πάντα τὰ ἀκάθαρτα πνεύματα εἰς φυγὴν τραπήσονται. καὶ τότε ἀοράτῳ δυνάμει κρατούμενοι, μὴ ἔχοντες πόθεν φυγεῖν, βρύξουσιν κατ' αὐτοῦ τοὺς ὀδόντας αὐτῶν λέγοντες αὐτῷ· ποῦ ἔστιν ἡ δύναμίς σου; πῶς ἡμᾶς ἐπλάνησας; καὶ ἐξεφύγομεν καὶ ἐξεπέσαμεν ἐκ τῆς δόξης ἧς εἴχομεν παρὰ τοῦ ἐρχομένου κρῖναι ἡμᾶς καὶ πᾶσαν φύσιν ἀνθρωπίνην. οὐαὶ ἡμῖν, ὅτι ἐν τῷ σκότει τῷ ἐξωτέρῳ ἐξορίζει ἡμᾶς.

17. Καὶ πάλιν εἶπον· κύριε, καὶ ἀπὸ τότε τί μέλλεις ποιεῖν; καὶ ἤκουσα φωνῆς λεγούσης μοι· τότε ἀποστελῶ ἄγγελον ἐξ οὐρανοῦ, καὶ κράξει φωνῇ μεγάλῃ λέγων· ἄκουσον γῆ καὶ ἐνισχύου, λέγει κύριος· πρὸς σὲ γὰρ κατέρχομαι. καὶ ἀκουσθήσεται ἡ φωνὴ τοῦ ἀγγέλου ἀπὸ περάτων ἕως περάτων τῆς οἰκουμένης καὶ ἕως ἐσχάτου τῆς ἀβύσσου. καὶ τότε σαλευθήσεται πᾶσα ἡ δύναμις τῶν ἀγγέλων καὶ τῶν πολυομμάτων, καὶ γενήσεται κρότος μέγας ἐν τοῖς οὐρανοῖς, καὶ σαλευθήσονται τὰ ἐννέα πέταλα τοῦ οὐρανοῦ, καὶ γενήσεται φόβος καὶ ἔκστασις ἐπὶ πάντας τοὺς ἀγγέλους. καὶ τότε σχισθήσονται οἱ οὐρανοὶ ἀπὸ ἀνατολῶν ἡλίου μέχρι δυσμῶν, καὶ κατέλθωσιν ἐπὶ τὴν γῆν πλήθη ἀγγέλων ἀναριθμήτων, καὶ τότε ἀνοιχθήσονται οἱ θησαυροὶ τῶν οὐρανῶν, καὶ κατενέγκωσιν πᾶν τίμιον καὶ τῶν θυμιαμάτων τὴν εὐωδίαν, καὶ τὴν Ἱερουσαλὴμ ὥσπερ νύμφην ἐστολισμένην κατενέγκωσιν ἐπὶ τὴν γῆν. καὶ τότε ἔμπροσθέν μου πορεύσονται μυριάδες ἀγγέλων καὶ ἀρχαγγέλων, βαστάζοντες τὸν θρόνον μου, κράζοντες· ἅγιος ἅγιος ἅγιος κύριος Σαβαώθ· πλήρης ὁ οὐρανὸς καὶ ἡ γῆ τῆς δόξης σου. καὶ τότε ἐξελεύσομαι ἐγὼ μετὰ δυνάμεως καὶ δόξης πολλῆς, καὶ πᾶς ὀφθαλμὸς ἐπὶ τῶν νεφελῶν ὄψεταί με, καὶ τότε κάμψει πᾶν γόνυ ἐπουρανίων καὶ ἐπιγείων καὶ καταχθονίων· καὶ τότε μείνῃ ὁ οὐρανὸς κενὸς καὶ κατέλθω ἐπὶ τῆς γῆς, καὶ κατενεχθήσονται πάντα τὰ ἐν τῷ ἀέρι ἐπὶ τὴν γῆν, καὶ πᾶσα φύσις ἀνθρωπίνη καὶ πᾶν πνεῦμα πονηρὸν μετὰ τοῦ ἀντιχρίστου, καὶ σταθήσονται ἐνώπιόν μου πάντες γυμνοὶ καὶ τετραχηλισμένοι.

18. Καὶ πάλιν εἶπον· κύριε, πῶς μέλλουσιν γενέσθαι οἱ οὐρανοὶ καὶ ὁ ἥλιος καὶ ἡ σελήνη σὺν τοῖς ἄστροις; καὶ ἤκουσα φωνῆς λεγούσης μοι· θεώρησον, δίκαιε Ἰωάννη. καὶ ἀτενίσας εἶδον ἀρνίον ἑπτὰ ὀφθαλμοὺς ἔχοντα καὶ ἑπτα κέρη. καὶ ἤκουσα πάλιν φωνῆς λεγούσης μοι· κελεύσω ἐλθεῖν τὸ ἀρνίον ἔμπροσθέν μου καὶ ἐρῶ· τίς ἀνοίξει τὸ βιβλίον τοῦτο; καὶ ἀποκριθήσονται πάντα τὰ πλήθη τῶν ἀγγέλων· δοθήτω τὸ βιβλίον τοῦτο τῷ ἀρνίῳ τοῦ ἀνοῖξαι αὐτό. καὶ κελεύσω τότε

power and great glory". [Mt. 24.30]. The Evildoer and his servants will see it with great *gnashing of teeth*. All the unclean spirits will turn to flight. But then, restrained by an unseen power and having no means of flight, they will gnash their teeth against the Evildoer with these words: "Where is your power? How did you deceive us? We fled and fell from the glory which we possessed in the company of the one who is coming to judge us and all humankind. Woe to us, because he banishes us in the outer darkness."'

17. I spoke again: 'Lord, what do you intend to do after this?' I heard a voice which said to me: 'Then I will send an angel from heaven; he will call out in a *loud voice*: "Earth, listen and regain your strength, says the Lord; for I am coming down to you". The angel's voice will be heard from end to end of the world and to the furthest part of the abyss. Then the whole power, of the angels and the *many-eyed ones*, will be shaken; there will be a great din in heaven, and the *nine heavenly spheres* will be shaken. Terror and confusion will affect all the angels. Then the heavens will be torn apart from east to west, and a host of angels—too many to count—will descend to earth. Since Heaven's treasures will be opened, they will bring down to earth everything valuable, the fragrance of incense, and *Jerusalem dressed as a bride*. Then before me will go many thousands of angels and archangels, carrying my throne and proclaiming: "*Holy, holy, holy* is the Lord of Hosts; heaven and earth are full of your glory". Then will I appear with power and great glory; on the clouds every eye will look upon me, and *every knee will bend* in heaven, on earth and under the earth. Then *Heaven will remain empty* and I will descend to the earth. Everything in the air will be brought down to the earth, all humankind, and every evil spirit, together with the Antichrist. All will have to appear "*naked and prostrate*" before me'.

18. Again I said: 'Lord, what will become of the heavens, the sun, the moon and the stars?' The voice I heard said to me: 'Observe, righteous John'. Looking intently I saw a *lamb with seven eyes and seven horns*. Again I heard a voice saying to me: 'I will tell the lamb to come to me, and I will say: "Who will *open this book*?" All the angelic host will answer: "Give this book to the lamb to open". Then I will command that the book be opened'.

ἀνοιχθῆναι τὸ βιβλίον. 19. Καὶ ὅταν ἀνοίξῃ τὴν πρώτην σφραγῖδα, πεσοῦνται οἱ ἀστέρες τοῦ οὐρανοῦ ἀπ᾽ ἄκρων ἕως ἄκρων. καὶ ὅταν ἀνοίξῃ τὴν δευτέραν σφραγῖδα, κρυβήσεται ἡ σελήνη καὶ οὐκ ἔσται ἐν αὐτῇ φῶς. καὶ ὅταν ἀνοίξῃ τὴν τρίτην σφραγῖδα, κατασταλήσεται τοῦ ἡλίου τὸ φῶς, καὶ οὐκ ἔσται φῶς ἐπὶ τὴν γῆν. καὶ ὅταν ἀνοίξῃ τὴν τετάρτην σφραγῖδα, λυθήσονται οἱ οὐρανοὶ καὶ ἔσται ὁ ἀὴρ ἀκατασκεύαστος, καθώς φησιν ὁ προφήτης· καὶ ἔργα τῶν χειρῶν σου εἰσὶν οἱ οὐρανοί· αὐτοὶ ἀπολοῦνται, σὺ δὲ διαμένεις, καὶ πάντες ὡς ἱμάτιον παλαιωθήσονται. καὶ ὅταν ἀνοίξῃ τὴν πέμπτην σφραγῖδα, σχισθήσεται ἡ γῆ καὶ ἀποκαλυφθήσονται πάντα τὰ κριτήρια ἐπὶ προσώπου πάσης τῆς γῆς. καὶ ὅταν ἀνοίξῃ τὴν ἕκτην σφραγῖδα, ἐκλείψει τὸ δίμοιρον τῆς θαλάσσης. καὶ ὅταν ἀνοίξῃ τὴν ἑβδόμην σφραγῖδα, ἀποσκεπασθήσεται ὁ ᾅδης.

20. Καὶ εἶπον· κύριε, τίνες μέλλουσιν ἐρωτᾶσθαι πρῶτον καὶ ἀπολαβεῖν τὴν κρίσιν; καὶ ἤκουσα φωνῆς λεγούσης μοι· τὰ πνεύματα τὰ ἀκάθαρτα μετὰ τοῦ ἀντικειμένου· κελεύω αὐτοὺς πορευθῆναι εἰς τὸ σκότος τὸ ἐξώτερον, ἔνθα εἰσὶν τὰ ὑποβρύχια. καὶ εἶπον· κύριε, καὶ εἰς ποῖον τόπον κεῖται; καὶ ἤκουσα φωνῆς λεγούσης μοι· ἄκουσον, δίκαιε Ἰωάννη· ὅσον δύναται ἀνὴρ τριακονταέτης κυλίσαι λίθον καὶ ἀπολῦσαι κάτω εἰς τὸν βυθόν, καὶ ὀλισθεὶς εἴκοσι ἔτη οὐ μὴ φθάσει εἰς τὸν πυθμένα τοῦ ᾅδου· καθὼς προεῖπεν ὁ προφήτης Δαυίδ· καὶ ἔθετο σκότος ἀποκρυφὴν αὐτοῦ.

21. Καὶ εἶπον· κύριε, καὶ ἀπ᾽ ἐκείνων ποία γλῶσσα μέλλει ἐρωτᾶσθαι; καὶ ἤκουσα φωνῆς λεγούσης μοι· ἄκουσον, δίκαιε Ἰωάννη· ἐρωτηθήσονται ἀπὸ τοῦ Ἀδὰμ οἱ γλῶσσαι ἐκεῖναι καὶ ὁ ἑλληνισμός, καὶ οἵτινες ἐπίστευον εἰς τὰ εἴδωλα καὶ εἰς τὸν ἥλιον καὶ εἰς τοὺς ἀστέρας, καὶ οἵτινες ἐν αἱρέσει τὴν πίστιν ἐμίαναν, καὶ οἱ μὴ πιστεύσαντες τὴν ἁγίαν ἀνάστασιν, καὶ οἵτινες οὐχ ὡμολόγησαν πατέρα καὶ τὸν υἱὸν καὶ τὸ ἅγιον πνεῦμα· τότε ἀποπέμψω αὐτοὺς ἐν τῷ ᾅδῃ, καθὼς προεῖπεν ὁ προφήτης Δαυίδ· ἀποστραφήτωσαν οἱ ἁμαρτωλοὶ εἰς τὸν ᾅδην, πάντα τὰ ἔθνη τὰ ἐπιλανθανόμενα τοῦ θεοῦ. καὶ πάλιν ὁ αὐτὸς εἶπεν· ὡς πρόβατα ἐν ᾅδῃ ἔθετο, θάνατος ποιμανεῖ αὐτούς.

22. Καὶ πάλιν εἶπον· κύριε, καὶ ἀπ᾽ ἐκείνων ποίους μέλλεις κρίνειν; καὶ ἤκουσα φωνῆς λεγούσης μοι· ἄκουσον, δίκαιε Ἰωάννη· τότε ἐρωτηθήσεται τὸ γένος τῶν Ἑβραίων, οἵτινες ὡς κακοῦργον τῷ ξύλῳ με προσήλωσαν. καὶ εἶπον· καὶ οὗτοι ποίας κολάσεως μέλλουσιν τυχεῖν καὶ ποίου τόπου, ὅτι τοιαῦτά σοι ἐποίησαν; καὶ ἤκουσα φωνῆς λεγούσης μοι· αὐτοὶ ἀπελεύσονται ἐν τῷ ταρτάρῳ, καθὼς προεῖπεν ὁ προφήτης Δαυίδ· ἐκέκραξαν, καὶ οὐκ ἦν ὁ σῴζων, πρὸς κύριον, καὶ οὐκ

19. *When he opens the first seal*, the stars will fall, from one end of heaven to the other. When he opens the second seal, the moon will be hidden, with no light in her. When he opens the third seal, the sunlight will be kept back, and there will be no light on the earth. When he opens the fourth seal, the heavens will be dissolved, and the air will be in chaos, just as the prophet said ("*and the heavens are the works* of your hands; they will perish, but you remain, and they will all grow old like a garment" [Ps. 102.25-26]). When he opens the fifth seal, the earth will be torn apart, and all the places of judgment throughout the earth will be revealed. When he opens the *sixth seal, half the sea* will not exist. When he opens the *seventh seal, the Underworld* will be uncovered'.

20. I said: 'Lord, who will be first to be questioned and to receive judgment?' The voice I heard told me: 'The unclean spirits, together with *the Adversary*—I command them to go into the outer darkness, where the watery depths are'. I said: 'Where are they located?' The voice I heard said: 'Listen, righteous John, imagine the biggest stone which a *fit man of 30* can roll and allow to topple down into the depths. If it falls for 20 years, it will not reach the *bottom of the Underworld*. As David prophesied: 'He made *darkness a place of concealment* for him' (Ps. 18.11)'.

21. I said: 'Lord, which people will be interrogated after them?' I heard a voice which said: 'Listen, righteous John. All those nations *descended from Adam* will be questioned, especially *the Greek*—those who were believers in idols, in the sun and the stars; heretics who defiled the faith by *not believing in the holy Resurrection*; those who did not confess *Father, Son and Holy Spirit*. These I will then send away to the underworld, just as David prophesied: 'Let the sinners turn away to *Sheol*; all the nations that forget God' (Ps. 9.17). David also said: 'Like sheep they are appointed for Sheol; death shall be their shepherd' (Ps. 49.14)'.

22. I spoke again: 'Lord, after those whom will you judge?' The voice I heard said: 'Listen, righteous John. Then *the Hebrew race* will be questioned, those who *nailed me to the tree* like a criminal'. I said: 'What sort of punishment will these receive, and where, because they did such things to you?' I heard a voice saying to me: 'They will go to *Tartarus*, just as David prophesied: 'They cried for help, but there was none to save; they cried to the Lord, but he did not answer them'

εἰσήκουσεν αὐτούς. καὶ πάλιν εἶπεν ὁ ἀπόστολος Παῦλος· ὅσοι ἀνόμως ἥμαρτον ἀνόμως καὶ ἀπολοῦνται, καὶ ὅσοι ἐν νόμῳ ἥμαρτον διὰ νόμου κριθήσονται.

23. Καὶ πάλιν εἶπον· κύριε, καὶ οἱ τὸ βάπτισμα λαβόντες τί; καὶ ἤκουσα φωνῆς λεγούσης μοι· τότε ἐρωτηθήσεται τὸ γένος τῶν Χριστιανῶν, οἱ τὸ βάπτισμα λαβόντες, καὶ τότε οἱ δίκαιοι ὑπὸ νεύματός μου ἔλθωσιν, καὶ πορευθήσονται οἱ ἄγγελοι καὶ ἐπισωρεύσουσιν αὐτοὺς ἀπὸ τῶν ἁμαρτωλῶν, καθὼς προεῖπεν ὁ προφήτης Δαυὶδ ὅτι οὐκ ἀφήσει κύριος τὴν ῥάβδον τῶν ἁμαρτωλῶν ἐπὶ τὸν κλῆρον τῶν δικαίων, καὶ σταθήσονται πάντες οἱ δίκαιοι ἐκ δεξιῶν μου καὶ λάμψουσιν ὡς ὁ ἥλιος. καθὼς ὁρᾷς, Ἰωάννη, τοὺς ἀστέρας τοῦ οὐρανοῦ, ὅτι ὅλοι ὁμοῦ ἐγένοντο, εἰς δὲ τὸ φῶς διαφέρουσιν, οὕτως ἔσται ἐπὶ τῶν δικαίων καὶ τῶν ἁμαρτωλῶν· οἱ γὰρ δίκαιοι λάμψουσιν ὡς φωστῆρες καὶ ὡς ὁ ἥλιος, οἱ δὲ ἁμαρτωλοὶ ἔστωσαν ζοφώδεις.

24. Καὶ πάλιν εἶπον· κύριε, καὶ πάντες οἱ Χριστιανοὶ εἰς μίαν κόλασιν ἀπέρχονται; βασιλεῖς, ἀρχιερεῖς, ἱερεῖς, πατριάρχαι, πλούσιοι καὶ πένητες, δοῦλοι καὶ ἐλεύθεροι; καὶ ἤκουσα φωνῆς λεγούσης μοι· ἄκουσον, δίκαιε Ἰωάννη· καθὼς προεῖπεν ὁ προφήτης Δαυίδ, ἡ ὑπομονὴ τῶν πενήτων οὐκ ἀπολεῖται εἰς τέλος. περὶ δὲ βασιλέων, ἐλασθήσονται ὡς ἀνδράποδα καὶ κλαύσουσιν ὡς νήπια· περὶ δὲ πατριαρχῶν καὶ ἱερέων καὶ λευϊτῶν τῶν ἁμαρτησάντων, διασκορπισθήσονται ἐν ταῖς κολάσεσιν κατὰ τὴν ἀναλογίαν ἑκάστου τοῦ ἰδίου πταίσματος, οἱ μὲν ἐν τῷ πυρίνῳ ποταμῷ, οἱ δὲ εἰς τὸν σκώληκαν τὸν ἀκοίμητον, ἄλλοι δὲ ἐν τῷ ἑπταστόμῳ φρέατι τῆς κολάσεως· ἐν ταύταις ταῖς κολάσεσιν διαμερισθήσονται οἱ ἁμαρτωλοί.

25. Καὶ πάλιν εἶπον· κύριε, καὶ οἱ δίκαιοι ποῦ μέλλουσιν αὐλίζεσθαι; καὶ ἤκουσα φωνῆς λεγούσης μοι· τότε ἀποσκεπασθήσεται ὁ παράδεισος, καὶ γενήσεται ὁ κόσμος ὅλος καὶ ὁ παράδεισος ἕν, καὶ ἔσονται οἱ δίκαιοι ἐπὶ προσώπου πάσης τῆς γῆς μετὰ τῶν ἀγγέλων μου, καθὼς προεῖπεν τὸ πνεῦμα τὸ ἅγιον διὰ τοῦ προφήτου Δαυίδ· δίκαιοι δὲ κληρονομήσουσιν γῆν, καὶ κατασκηνώσουσιν εἰς αἰῶνα αἰῶνος ἐπ᾽ αὐτῆς.

26. Καὶ πάλιν εἶπον· κύριε, πόσον ἐστὶν τὸ πλῆθος τῶν ἀγγέλων; καὶ ποῖόν ἐστι πλέον, τῶν ἀγγέλων ἢ τῶν ἀνθρώπων; καὶ ἤκουσα φωνῆς λεγούσης μοι· ὅσον ἐστὶν τὸ πλῆθος τῶν ἀγγέλων, τόσον ἐστὶν τὸ γένος τῶν ἀνθρώπων, καθὼς εἶπεν ὁ προφήτης· ἔστησεν ὅρια ἐθνῶν κατὰ ἀριθμὸν ἀγγέλων θεοῦ.

27. Καὶ πάλιν εἶπον· κύριε, καὶ ἀπὸ τότε τί μέλλεις ποιεῖν; καὶ πῶς μέλλει εἶναι ὁ κόσμος; ἀποκάλυψόν μοι πάντα. καὶ ἤκουσα φωνῆς

(Ps. 18.41). Elsewhere the apostle Paul said: "All who sinned apart from the law will also perish apart from the law; all who sinned under the law will be *judged by the law*" (Rom. 2.12)'.

23. I spoke again: 'Lord, what about *the baptized*?' I heard a voice telling me: 'Then the "race" of Christians, the baptized, will be questioned; the righteous will come then at my command, and the angels will go and make a great collection of them from among the sinners, just as David prophesied that 'the Lord will not allow the *sceptre of the sinners* to rest upon the land allocated to the righteous' (Ps. 125.3). All the righteous "will be placed at [my] right hand" (Mt. 25.33) and 'will shine like the sun' (Mt. 13.43). Just as you, John, see the stars of heaven, that they were all created together but in terms of light "*star differs from star*" (1 Cor. 15.41), so it will be with the righteous and the sinners: for as lights "the righteous will shine like the sun", but let the sinners be in the dark'.

24. And again I said: 'Lord, and do all Christians go to *one kind of punishment*—kings, high priests, priests, patriarchs, rich and poor, slave and free?' And I heard a voice saying to me: 'Listen, righteous John. As the prophet David spoke before, "*the hope of the poor* shall not perish for ever" (Ps. 9.18). But as for kings, they will be driven like slaves and cry like babies; as for *patriarchs, priests and levites* who have sinned, they will be punished *differently, in proportion* to each individual error: some in *the river of fire*, some to *the worm that does not die* (Isa. 66.24; Mk 9.48), others in the *seven-mouthed punishment pit*. The sinners will be divided among these punishments'.

25. Again I said: 'Lord, where will the righteous live?' I heard a voice which told me: 'Then paradise will be revealed. The whole world and *paradise* will become one; and the righteous, together with my angels, will be spread over the whole earth, just as the Holy Spirit said before, by David the prophet: "*The righteous shall inherit the earth, and dwell upon it for ever*" (Ps. 37.29)'.

26. I said again: 'Lord, how great is the *number of the angels*? Which are more numerous, angels or human beings?' The voice I heard told me: 'The human race is as numerous as the angels, just as the prophet said: 'He fixed the bounds of the peoples according to the number of God's angels' (Deut. 32.8 LXX)'.

27. Again I spoke: 'Lord, after that what do you intend to do? How will the world be? Reveal everything to me'. I heard a voice which said:

λεγούσης μοι· ἄκουσον, δίκαιε ᾿Ιωάννη· ἀπὸ τότε οὐκ ἔστιν πόνος, οὐκ
ἔστιν λύπη, οὐκ ἔστιν στεναγμός, οὐκ ἔστιν μνησικακία, οὐκ ἔστιν
δάκρυα, οὐκ ἔστιν φθόνος, οὐκ ἔστιν μισαδελφία, οὐκ ἔστιν ἀδικία, οὐκ
ἔστιν ὑπερηφανία, οὐκ ἔστιν καταλαλία, οὐκ ἔστιν πικρία, οὐκ ἔστιν
μέριμνα βίου, οὐκ ἔστιν πόνος γονέων ἢ τέκνων, οὐκ ἔστιν πόνος χρυ-
σίου, οὐκ εἰσὶν πονηροὶ λογισμοί, οὐκ ἔστιν διάβολος, οὐκ ἔστιν θάνατος, οὐκ ἔστιν νὺξ ἀλλὰ πάντα ἡμέρα. καθὼς προείρηκα· καὶ ἄλλα
πρόβατα ἔχω, ἃ οὐκ ἔστιν ἐκ τῆς αὐλῆς ταύτης, τουτέστιν τοὺς
ἀνθρώπους τοὺς ὁμοιουμένους τῶν ἀγγέλων διὰ τῆς ἐναρέτου αὐτῶν
πολιτείας, κἀκεῖνά με δεῖ ἀγαγεῖν, καὶ τῆς φωνῆς μου ἀκούσωσιν, καὶ
γενήσεται μία ποίμνη, εἰς ποιμήν.

28. Καὶ πάλιν ἤκουσα φωνῆς λεγούσης μοι· ἰδοὺ ταῦτα πάντα
ἤκουσας, δίκαιε ᾿Ιωάννη· ταῦτα παράθου πιστοῖς ἀνθρώποις, ἵνα καὶ
ἐτέρους διδάξωσιν καὶ μὴ καταφρονήσωσιν, μηδὲ τοὺς μαργαρίτας
ἡμῶν ῥίψωσιν ἔμπροσθεν τῶν χοίρων, μή ποτε καταπατήσουσιν αὐτοὺς
ἐν τοῖς ποσὶν αὐτῶν.

Καὶ ἔτι μου ἀκούοντος τῆς φωνῆς ταύτης, κατήνεγκέ με ἡ νεφέλη
καὶ ἀπέθετό με ἐν τῷ ὄρει Θαβώρ. καὶ ἦλθεν φωνὴ πρός με λέγουσα·
μακάριοι οἱ φυλάττοντες κρίσιν καὶ ποιοῦντες δικαιοσύνην ἐν παντὶ
καιρῷ. καὶ μακάριός ἐστιν ὁ οἶκος ὅπου κεῖται ἡ διάθεσις αὕτη, καθὼς
εἶπεν ὁ κύριος ὅτι ὁ ἀγαπῶν με τοὺς λόγους μου τηρεῖ ἐν Χριστῷ
᾿Ιησοῦ τῷ κυρίῳ ἡμῶν· αὐτῷ ἡ δόξα εἰς τοὺς αἰῶνας, ἀμήν.

'Listen, righteous John: after that there is "no pain" (Rev. 21.4), no grief, no groaning, no bearing a grudge, no tears, no jealousy, no hatred of one's brother, no injustice, no arrogance, no slander, no animosity, none of the anxieties of life, no suffering for parents or children, no money-worries, no malicious thoughts, no devil, 'no death' (Rev. 21.4), and 'no night' (Rev. 21.25), but everything is daylight. As I have said before: 'And I have other sheep, that are not of this fold' (that is, *human beings made like angels* because of their *virtuous* way of life); 'I must bring them also, and they will heed my voice. So there shall be one flock, one shepherd' (Jn 10.16)'.

28. Once again I heard a voice which said: 'Take note, righteous John: you have heard all this; entrust it to faithful people, that they may teach others as well, not treating it with contempt, nor throwing our '*pearls before swine*, lest they trample them underfoot' (Mt 7.6)'.

As I still heard this voice, the cloud carried me down and deposited me on *Mt Tabor*. A voice came to me with these words: "*Blessed are they who observe justice*, who practise righteousness at all times" (Ps. 106.3). And *blessed is the house* where this attitude of mind prevails, in accord with the Lord's saying (Jn 14.23), '"If a man loves me he will keep my words" in Christ Jesus our Lord; to him be glory for ever, Amen'.

Explanatory Notes

1.

Mt Tabor: a steep-sided mountain rising from the Plain of Jezreel, with splendid views from the summit. Since the fourth century CE it has been regarded as the traditional site of the Transfiguration (Mk 9.2-8; Mt. 17.1-8; Lk. 9.28-36). It can be argued that the Transfiguration story anticipates, or is a misplaced version of, Christ's appearances after the Resurrection. In the canonical Apocalypse the site of the Revelation to John was the island of Patmos (1.9-10), but the experience was similarly overwhelming. The Mount of Olives is a much more usual setting in the tradition for such a post-Resurrection encounter, preceding Christ's Ascension (see Acts 1.12; *Apocryphon of John*).

undefiled fulness: cf. *Jn Chrys. Apoc.* 32 for the use of ἄχραντος. For the meaning 'undefiled by sin', applied to Christ's incarnation, see Athanasius, *Sermo major de fide* 13: τὸ χωρῆσαι δυνάμενον ἄχραντον σῶμα πᾶν τὸ πλήρωμα τῆς θεότητος σωματικῶς.

unable to stand: cf. Rev. 1.17. Extreme awe and involuntary prostration are a regular feature in accounts of theophanies and angelophanies (see, e.g., *2 En.* 1.7; Mt. 28.4).

2.

seven days: the conventional time measurement in apocalyptic of 'the week'.

cloud: cf. the guiding function of the pillars of cloud and fire for Israel during the wilderness wanderings (Exod. 13.21).

voice: the voice from whom John receives revelation, and with whom he engages in dialogue is indefinite and unidentified throughout the work. But it clearly belongs within the Jewish tradition of the *Bath qol* and should be regarded as the voice of God. The interventions of this voice are decisive and authoritative in the same way as the voice from the whirlwind answers Job (Job 38.1). A modern reader naturally might equate it with the powerful voice of conscience, or the 'independent inner voice' of aesthetic inspiration referred to by Harold Bloom (*Ruin the Sacred Truths: Poetry and Belief from the Bible to the Present* [Harvard: Harvard University Press, 1989] p. 32). But care must be taken not to diminish the transcendence of the voice, over which even the righteous John can have no control.

incense: cf. Rev. 8.3-5. But in *2 Apoc. Jn* the incense clearly belongs in the tradition of Old Testament sacrifice. It is debated to what extent the death of Christ was seen in Revelation as the fulfilment of Old Testament sacrificial prototypes (contrast the letter to the Hebrews).

3.

righteous John: δίκαιε has the primary connotation of 'righteous', on analogy with Old Testament saints and prophets; the term was applied quite widely by the Patristic writers to faithful Christians. As a special title it is better known as applied to St James (cf. *3 Apoc. Jn*).

book with seven seals: the basis is the 'scroll with seven seals' which only the Lamb can open (Rev. 5–6). In *2 Apoc. Jn* the dimensions of the book are exaggerated to be inconceivable, just as the revelation is immense and all-encompassing (see *2 Apoc. Jn* 4). One might give an approximation of the size as seven times that of Mt Tabor; an alternative reading describes a book 'seven hundred cubits thick'.

4.

abyss: cf. Rev. 9.11; 11.7; 17.8; 20.3. The underworld is contrasted with heaven and earth.

righteousness: cf. Jn 16.8. One manuscript clarifies the reference to judgment ('verdicts') in *2 Apoc. Jn* by adding a brief description of the Last Judgment, as seen by the prophet Daniel (7.9-10), and citing Jesus' promise to the 12 apostles that they would take part in the process of judgment (Mt. 19.28; Lk. 22.30).

5.

righteous John: one manuscript inserts a quotation of Lk. 21.11 at this point.

corn and wine: this single year of plenty could be related to the seven good years in Pharaoh's dream (Gen. 41); in the same way it will be succeeded by famine conditions.

The predicted blessing of a time of paradise and cornucopia is attributed to Jesus himself, on the authority of John the Lord's disciple, as reported by Papias and other elders:

> The days will come, in which vines shall grow, each having ten thousand branches, and in each branch ten thousand twigs, and in each true twig ten thousand shoots, and in each one of the shoots ten thousand clusters, and on every one of the clusters ten thousand grapes, and every grape

when pressed will give five and twenty metretes of wine. And when any one of the saints shall lay hold of a cluster, another shall cry out, 'I am a better cluster, take me; bless the Lord through me.' In like manner the Lord declared that a grain of wheat would produce ten thousand ears, and that every ear should have ten thousand grains, and every grain would yield ten pounds of clear, pure, fine flour; and that all other fruit-bearing trees, and seeds and grass, would produce in similar proportions; and that all animals feeding on the productions of the earth, should in those days become peaceful and harmonious among each other, and be in perfect subjection to man. And these things are borne witness to in writing by Papias, the hearer of John, and a companion of Polycarp, in his fourth book (Irenaeus, *Adv. Haer.* 5.33.3-4).

Cf. *2 Bar.* 29.5: The earth will also yield fruits ten thousandfold. And on one vine will be a thousand branches, and one branch will produce a thousand clusters, and one cluster will produce a thousand grapes, and one grape will produce a cor of wine (translation by A.F.J. Klijn, *OTP*, I, p. 630).

In the following year: the corresponding scenario is of the lean years of famine. It closely resembles the projection of the world's end, as in the book of *Jubilees*:

Behold, the land will be corrupted on account of all their deeds, and there will be no seed of the vine, and there will be no oil because their works are entirely faithless. And all of them will be destroyed together. (23.18, translation by O.S. Wintermute in *OTP*, II, p. 101).

6.

what do you intend: the answer to this question is deferred to the latter part of ch. seven.

Denier: ἀρνητής does not seem to be widely used as an alternative name for the Antichrist, although it was later used of iconoclasts and Saracens. But *2 Apoc. Jn*'s use is appropriate, because the root verb is widely used from the New Testament onward of the act of denying Christ or God or the truth and power of religion (see Rev. 2.13; 3.8). In the spurious work *de consummatione mundi* (ch. 28), attributed to Hippolytus, it is recognised that in gematria the letters APNOYME total 666 (Rev. 13.18).

7.

on his forehead: see Rev. 13.16; 17.5; 20.4. This is the place where a slave is branded to indicate the master's name.

Antichrist: the actual name is found in the New Testament in the

Johannine letters (1 Jn 2.18, 22; 4.3; 2 Jn 7); the concept and the characterization, without the actual name, is found in Rev. 12–13; 17 and
2 Thess. 2. It is scarcely surprising that in the various manuscripts of
2 *Apoc. Jn* the description of Antichrist has been enhanced and developed in a number of ways. The longest addition reads:

> He holds in his hand a cup of death; all his worshippers drink from it.
> [His two eyes do not match because] when he was taken prisoner by
> Michael [cf. Rev. 12.7-8], the archangel took his divine status from him;
> and I was sent from the bosom of my Father, and I snatched up the head
> of the defiled one and his eye was extinguished. Here they will worship
> him, and he writes on their right hands, so that they may sit with him in
> the outer ring of fire. Otherwise it is not possible to be protected: all who
> have not been initiated—the unbelievers [as far as the Antichrist is con-
> cerned]—for them is reserved all anger and wrath. I said, 'My Lord,
> what miracles does he perform?' 'Listen, righteous John: he will remove
> mountains and hills. He will gesture with his defiled hand, "Come to me,
> all of you." Through display and deceit they are gathered in his own
> place; he raises the dead and in everything creates the impression of
> being god.

manifestations: at this point one manuscript adds an anti-Semitic
reference—'he will love especially the race of the Hebrews; but the
righteous will hide themselves and flee to hills and caves. He will pun-
ish many of the righteous. Happy is the one who will not believe in
him.' (cf. Mk 13.14 and //s; Rev. 6.15)

brazen: metaphorical from the imperviousness of a vessel made of
metal—for the metal in Rev. see 1.15; 2.18; 9.20; 18.12 and Colin J.
Hemer, *The Letters to the Seven Churches of Asia in their Local Setting*
(JSNTSup, 11; Sheffield: JSOT Press, 1986), pp. 111-17.

wind will not blow: see Rev. 7.1

8.

three years: the reduction in the waiting-time expresses in a somewhat
literalistic manner the idea from Mt. 24.22; Mk 13.20 that 'the days are
shortened...for the sake of the elect'.

Enoch and Elijah: the two witnesses in Rev. 11 have often been identified as Moses and Elijah; but an important alternative for Christian
exegetes since Irenaeus and Hippolytus was to see them as Enoch and
Elijah). It is easier to think of Enoch and Elijah as returning at the last
day, to play a key role in the confrontation of the Antichrist/Beast,

because at the end of their earthly lives they were both 'taken' by God, and translated to heaven, rather than dying and being buried in the normal way (Gen. 5.22, 24; *1 En.* 90.31; Heb. 11.5; *1 Clem.* 9.3; 2 Kgs 2.11; Mal. 4.5; *1 Clem.* 17.1; Rev. 11.12). The encounter between Enoch, Elijah and the Antichrist is described in *Apoc. Elij.* 4–19:

> Then when Elijah and Enoch hear that the shameless one has revealed himself in the holy place, they will come down and fight with him... They will scold him saying, 'O shameless one, O son of lawlessness. Are you indeed not ashamed of yourself since you are leading astray the people of God for whom you did not suffer? Do you not know that we live in the Lord?' (trans. O.S. Wintermute, *OTP*, I, pp. 747-48).

The *Apocalypse of Elijah* seems to be a composite of Jewish and Christian traditions; the Christian developments, including the probable use of Revelation and 1 John, may well be from the third century CE.

prophet: the quotation attributed to 'the prophet' is from Ps. 51. But David, as the traditional author of the Psalms, is consistently regarded as a prophet in *2 Apoc. Jn* (see the verb 'prophesied' with the quotation from Ps. 89 above). The substantial use in this work of formula quotations from the Psalms (see table of quotations in Conclusion) is the more understandable if they are regarded both as a living part of the community liturgy and also (along with much else from the Old Testament) as having prophetic importance for Christians. An interesting comparison (and possible precedent) for such usage can be found much earlier in Mt. 13.35, where the quotation is attributed to a prophet (or Isaiah), while the actual quotation is substantially Ps. 78.2 (admittedly with some influence from Isa. 29.14).

The reference to the sacrifice of bulls in Ps. 51.19 is applied to the great sacrifice of the martyred witnesses who dared to confront the Antichrist.

9.

no human being is alive: one manuscript has substantial additions, e.g.:

> Those who have gold and silver will throw them into the streets, and into every inhabited place, and nobody will pay any attention. They will throw into the streets ivory vessels and robes decorated with stones and pearls. Kings and rulers waste away with hunger, as do patriarchs and abbots, priests and people. Where is the fine wine, the banquets and pomp of the world? Nowhere in the world shall they be found. Men will die on the mountains, in the streets, and everywhere in the world. The

living will die from the stench of the dead... Whoever does not worship
that beast and his apparitions, will be called a witness/martyr in the kingdom of heaven, and will inherit eternal life with my saints.

ram's horns: the Jewish *shofar* sounded on ceremonial occasions and
for a formal proclamation. It may now seem too late for the call to
penitence with which these horns are often associated (cf. Num. 29.1;
Lev. 23.24, traditionally linked with the horn of the ram in Gen. 22.13).
Rather this is the eschatological day on which 'a great trumpet will be
blown' (Isa. 27.13). The entire human species is being summoned by
the penetrating blasts of these horns.

Michael and Gabriel: the two archangels are named here, as Michael
(Dan. 10.13, 21; 12.1; Jude 9; Rev. 12.7 [see note on *2 Apoc. Jn* 7,
above]) and Gabriel (cf. Dan. 8.16; 9.21; *1 En.* 9.1; Lk. 1.19, 26).

10.

thirty-year-olds: for reference to this age see also *2 Apoc. Jn* 20. Such
an age is chosen for two reasons, one commonplace, the other theological. Aged 30 a man is assumed to be at the peak of maturity and
physical powers. Since this is also how old Jesus was at his crucifixion,
the age is consecrated as the symbol of manhood made perfect.

One might compare C.S. Lewis's description of heaven (*The Great
Divorce* [London: Bles, 1945], p. 29):

> Some were bearded but no one in that company struck me as being of
> any particular age. One gets glimpses, even in our country, of that which
> is ageless—heavy thought in the face of an infant, and frolic childhood
> in that of a very old man.

Notice also the characterization as cherubim of the inhabitants of
the 'Citie...in Eden'—'Sparkling Eys fair Skins and ruddy faces'—in
Thomas Traherne's *Centuries of Meditations* 3.3, quoted above in the
Introduction to this Apocalypse.

11.

at the resurrection: see 1 Cor. 15.35 for the prototype of this question.
The answer given in *2 Apoc. Jn* has unusual features, particularly the
analogy with bees. One is uncertain whether to use this as evidence of a
rural context for the work, or, conversely, to argue that a countryman
would know better and could tell bees apart. There is clearly no risk of
racial discrimination in heaven, whatever may be the reality on earth.

Compared with Paul's questioner, the curiosity about the nature of resurrection is increased; but the question is no longer focused on bodily resurrection, and the answer uses the quotation from Matthew to exclude the relevance of any shape or form of body.

12.

recognition: the ability to recognize one another is a privilege of the righteous in the heavenly world; such identification clearly does not depend on external characteristics. For sinners, resurrected for the last judgment, it is part of their punishment that they cannot recognise each other. To my knowledge this idea is unique to *2 Apoc. Jn.*

recollection: the two proof-texts from the Psalms are used to exclude ultimately any positive answer to John's wistful question. All that one 'remembers' is one's own mortality; the context and ambitions of this ephemeral existence are not transferable. This excludes the possibility of stray recollections that can be used as proof for reincarnation, and any theory of anamnesis such as Plato developed in the dialogues of Socrates.

13.

the churches' holy things: what is now made explicit for the first time is the existence of church-treasures and the valuables belonging to religious institutions. Unlike the ephemera of human life, these spiritual jewels are raised on the clouds for the Parousia.

venerated sceptre: the specific inclusion of the 'true cross', in the list of ecclesiastical valuables, is a positive help in the dating of this document (see Introduction). In later church tradition the 'true cross' refers particularly to the double-barred or 'patriarchal' cross, as in the Liudhard Medalet (Liverpool Museum M7018)—the inscription on this coin refers to Bishop Liudhard, the Frankish chaplain of Queen Bertha of Kent.

meet the Lord in the air: the description of the Parousia, or triumphal second coming of Jesus Christ, is modelled explicitly on the early concept found in 1 Thessalonians. Its great advantage for later imaginative development seems to be its 'in-between' location (neither earth nor heaven). There can be a parallel resurrection of Antichrist and his adherents, without admitting them to heaven itself. And the surrounding world can be swept as in a cosmic spring-cleaning, so that the entire universe, earth and heaven, is rigorously destroyed or purified.

14.

depth of 4250 metres: the measurement is given in the text in 'cubits'—
a measure of length, two of which approximately equal a metre. Two
manuscripts read 'eight thousand five hundred cubits', but there are
variant readings of 'five hundred', 'one thousand eight hundred', and
'thirty', all 'cubits', and also a proportion 'sixty per cent' of the earth.
Since a general destruction on the earth's surface is next referred to, it
seems more likely that the present measurement describes the depth of
the universal scorching (so preventing the continuance of life), rather
than a selective burning over a certain radius 4250 metres distant from
an unknown point.

Ancient measurements are notoriously variable: if the Roman standard cubit is used, the distance/depth is slightly over 2½ Roman miles;
with the Royal cubit we reach 3 Roman miles; if the cubit is 2ft. the
measurement would be 3½ Roman miles. Perhaps it is more relevant to
explore the possible significance in symbolism (or even gematria) of
such a dimension in the present context. There is a Jewish tradition that
a replica of the heavenly Jerusalem will appear in the clouds, 18 miles
above the site of the earthly Jerusalem. In the present context which
speaks of a reunion 'in the air', it may be intended to ensure that the
earth beneath is purified with fire to at least a corresponding depth. This
might explain the reading of 1800 cubits. The majority reading of 8500
cubits might be explained as the result of multiplying the mathemati-
cally interesting number 17 by 500 (compare the symbolic number of
153 fish in Jn 21.11). Adding religious to mathematical interest, 17 is
itself the sum of 7 and 10, both of which figure in Revelation. Any
solution in terms of gematria for 8500 has yet to be discovered, and is
fairly unlikely because of the size of the total.

all livestock: in this description there is a clear reversal of the process
of creation (see, e.g., Gen. 1.30).

15.

four great winds: see Rev. 7.1; Mk 13.27; Mt. 24.31

scatter like chaff: the image is the agricultural one of winnowing on
the threshing floor.

white as snow: snow is a traditional symbol of perfect whiteness.
Here whiteness is surely intended as the absence of colour; in contrast
its meaning is much more positive in Mt. 28.3 and Rev. 1.14

sinless virgin: see Rev. 14.4

'*Every valley*': notice that the quotation from Isaiah is introduced (inadvertently?) by a formula which attributes it to David ('the prophet' —see note to *2 Apoc. Jn* 8, above). One manuscript corrects the mistake by reading 'Again another prophet has said'.

16.
sceptre: see note to *2 Apoc. Jn* 13, above.

as I have said previously: with an appropriate simplicity this formula is used to introduce Gospel quotations of Jesus' words. See also *2 Apoc. Jn* 27.

'*sign of the Son of Man*': in this context the 'sign' (quotation from Mt. 24.30—*not* Mk 13.26) is applied directly to the cross itself, as the instrument of Jesus' suffering and glorification. Beyond the imagery of Dan. 7, Matthew seems to have thought of some heavenly phenomenon to balance the star at Christ's birth. But in apocryphal texts (e.g. *Apocalypse of Peter*) the cross plays an active role in Christ's resurrection; it therefore becomes conventional in patristic writers to interpret Matthew's reference as being to the cross as the symbol of what Christ's death represents (cf. Jn 3.14).

gnashing of teeth: the verb βρύχω is used in the adversarial sense of Acts 7.54, while Matthew's use of the noun βρυγμός (8.12; 13.42, 50; 22.13; 24.51; 25.30) is at least as much to do with grief as anger.

17.
loud voice: for the loud voice of angelic pronouncement to the whole world compare Rev. 14.6-7.

many-eyed ones: designates a distinct order in the angelic hierarchy, often identified with the cherubim and seraphim found in the visions of Isaiah and Ezekiel.

nine heavenly spheres: the word translated 'sphere' is πέταλον (usually 'leaf' or 'plate', as for the golden plate on the breast or the mitre of the High Priest—Exod. 28.36 [32 LXX]); πέταλα πύρινα refers to the stars in a single text in Aelius Arabus, *Placita Philosophorum* 2.14.4; it is also used of a heavenly sphere in a fragment of the *Gospel of Bartholomew* 4.30, with reference to the first of the seven heavens, where are located the powers which operate on human beings. In terms of a mystic or gnostic ascent through the heavens to the highest realm, the actual number of heavens varies between three and seven (cf. *T. Levi* 2.7-10; 3.1-4; *Asc. Isa.* 7–9). There are then twin possibilities: either

2 Apoc. Jn uses nine instead of seven as an exaggeration, so as to be fully comprehensive of the entire universe; or these nine spheres are the full total of the powers which operate in the first level of heaven (where, perhaps, the mid-air encounter of the Parousia is thought to happen).

Jerusalem dressed as a bride: see Rev. 21.2, 9.

'Holy, holy, holy': see Isa. 6.3; Rev. 4.8.

every knee will bend: see Isa. 45.23 (LXX); Phil. 2.10.

Heaven will remain empty: just as the earth was evacuated at an earlier stage (*2 Apoc. Jn* 13), so now Heaven is literally emptied as all heavenly realities are manifested on a purified earth.

naked and prostrate: the quotation is from Heb. 4.13 ('Before him no creature is hidden, but all are naked and laid bare to the eyes of the one to whom we must render an account'). This text was naturally applied in patristic exegesis to the specific occasion of the Last Judgment. The root of the word translated 'prostrate' is τράχηλος ('neck'); the literal meaning is 'seized by the neck' (or twisted, even chained, by the neck). The image could be of captives in the victor's triumph. But Hesychius and Oenomaus both explain τραχηλίζειν as a synonym of 'open' or 'reveal'; perhaps the idea is of something being revealed by having its cover 'unscrewed'.

18.

Lamb with seven eyes and seven horns: see Rev. 5.6, quoted here with only slight alteration.

open this book?: see Rev. 5.2, quoted with one alteration. The book was described, with exaggerated dimensions, in *2 Apoc. Jn* 3 above.

19.

When he opens the first seal: the ensuing sequence, the consequences of opening the seven seals individually, is retained from Rev. 6.1–8.1, but much of the detailed contents (especially the four horsemen) is missing. In *2 Apoc. Jn* the material derives substantially from one seal, the sixth, in Rev. 6.12-17. The order of the elements is also varied, because Revelation's sixth seal begins with the earthquake and the eclipse of the sun. The selection of material from the sixth, rather than any previous, seal is not accidental: as has been observed, it is at this point that the plague sequence reaches a cosmic dimension. 'With the opening of the sixth seal the perspectives have altered. No longer is the subject-matter concentrated on the special circumstances of the Asia Minor congregations, but a cosmic dimension is opened up for the first time by the decription of the great earthquake and the cataclysmic portents in the heavens. The pattern is substantially that of the Synoptic apocalyptic tradition, with the qualification Charles noted, namely that the earthquake has been placed in the context of a cosmic, rather than a local, dimension'. (J.M. Court, *Myth and History in the Book of Revelation* [London: SPCK, 1979], p. 67)

The material can be tabulated as follows:

2 Apoc. Jn *19*	*Themes*	*Revelation 6*
First	Falling of stars	Stars fall (6.13)
Second	Eclipse of moon	Moon as blood (6.12) Eclipse cf. Mk 13.24, Mt.24.29
Third	Eclipse of sun	Eclipse of sun (6.12)
Fourth	Heavens dissolved Chaos of the air	Sky vanishes (6.14)
Fifth	Earthquakes	Great earthquake (6.12)
	Sites of judgment revealed	Mountains and islands moved (6.14)
		Hiding from judgment (6.16-17)

'and the heavens are the works': yet again a Psalm text is introduced as a prophetic quotation. Ps. 102.25-26 is also quoted in Heb. 1.10-11, which may be more significant because of the use of Hebrews at the conclusion of *2 Apoc. Jn* 17.

sixth seal, half the sea: with the opening of this sixth seal, the dependence upon the material of Revelation's sixth seal is at an end. But there are still more general echoes of Revelation here, in two respects. The proportion of the sea affected is one half; this might be related to the fractions which are part of Revelation's significant symbolism of numbers, showing the increasing range of the destructive forces. In Rev. 11.13 (during a flashback) the fraction is one tenth; with the sounding of the second trumpet (8.8-9) one third of the sea turns to blood; while at the pouring of the second bowl (16.3) the totality of the sea is polluted and all its life dies. If the reminiscence of Revelation is intended, then the action has not yet reached that ultimate stage. In Revelation, as in Hebraic traditions, the underlying thought is of the sea as an alien element, associated with Tiamat in the Babylonian antecedent of the creation myth. It is not therefore surprising that Rev. 21.1

proclaims the total absence of the sea in the new heaven and earth (cf. *T. Levi* 4.1).

seventh seal, the Underworld: here the series might seem to have parted company with Revelation entirely. But Hades is mentioned in Revelation: the risen Christ has the keys to unlock the realm of death and Hades (1.18); the pale horse, revealed as the fourth seal is opened, has death as its rider and Hades as accompanying shadow (6.8); but the significant reference—for this and the previous seal in the sequence of *2 Apoc. Jn* 19—is Rev. 20.13. Both the sea and death/Hades are to surrender, for the last judgment, the dead in their respective realms. (See R. Bauckham, 'Resurrection as Giving Back the Dead', in J.H. Charlesworth and C.A. Evans [eds.], *The Pseudepigrapha and Early Biblical Interpretation* [JSPSup, 14; SSEJC, 2; Sheffield: Sheffield Academic Press, 1993], pp. 269-91). Exactly this stage has now been reached in the present apocalypse.

20.

the Adversary: the term, literally 'someone in opposition', is applied to the devil (*1 Clem.* 51.1) and to the Antichrist (2 Thess. 2.4).

fit man of thirty: cf. note to *2 Apoc. Jn* 10.

bottom of the underworld: see Rev. 20.2-3 for the 'bottomless pit'. Here the point is laboured: with the greatest athlete hurling it, the heaviest weight will not have reached the bottom after falling for 20 years.

'darkness a place of concealment': in the Old Testament the Hebrew 'Sheol' is usually rendered in the Septuagint by 'Hades' (see note on *2 Apoc. Jn* 19 above). 'Hades' then represents the darkness, the temporary or permanent realm of the dead (particularly, but not always, the evil spirits) that is located under the ocean (Job 10.21-22; 26.5) or at the heart of the earth (cf. Mt. 12.40), in either case at the maximum depth (cf. Mt. 11.23; Lk 10.15). The prophetic proof-text from Ps. 18.11 bristles with problems of its own (although none are of great relevance to the present application). 2 Sam. 22 and Ps. 18 run parallel, though they diverge at this verse which is thought to be corrupt (see F.M. Cross and D.N. Freedman, 'A Royal Song of Thanksgiving 2 Samuel 22= Psalm 18', *JBL* 72 [1953], pp. 15-34). The general tenour of the Psalm is of thanksgiving that the psalmist (a royal person) has been rescued by a theophany. God's action in 'coming down' is described in terms reminiscent of Baal in the Ugaritic texts. Thus God seems to wrap himself in the dark storm clouds. Peter C. Craigie translated this verse: 'He

made darkness his den; his lair round about was dense clouds, dark with water' (*Psalms 1–50* [WBC, 19; Waco, TX: Word Books, 1983], p. 166). The apocalyptic use takes it out of context, for the only links are the darkness, the associated watery depths, and being enveloped.

21.

descended from Adam: cf. the genealogy of Jesus in Lk. 3.38. Luke's divergence from the genealogy traced to Abraham in Matthew has at least two explanations. In the context of Jesus' baptism (see 3.22) Luke is exploring what it means to talk of 'son of God'. But Luke also sees the descent from Adam as that which relates Jesus to the whole of humanity. The latter is clearly the point in *2 Apoc. Jn* where the universal nature of this interrogation is stressed.

the Greek: it has already been observed how this writer keeps a distance from the Greeks—although he writes in Greek he will not identify with the philosophical or religious traditions which he regards as idolatrous, pagan or heretical.

not believing in the holy Resurrection: see also Apocalypse of Paul 42: in the place of punishment are 'those who say that Christ has not risen from the dead and that this flesh does not rise' (*New Testament Apocrypha* [ed. W. Schneemelcher; Cambridge: James Clark, 1992], II, p. 735). Greek difficulties with the doctrines of Resurrection (the relationship between the resurrection of Christ and the future hope of a general resurrection) were indicated in St Paul's Corinthian correspondence (1 Cor. 15.12-13). Subsequently in Christian history there is a wide variety of groups who denied the physical resurrection, beginning from the Docetists who are Ignatius's concern, and including the Marcionites, a number of gnostic sects, and the Manichees. The particular association in the present text with a Trinitarian heresy may assist a more precise identification (for this see the discussion in the Introduction).

Father, Son and Holy Spirit: the full Trinitarian confession. Especially after Arius there was a rich assortment of heresies about the doctrine of the Trinity.

Sheol: see note on Hades at *2 Apoc. Jn* 20 above.

22.

the Hebrew race: New Testament usage of Ἑβραῖος regularly denotes those who speak Hebrew (or Aramaic) as opposed to those who speak

Greek (Acts 6.1). In Greek Patristic writings it is the usual synonym for
'Jew'.

nailed me to the tree: see Acts 5.30; 10.39-40; Gal. 3.13; 1 Thess.
2.15; Deut. 21.22-23.

Tartarus: the Greeks thought of Tartarus as a subterranean place
(deep and dark but not wet), the ultimate place of divine punishment,
even lower than the realm of Hades (Homer, *Iliad* 8.13, 481; Hesiod,
Theog. 807). It is as far beneath Hades as the earth is below heaven.
A similar idea is reflected in Jewish apocalyptic (see Job 41.24 LXX;
2 Pet. 2.4; *Apoc. En.* 20.2; Philo, *Exsecr.* 152; Josephus, *Apion* 2.240;
Sib. Or. 2.302; 4.186)

'judged by the law': Paul's conclusions about universal sinfulness are
quoted unsophisticatedly here, with emphasis—one might feel—on the
poetic justice of the final clause.

23.

the baptized: the fourth category to come to interrogation, after evil
spirits, Greek heretics and Jewish sinners, are baptized Christians. The
collective noun for Christians is γένος, in the sense of the 'third race'
after pagans and Jews (cf.1 Pet. 2.9; *Mart. Pol.* 3.2; 14.1; 17.1; *Letter to
Diognetus* 1; Hermas, *Similitudes* 9.17.5; Clement of Alexandria, *Stro-
mateis* 6.5)

'sceptre of the sinners': the quotation comes from a Psalm (125.3)
which originally had a political orientation on historical Israel and its
confidence in God's kingship in Jerusalem. The power of the wicked
(the enemy) will prove ineffectual in any attempt at conquest. Out of
this context, the reapplication simply concerns the separation of the sinners and the righteous, like the goats and the sheep at God's seat of
judgment (Mt. 25.33).

'star differs from star': St Paul's argument in 1 Cor. 15.41 concerns
the distinctiveness between heavenly bodies (sun, moon and stars) as
the basis for his hope that God will allocate an appropriate range of
'heavenly' bodies at the resurrection from the dead. This text is distorted, as applied in *2 Apoc. Jn*, and simply means that sinners and righteous are distinct and separable. If Paul's argument had been applied
more directly, it would have been at odds with *2 Apoc. Jn* 11 and 12.

'the righteous will shine like the sun': Matthew's text (13.43) is more
appropriate since it is the conclusion of a parable of judgment concerning the weeds. But in *2 Apoc. Jn* there is a simple dualism between light

and darkness (which has been in the author's mind since ch. 20), rather than the sun of God's kingdom contrasted with the fire of judgment.

24.

one kind of punishment: if all those resurrected appear identical, should there not be egalitarian terms of punishment for sinners? But clearly Greeks, Jews and Christians are processed separately, and there also appear to be social distinctions among the Christians. But as in some Old Testament justice, there may be an idea of revenge within the punishment; thus sinners with the greatest resources, such as political or spiritual power, will suffer the most. It is not just redressing the balance, like Dives and Lazarus (Lk. 16.19-31); there could be a measure of anti-clericalism as well.

'the hope of the poor': Craigie (*Psalms 1–50*, p. 114) translated the Hebrew of Psalm 9.18: 'for the poor will not always be forgotten, nor will the hope of the afflicted perish forever.' God does not forget his own, in contrast to the way the nations forget God (v. 17). Craigie commented: 'the word "poor" is synonymous with "afflicted", in this context, and refers not to the absence of wealth, but to those righteous servants of God who suffer unjustly at the hands of evil persons, yet whose "hope" (or "expectation" of God's intervention) does not "perish"—though the enemies who are the cause of such suffering shall indeed "perish" (v. 4)'. Such sentiments persist in the application in *2 Apoc. Jn*, but it is clear from the contrast with wealth and privilege that poverty is taken more literally. The force of the Psalmist's 'prophecy' is needed to supply the positive idea of restoration for the poor in the apocalyptic scenario.

patriarchs, priests and levites: πατριάρχης is used in the Septuagint of the fathers of the Hebrew nation, such as Abraham; from the sixth century CE the term referred to the superior of the metropolitans in the five original patriarchates of the Christian church. Earlier it is used more generally, as here, of senior bishops. The preference for Old Testament terminology for all three orders indicates a church which stresses theological continuity with the Hebraic traditions (as is found for example in *Didache* 11–13). In such a tradition 'Levite' is a synonym for 'deacon' (*Apostolic Constitutions* 2.26.3).

differently, in proportion: the general idea of proportionality, or of the punishment fitting the crime, seems to be in the author's mind. But there is no detailed account of how this works out, unless we are meant to think of a hierarchy of punishment designated for the three religious orders.

river of fire: cf. Dan. 7.10, but see the details of these punishments in *3 Apoc. Jn*. There is no indication of which sins qualify for which punishment (in contrast to e.g. *Apoc. Pet.* 8-11).

worm that does not die: according to Isa. 66.24, the damned will be tormented by a twisting and never-dying worm (cf. Jud. 16.17; Sir. 7.17; Mk. 9.48; *2 Clem.* 7.6; 17.5; *Apoc. Pet.* 9; *Apoc. Paul* 42 ['the worm was a cubit in size and it had two heads']; Gregory of Nyssa, *Oratio Catechetica* 40). The thought that the body is destined for corruption can be a motive for humility (see Sir. 7.17); but here the apocalyptist imagines a living punishment (comparable to drawing and quartering as part of hanging?) for his enemies.

seven-mouthed punishment pit: φρέαρ literally means a well, that is a pit dug for a purpose; but here it is used of the depths of hell, as in Rev. 9.1-2 (the well of the abyss or bottomless pit); *Apoc. Paul* 41 (the well sealed with seven seals which is the place of all punishment).

25.

paradise: the Persian enclosed and formal garden, transformed into the image of ultimate blessedness, corresponding to the promise of the Garden of Eden. See Isa. 51.3; Ezek. 36.35; Rev. 2.7; 22.2, 14, 19; also 2 Cor. 12.4; *2 Bar.* 73.1–74.1; *4 Ezra* 2.12; 8.52. The Church Fathers debated extensively whether 'paradise' was in heaven or on earth. In the present author's apocalyptic fusion this is no longer a problem. God's hosts from heaven have descended to earth (16-17) and the perspectives of this world merge with those of eternity.

'the righteous shall inherit the earth': Ps. 37 is in origin an acrostic psalm of instruction within the Hebrew tradition of Wisdom. It teaches a moral life, conventionally based on the traditional themes of retribution and recompense, recognizable in experience. The practical message urges the longer perspective: the righteous ('they that hope in the Lord' 37.9) will inherit the land, just as their ancestors did, as a result of God's action. The Qumran community interpreted the Psalm to refer to the Elect, the Teacher of Righteousness, and the eventual apocalyptic destruction of evildoers. (J.M. Allegro, 'A Newly Discovered Fragment of a Commentary on Psalm XXXVII From Qumran', *PEQ* 86 [1954], pp. 69-75). The application in *2 Apoc. Jn* appears closer to Qumran than to the Sermon on the Mount (Mt. 5.5, cf. Ps. 37.11).

26.

number of the angels: this seems like another instance of the author satisfying his curiosity. Will the righteous human beings be outnumbered by God's angels? But it appears that the number of the Elect community is controlled by the number of the angels. And the 'prophetic' text, based on the Septuagint and Qumran reading (ctr. MT), of Deut. 32.8 is adduced to prove this. The original meaning would be 'that the nations were divided up and given their land in such a way that to each was assigned its divine protector' (A.D.H. Mayes, *Deuteronomy* [New Century Bible Commentary; London: Marshall Morgan & Scott, 1979], p. 384). This forms the basis of the idea, found in Dan. 10.13, 20-21; 12.1, that for example Israel is looked after by the archangel Michael. In *2 Apoc. Jn* such symbolism has been reapplied, so as to mean that each individual member of the elect/righteous 'human race' will be looked after by a 'guardian angel'.

27.

human beings made like angels: with references to the text of Revelation 21, this chapter describes those who already live an 'angelic' life, free from family cares. An explicit use is made of the traditional material in the catalogues of virtues and vices (see e.g. Col. 3.5-11; Eph. 5.3-11). Jn 10.16 is then interpreted in this particular sense of the angelic life. I believe that Stuart Hall is correct in identifying this description as belonging to the period of monastic developments (see 'Introduction', above, pp. 28-29). But there may also be some hint here, unusually for apocalyptic texts, of the possibility of repentance (contrast *2 Apoc. Jn* 9 above)

virtuous: ἐναρέτος was a favourite Stoic word; compare also its use in *1 Clem.* 62.1 and Ignatius, *Phld.* 1.2.

28.

'pearls before swine': (Mt. 7.6)—one of five quotations from this Gospel, the most quoted Gospel source in *2 Apoc. Jn*. This would be natural if this apocalypse belongs within a Syrian tradition including not only Ephraem but also the Didache which has a special relationship with Matthew's Gospel. As in the commissioning at the end of the Gospel (Mt 28.19-20), the teaching component is vital; it must be safeguarded through faithful teachers, so that it is not treated with contempt (as by heretics).

Mt Tabor: the heavenly tour returns to its starting point, as in ch. 1.

'blessed are they who observe justice': this macarism, quoted from Ps. 106.3, originates in a context of covenant renewal for the community of Israel; as such it was naturally adopted at Qumran in the liturgy of the Manual of Discipline. It is equally appropriate in the apocalyptic teachings of a Christian monastic community.

blessed is the house: it would be possible to read this of a monastic community, rather than of individual families and their domestic arrangements. The quotation from Jn 14.23 then follows on from the interpretation of Jn 10.16 in ch. 27; the relationship of the faithful disciple to the Lord is one with that of the single flock in obedience to its shepherd.

Figure 4: *St John Chrysostom (own photo).*

Chapter 4

THE APOCALYPSE OF ST JOHN CHRYSOSTOM

Introduction

St John Chrysostom has already made a brief appearance, in the introduction to *2 Apoc. Jn.* In describing the possibility of a Syrian monastic
setting for the work, mention was made of Chrysostom's observation
that the Syrian monks, when they came in from the desert, were 'like
heavenly visitants at church festivals'. That is a tenuous but colourful
connection. John Chrysostom's actual connection with this apocalypse,
for all that it is attributed to him, may be no less tenuous. But the explanation of the attribution is most probably to be found in the substantial
amount of ecclesiastical, and particularly liturgical, material incorporated within it. A further suggested explanation comes from its potential
as a vehicle for Nestorian thought; this Apocalypse was actually redis-
covered as part of a trawl through unpublished texts of John Chrysostom, looking for Nestorian writings which might have been promul-
gated under his name.

John Chrysostom
John Chrysostom was the most celebrated preacher of his day as well
as a theologian, liturgist and ascetic. His epithet ('golden mouthed')
reflects his preaching skills; from the Middle Ages he was included
among the pre-eminent 'Doctors of the Church'. Born c. 347 CE, he
died in 407; from 398 he reluctantly became Bishop (Patriarch) of Constantinople. His frequent representation in icons is of course stylized,
but may contain authentic details in the receding hair, sparse beard and
emaciated ascetic face.
John was well-trained in Greek culture and rhetoric by Libanius, and
he studied Scripture in the Antiochene School under Melitius of Antioch and Diodore of Tarsus. Between 373 and 381 CE, before ordination,
he lived as a hermit under the Pachomian Rule; his excessive asceticism

is thought to have undermined his health at this stage.

His writing includes a significant early work *On the Priesthood* (De Sacerdotio), and several series of his celebrated sermons: *On the Statues* (occasioned by civic violence against the Emperor and his family); *On the Incomprehensibility of God* (against Arian Christians); and *Against Judaising Christians* (on the dangers for Christians of participating in Jewish festivals—a series with anti-Semitic potential). But his major works are exegetical homilies on the Bible, expounding Genesis, Matthew, John, Romans, Galatians, 1 and 2 Corinthians, Ephesians, Timothy and Titus. It seems significant that there is no exposition of apocalyptic texts, such as Revelation.

While Chrysostom was predictably opposed to allegorical exegesis, his exposition combines spiritual insights with practical applications. A quotation will demonstrate his great zeal for social righteousness:

> You honour the altar in church, because the Body of Christ rests upon it, but those who are themselves the very Body of Christ you treat with contempt, and you remain indifferent when you see them perishing. This living altar you can see everywhere, lying in the streets and market places, and at any hour you can offer sacrifice upon it.

He had always been a passionate critic of the wealth and luxury of the ruling classes, a defender of the poor in his demands of both justice and generosity for them.

Chrysostom's career as a Bishop was coloured by political rivalry with Theophilus of Alexandria and by dissensions with the Empress Eudoxia, no doubt fostered by John's tactlessness, or concern for free speech, especially in his denunciations of corruption in the royal court. Undoubtedly the malice and jealousy of his fellow bishops contributed to his being brought to trial. Among the rich in Constantinople there were plenty to help secure his condemnation and guarantee a savage punishment. In 403 at the Synod of the Oak (Chalcedon) Chrysostom was removed from his see, exiled and hastened to death on 14 September 407, his health already broken by constant privation and ill-treatment.

In his lifetime he was noted for liturgical reforms, redefining the boundaries of sacred and profane. The liturgy which bears his name is now in general use in the Eastern Orthodox Churches, except for the few days on which the Liturgy of St Basil is appointed. In its present form the liturgy is much later than Chrysostom's time, and it is debatable how closely it should be connected with him. Presumably it was so influential because it was the liturgy of Constantinople; it assimilated and superseded the older liturgies of St James (Jerusalem and Antioch) and St Mark (Alexandria). Archbishop Cranmer drew the Prayer of St Chrysostom in the Book of Common Prayer from this Liturgy:

> Almighty God, who hast given us grace at this time with one accord to make our common supplications unto thee; and dost promise, that when two or three are gathered together in thy name thou wilt grant their requests: Fulfil now, O Lord, the desires and petitions of thy servants, as may be most expedient for them; granting us in this world knowledge of thy truth, and in the world to come life everlasting. Amen.

The Church was God's creation, the place where the image of God was being revealed and restored. Therefore the structures of the Church and of the social order must always be tested and judged by the degree of honour, and the fulness of Christian liberty, which they allow to human beings. St John Chrysostom's vision of heaven on earth, to be realized in liturgical form, became one of the main inspirations of Orthodoxy: 'The Church is the place of the angels, of the archangels, the kingdom of God, heaven itself'.

Greek Orthodox Christians today would readily say that when they stand within an Orthodox church—the walls and iconostasis dense with icons, and the ceilings painted with stars and pictures of the Pantocrator—they stand in Paradise, in the presence of God, the Virgin Mary and all the saints. The entry into the holy space serves, in effect, to presage their entry at death into eternity. A special event, such as a group pilgrimage to the Holy Land, would represent a preparation for death, both by individual self-purification, and by collective participation in eternity, this being represented by the churches that stand on the sacred sites where Christ had worked. The essential process of meta-stoicheiosis, or trans-elementation, is symbolized by the icons of Christ and his mother in such pilgrimage churches. The redemptive potential of Christ is cosmological, and hence eventually universal, as summarized in the words of St Gregory of Nyssa in his *Catechetical Oration*:

> As the principle of death took its rise in one person and passed on in succession through the whole of the human nature, so the principle of the Resurrection extends from one person to the whole of humanity... This is the mystery of God's plan with regard to His death and His resurrection from the dead.

The truth that St John Chrysostom symbolizes in his own person the noblest vision of Orthodoxy and the greatest powers of the Byzantine empire is well illustrated by a Pontic folk-song, composed 500 years ago, when the news of the fall of Constantinople reached Trebizond:[1]

> A bird, a good bird, left the City [Constantinople],
> it settled neither in vineyards nor in orchards,
> it came to settle on the castle of the Sun.
> It shook one wing, drenched in blood,
> it shook the other wing, it had a written paper.
> Now it reads, now it cries, now it beats its breast.
> 'Woe is us, woe is us, Romania [Byzantium] is taken.'
> The churches lament, the monasteries weep,
> and St. John Chrysostom weeps, he beats his breast.
> Weep not, weep not, St.John, and beat not your breast.
> Romania has passed away, Romania is taken.
> Even if Romania has passed away, it will flower
> and bear fruit again.

The Apocalypse attributed to John Chrysostom

The text of this Apocalypse, with introduction, translation into French, and some notes, was published by F. Nau.[2] Nau had discovered it in a Greek manuscript (Paris 947, fol. 276-82). This manuscript is a typical miscellany of items; one might just call it an anthology, on the strength of the fact that much of the material has a scriptural connection, so that this might have served as a principle of arrangement, just as other manuscripts contain predominantly ethical material. This Apocalypse is the final item, numbered 263, in the collection. What follows it in manuscript 947 belongs to another volume, a Menology or calendar of saints' days in the Greek Church.

The manuscript was purchased at Nicosia in Cyprus in June 1671, as part of a sustained programme of purchasing by the French between 1646 and 1685. The provenance of the manuscript is the island of Cyprus, where it was written between 1523 and 1574 (at which point the island had just been conquered by the Turks). The scribe is named George Korphiate, who describes himself as 'uneducated' (ἀμαθής). If Codex Vaticanus of the Bible can be rightly celebrated for its consistency of spelling and presentation, then our text of this Apocalypse represents the complete opposite. The Greek of the manuscript is unimag-

---

1.   Neal Ascherson, *Black Sea—The Birthplace of Civilisation and Barbarism* (London: Random House, 1996), p. 182.
2.   'Une deuxième apocalypse apocryphe Grecque de Saint Jean', *Revue Biblique* NS 11 (1914), pp. 209-21.

inably atrocious, with apparent fluidity in the use of vowels, consonants, breathings and accentuation. As you will observe, the commonest
words (for example 'speak') are spelt in an amazing variety of permu-
tations, with accents applied seemingly at random, or at least in ignor-
ance of classical rules. I seriously considered the possibility of including in this volume a corrected and standardized version of the Greek
text, but recognized that it would be an enormous and highly conjec-
tural task, and as a work of restoration comparable to that of Victorian
'conservation' of a Gothic church.

Despite its bewildering array of errors and inconsistencies, Nau
remained convinced that the copyist George Korphiate was not himself
the author of the texts in this manuscript. Their state was comparable
with that of others preserved elsewhere (one of the best comparisons
is with a fifteenth-century Cypriot work, *Makhairás's Chronicle*, found
in manuscripts in Venice and Oxford). In fact our Apocalypse has only
three indecipherable passages, while the scribe's own composition,
when he appends his signature to the manuscript, is quite unintelligible!
The appropriate comparison for the language of the Apocalypse is with
kinds of popular Greek; the puzzle is whether the present state of the
text reflects the Cypriot Greek of the last time when it was copied, or if
it is a faithful copy of a significantly earlier stage of popular Greek. A
colleague teaching Classics assures me that the character of the text
would fit well with a Cypriot variety of Greek, either of the fifteenth/
sixteenth century, or even with that of a significantly earlier period.
The history of Cyprus is a history of marginalization, varying in degree
according to those who controlled the area, whether Venetians or Cru-
saders. And so it was inevitable that some major changes to the Greek
language and its orthography should have taken place both in the sixteenth century and earlier, because of the distance from the Byzantine
tradition that resulted from so long a period of western rule.

Modern research into the original Greek dialects has confirmed the
existence of a fourth grouping, Arcadian and Cypriot, beside the three
long-recognized 'tribal' groupings Ionian (the context of the classical
Attic dialect), Dorian and Aeolian. There is evidence for a distinctive
form of Eastern Koine Greek in the Hellenistic world, which was spo-
ken in Cyprus and Asia Minor. A particular feature is the retention of
the final 'v' in Cypriot dialect then, and now, while other forms of
Greek are shedding the final nasal consonants. In the later centuries the
Greek of Cyprus is marked by a striking flexibility (or absence of

norms), both preserving features of Eastern Koine and developing local vernacular forms. It seems that the educated Cypriot of the fifteenth century would be able to tolerate a free variation between older vernacular and local innovation. Almost every possibility in form of declined endings and spelling of particles and prepositions seems permissible. It is a matter of conjecture whether the pronunciation would be as varied as the spelling suggests. The more learned language forms would be almost entirely confined to scriptural quotation. Among the characteristic dialect features to be found in this text of the Apocalypse and comparable works are:

—assimilating a vowel to the syllable which follows;
—losing consonants, especially fricatives, between vowels;
—spelling confused by palatal articulation of 's';
—retaining final 'n' and assimilating it to the start of the next word;
—emphasising double consonants and doubling single consonants.[3]

At some point this Apocalypse could well have been translated from a Koine or Byzantine Greek original. The question then would be how much, in both quantity and substance, has been preserved of an earlier Byzantine apocalyptic text? But there is an alternative, which Nau favoured, of an actual origin on Cyprus in the fifth century, when a number of apocryphal texts were used to establish the apostolicity of the church on Cyprus and to achieve independence from Antioch. The actual subject-matter of the Apocalypse lacks the kind of specific reference to assist with an exact dating (in contrast to the references to the Cross in *2 Apoc. Jn*). The range of possible dating, as Elliott notes,[4] is from the sixth to the eighth centuries CE. The interests of the work in the stipulations of canon law about sins, the monastic life and the liturgy, make a date before the fifth century unlikely. Equally there are no traces in the Apocalypse of preoccupations later than the eighth century (e.g. Iconoclast controversies; Arabic or Latin influences).

The most striking feature of the structure of this Apocalypse is the routine of question and answer between 'John' and the Lord Jesus Christ, identical in style with that of *2 Apoc. Jn*. In both works, Christ's replies begin with the address Ἄκουσον, δίκαιε Ἰωάννη. But the most

3.   Further discussion of the historic matters of Cypriot dialect can be found in Geoffrey Horrocks, *Greek: A History of the Language and its Speakers* (London: Longman, 1997).
4.   Elliot, *The Apocryphal New Testament*, p. 684

striking difference between the texts lies in the nature of the subject matter. This Apocalypse seems preoccupied with the practical concerns of church life: sinning, Sunday observance, fasting, ascetic practices, church services and the mystical meaning of the liturgy, respect due to priests, baptism, length of hair and teaching on love.

The basic literary form of dialogue/interrogation is certainly ancient, and can be traced back to the second century. The saint wishes to satisfy his curiosity, or penetrate the mysteries; this yields fresh, if often derivative and culturally-conditioned, revelations. It is also an effective means of inculcating, or refining, practical guidelines from the ultimate source of authority. Nau mentions formal comparisons with six versions of a *Testament of our Lord Jesus Christ* and with the *Didascalia XII Apostolorum* (where the disciples question Christ in the Valley of Jehoshaphat). In the Coptic Apocalypse, which begins and ends on the Mount of Olives, John asks the Lord about natural and heavenly phenomena. In a Latin Apocalypse, Christ is interrogated about the creation of human beings and about Satan's glory before his Fall. Christ himself is not always one of the participants in dialogue. In the Pseudo-Clementines the questioning is between Clement and Peter. Similarly in *3 Apoc. Jn* James, the Lord's brother, asks copious questions of John the theologian about the future destinies of souls.

Τοῦ ἐν ἁγίοις πατρὸς ἡμῶν Ἰωαννοῦ ἀρχιεπησκόπου Κοσταντίνου πόλεος του Χρισοστόμου. Λόγος περὶ ὀφέλιας των ἀκοῦὅντον αὐτῶν. Ἐλόγησων πάτερ.

1. Προσελθὸν Ἰωαννης ὁ θεολόγος τω κυριω ἡμῶν Ἰησοῦ Χριστῷ, εἶπεν· Κύριε, ὑπέ μοι πόσε ἀμαρτίαι ἡστὶν, καὶ πεία ἀμαρτία ἀσυγχώριτος ἐστὶν τοὶς ἀνθρώποις. 2. Ἐὰν τὰ δαιμόνια ἐξαγορευσεται· καὶ ἀρνίσιτε τὸν κύριον, καὶ σηνὲργῇ τὸ διαβολο καὶ τοῖς δέμοσην αὐτοῦ· οὐ κρίνη αὐτὸν ὁ Θεὸς εἰς τὸν αἰῶνα τοῦ αἰῶνος. 3. Δευτέρα ἀμαρτία ἐστὴν· ἐὰν τὶς θηγατρος ἢ μητρος, ἢ σηντέκνησας, ἢ ἀδελφῆς, ἢ θήας, ἢ ἀνιψύας, μηᾶνι (μιαίνη) κοίτην. πῶς κρίνη αὐτοὺς ὁ Θεός· ὡς τῶν Ἰούδαν ἐν τῷ πυρίνῳ ποταμῷ. 4. Τρίτη ἀμαρτία ἐστὶν. ἐὰν τῆς τὰς ἕξ ἡμέρας ἀναπαύση τὸν κάματον αὐτοῦ, καὶ φυλάττη τὸν μίλον αὐτοῦ, καὶ τὰς ἀποκρίσης αὐτοῦ ἕως τῆς κυριάκῆς· πῶς κρίνη αὐτὸν ὁ Θεός· ὃς τὸν Ἰούδαν τὸν προδότην.

5. Ὁ δὲ Ἰωάννης ἠρώτησεν τῳ Κυρίῳ λεγων· Εἰπέ μοι καὶ περὶ τῆς ἁγίας κυριάκῆς.

6. Ὁ δὲ Κύριος εἶπεν· Ἄκουσον δήκεε Ἰωάννη· Κυριάκή ὁ Κύριος, καὶ ὁ Κύριος κυριάκή. Ὁ τημῶν τὴν ἁγίαν κυριάκήν, τῆμὰ αὐτὸν ὁ Κύριος ἐνόπιον ἀγγέλων καὶ ἀνθρωπῶν. 7. Ὁ τημὸν τὴν κυριάκὴν μετὰ παντὸς τοῦ οἴκου αὐτοῦ, ἀπὸ ὥρας θ' του σαμβάτου ἀφήει το ἔργον αὐτοῦ, καὶ ὑπάγι εἰς τὴν ἐκλησίαν καὶ εὐχαρίστι τῳ Θεῷ, καὶ εἰς τὴν θείαν λυτουργίαν τὸ αὐτὸ τρόπω, καὶ ἑσπέρας τῆς ἁγίας κυριάκῆς, λυτροῦτε τῶν ἐξ ἡμερῶν τὰ πταῖσματα, εὐλογῆ αὐτὸν ὁ Θεὸς ὡς τὸν Ἀβραὰμ, εὐλογῆ τὸν οἴκον αὐτοῦ, και τοὺς καμάτους αὐτοῦ.

8. Ὁ δὲ Ἰωάννης εἶπεν· Ἐὰν τις τὰς ἐξ ἡμέρας νηστευων καὶ προσεύχεται τὴν ἁγίαν κυριάκὴν οὐ τῆμὰ, τί μηστὸν λύψεται; 9. Ἄκουσον, δίκαιε Ἰωάννη· τὸν δρόμον ὅλον τῆς ἡμέρας ἐὰν βόσκει τις τὰ πρόβατα αὐτοῦ καὶ τῆνικτα [τὴν νύκτα] οὐκ ἀποκλήσι αὐτα τί ὄφελος; 10. Οὕτω ἔσται καὶ ὁ νυστεύων προσευχόμενος, τὴν ἁγίαν

THE APOCALYPSE OF ST JOHN CHRYSOSTOM

(From our father John Chysostom, archbishop of Constantinople, who is now among the saints, a word about the benefit for his hearers. Give us your blessing, Father.)

1. *John* the theologian *approached our Lord* Jesus Christ and said: 'Lord, tell me *how many sins* there are, and *what kind of sin is unforgivable* for human beings.' 2. 'If one publicly acknowledges demons and denies the Lord, and collaborates with the devil and his demons, God will never finish judging that person. 3. This is the *second sin*: if anyone defiles incestuously the bed of daughter or mother, sister or twin, aunt or cousin. How does God judge them? *Like the Jews in the river of fire.* 4. This is the third sin: if one relaxes from work during the six weekdays, and avoids his grindstone and his business affairs *until Sunday*. How does God judge him? Like Judas the betrayer.'

5. John asked the Lord: 'Tell me also about Sunday, the *holy day of the Lord.*' 6. The Lord said: 'Listen, righteous John, *Sunday is the Lord* and the Lord Sunday. The Lord honours, before angels and men, the man who honours Sunday. 7. The man who honours Sunday with his whole household, leaves work *at the ninth hour on Saturday*, goes to church and gives thanks to God, and similarly goes to the divine liturgy, and on Saturday evening cleanses himself from the sins of six days, this man is the one *God blesses like Abraham*, blesses his house, and his labours.'

8. John said: '*If someone fasts* and prays for the six weekdays, but does not honour Sunday, what punishment will he receive?' 9. 'Listen, righteous John: if someone feeds his sheep throughout the day, but doesn't shut them up at night, what good is it? 10. So will he be who fasts and prays, but does not honour holy Sunday and the good

κυριάκὴν οὐ τιμᾶ, τὴν καλὴν ὁμολογὶαν· καὶ ὥστις λέγει ὅτι ἀγαπᾶ
τὸν Θεὸν, καὶ τὴν ἀγίαν κυριάκὴν οὐ τιμᾶ, ψεύστος ἐστὶν.

11. Ὁ δὲ Ἰωάννης εἶπεν· Ἠπε μει καὶ περι τῆς αὐτῆς νιστίας.
12. Μεγάλη γὰρ χάρης ἐστὶν ἡ νηστεία· πολλοὶ διὰ τῆς νηστείας,
ὑπερέβησαν μετα τὰ οὐρανία, καὶ μετὰ ἀγγελῶν ἔχουσιν τὴν μερίδαν
καὶ τὴν συνομιλίαν. Μεγάλι γὰρ χάρης ἐστὴν εἰ νιστία ὅτι σύ πινὰς
καὶ ὁ πένης χορτασθύσεται ἐκ τῶν σῶν ἄρτων, ἐγκαρπος ἐστὶν ἡ
νιστεία σου.
13. Ὁ δὲ Ἰωάννης· Εἶπε μοι ὅτι ὁ μοναχὸς, μήτε ἄρτων ἔχων,
μοίτε οἶνον, μήτε ἔλαιον, τί ποιεὶ σοι; 14. Ἄκουσον, δίκαιε Ἰωάννη,
τῶν μοναχῶν ὑπενήα ἵνα διὰ τῆς ταπεινόσεως τοῦ αὐτοῦ σώματος
ἥξει· τοῖς δὲ κοσμικοῖς ἐπιτελύσθη, ἵνα μεταδοσο ποίοσιν τοῖς πτωχοῖς.
15. τοῦ [πῶς?] θέλη ὁ Θεὸς τιᾶν [τὴν] νηστείαν. 16. Ἄκουσον, δικ-
αίε Ἰωάννη, ποίαν νηστεῖαν ἀγαπᾶ ὁ Θεός· Ἄλεψε σου τὸ πρόσωπον καὶ τὴν κεφαλὴν σου νήψαι, ὅπως μὴ φανοῖς τοῖς ἀνθρώποις
νηστεύων. Ἡσελθὲ εἰς τὸ ταμίο σου, καὶ κλύσον τὴν θήραν [θύραν]
σου, καὶ προσεύξου τῷ πατρί σου ἐν τῷ κριπτῷ, καὶ ὁ πατήρ σου ὁ
βλέπον σε ἐν τῷ κρηπτῷ, ἀπῶδῶσοι σει ἐν τῷ φανερῷ. καὶ ἐν τὲς
μνήαις τῶν ἀγίον σου μὴ παρίδης ὅτι πρεσβείαις αὐτῶν λυτροῦτε
ἄνθρωπος ἐκ θανάτου πονηροῦ καὶ ἐκ πτεσματῶν. Ὅτε γὰρ νηστεύης
προ πάντον τὴν γλῶττα ἐγκρατεύου τοῦ μι λαλὴν πονηρὰ, μηδὲ
ἀκοῦον τὰ ὦτα σου λαλήσουσιν, τὰ χείλη σου μὴ καταλαλήσουσιν,
ἐὰν μὴ εἴδοσιν οἱ ὀφθαλμοὶ σου μὴ ἤπης. Ὅταν εἴδης τότε λάλη ὅ
ἐωράκασιν ἀληθές.

17. Καὶ πάλην λέγει ὁλήος [ὀλίγος] οἶνος ἀγιάζει, ἰδαῖ πολῆς
δαίμονοι, οὐχ ἡμῶν ἀποχὴ τῶν βρομάτων καλεῖται, ἀλλὰ πάντων τῶν
κακῶν. 18. Ὁ γὰρ νιστεύεις, πάντων ἐνγκρατεύου, τῇ τετράδι καὶ τῇ
παρασκευῇ· μηδόλος τὰς ἡμέρας τῆς ἀγίας πεντικοστῆς, καὶ τῶν
ἀγίον καλλινίκων· μνήμασιν γὰρ καὶ ιβ' ἡμερῶν καὶ παρα τῶν κανων
ὡς γέγονη, ἐπιβλάβία ἠσὶν· 19. μεγάλη γὰρ χάρης ἐστὴν ἡ νιστία,
καὶ λυτροῦτε ἄνθρωπος ἐκ πυρὸς, καὶ ὕδατος, καὶ θηρίων ἀγρίων, και
ἐκ παντὸς κακοῦ, καὶ ἐκ θανάτου πονιροῦ.

20. Ὁ δὲ Ἰωάννης ὁ χρ εἶπεν· Κύριε, τὰ ἀντίτηπα τῆς ἐκλισίας.
21. Ὁ δὲ Κύριος εἶπεν· Ἄκουσον, δίκεε Ἰωάννη, οἱ κοχοὶ τῆς ἐκλη-
σίας ἐστὶν ἡ κοριφὴ τοῦ Θεοῦ, τὸ βῆμα ἐστιν το μνεῖμα τοῦ Κυρίου, ἡ
τράπεζα τὸ στῆθος τοῦ Κυρίου, ὁ δὺσκος ὁ λύθος ὁ ἀποκυλησθῆς ἐκ
τῆς θύρας τοῦ μνημείου, καὶ οὐκ ἐστιν ἄξιος ὁ λαϊκὸς ἀποδίσε ἠσαυ-
τῶν. καὶ οὐκ ἐστιν ἄξια ἡ γηνὶ τοῦ εἰσελθεῖν ἀμβόνων ἔμπροσθεν.

confession. *Whoever says that he loves God, and does not honour Sunday, is a liar.*'

11. John said: 'Tell me also about the fasting itself.' 12. '*Fasting* is rich in divine grace; for many people through fasting have *ascended to the heavens*, and share in the fellowship of the angels. For the fasting is rich in grace because, when you go hungry and the poor man is satisfied from your bread, your fasting is fruitful.'

13. John said: 'Tell me what *the monk*, who does not have *bread, wine or olive oil*, does for you?' 14. 'Listen, righteous John; monks expect to come to God through the humiliation of their bodies. This is perfected for the *seculars* when they share with the poor.'

15. 'What kind of fast does God wish for?' 16. 'Righteous John, listen to what kind of fast God loves: *anoint your face* and wash your head, that your fasting may not be seen by men. *Go into your room* and shut the door, and pray to your Father who is in secret; and your Father who sees in secret will reward you openly (Mt. 6.17-18, 6). And in the *commemorations of your saints*, do not forget that by their advocacy man is redeemed from a wicked death and from sins. When you fast, guard your tongue before all so as to say nothing bad; what your ears have not heard, they will not say; your lips will utter no *slander*; you will not speak of whatever your eyes have not seen. When you see, then speak what your eyes have truly seen.

17. Again God says that *a little wine* sanctifies (1 Tim. 5.23); it is our abstinence from all evil, rather than from food, that is called the *demon's defeat* (?). 18. When fasting, abstain totally on *Wednesday and Friday*, except for the days of holy *Pentecost* [*Did.* 8.1] and of the *martyr-saints*; but it is harmful to eat at the *burial*, and for 12 days afterwards, which is against the Rule. 19. *Fasting is rich in divine grace*, and redeems mankind from fire, water, wild beasts, from every evil and from a wicked death.'

20. John (*Chrysostom*) said: 'Lord, what are the *symbols of the church*?' 21. The Lord said: 'Listen, righteous John—the *chancel gates* are the head of God, the *sanctuary* is the remembrance of the Lord, the holy-table *the Lord's breast*, the *paten* the stone which was rolled away from the door of the tomb; and the *layman is not worthy* to enter within the sanctuary, and the woman [*deaconess*] is not worthy to go before the *reading-desk*.'

22. Ὁ δὲ Ἰωάννης ἤπεν· Κύριε, ὑπέ μοι οἱ ἀναγνῶσται τίνες εἰσὶν, ὅταν ἔλθωσιν ἐν ἀμβόνῳ ψαλλοντες; 23. Ἄκουσον, δίκεε Ἰωάννη, ὁ πρεσβύτερος ἐστὶν προτάγγελος Μιχάηλ διὰ νεφέλης, ὅτι διαβάζῃ τὰ ἄγια δῶρα διὰ νεφέλης ἐν τῇ τραπέζῃ καὶ εἰσοδεύει, καὶ οὐκ ἔστην ἄξιος ὁ λαϊκὸς ἐτρανίσε αὐτὸν ἀπὸ τὰ γόνατα τὴν ἄνω.

24. Ὁ δὲ Ἰωάννης εἶπεν· Ὑπέ μοι, Κύριε, καὶ περὶ τῆς λυτουρ-γίας, ὅταν ποιεῖσῃ ὁ ἱερευς τὴν εὐχὴν τῆς προθέσεως, καὶ ἀπὲρχετε ἱερουργήν. 25. Ἄκουσον, δίκαιε Ἰωάννη, τότε ἀπέρχετε ἄγγελος Κυρίου φυλάττον τὰ ἄγια δῶρα. 26. Κύριε, οἰπέ μοι κὲ περὶ τῶν ἀντίφωνων, τίνες εἰσὶν; 27. Ἄκουσον, δίκαιε Ἰωάννη, ὅταν ἠσήλθεν ὁ Κύριος εἰς τὴν Ἄδην, καὶ σηνἔτρεψεν τοὺς μοχλοὺς καὶ τὰς πύλας, καὶ σηνήγηρεν τοὺς ἀπεῶνων νεκρούς· τότε εὐφράνθη ὁ Δαυὶδ, καὶ οἱ προφύτε ἔψαλλον ταῦτα.

28. Ὑπέ μει καὶ περὶ τῆς εἰσόδου. 29. ὅταν ἄρη πρεσβίτερος τὸ ἄγιον ἐβαγγέλιον, κατεβέννι ἄγγελος εἰς τὸν τράχιλον τοῦ ἱερέως· ἢ ὡς εἴπη ἐν εἰρήνη προὲλθομεν.

30. Ὁ δὲ Ἰωάννης εἶπεν· Ὑπέ μει, Κύριε, καὶ περὴ τοῦ προκή-μενου· καὶ τοῦ Ἀλληλουϊά καὶ τοῦ ἀποστόλου, καὶ περὶ τοῦ εὐαγ-γελοίου, καὶ τῶν κατιχουμένων, τοῦ χερουβικοῦ, καὶ τῶν μυστηρίων, τῆς ἀγαπίσεως, καὶ τῶν ἁγίων θυρῶν, περὶ τοῦ ἐνσυμβόλου, το πῶς ἔκαστον διλῇ.

31. Ἄκουσον, δικαὶε Ἰωάννη· Τὸ προκήμενον ψάλλει Δαυίδ προέρ-χεται τὸ πνευμά σου τῷ ἁγίῳ· Τὸν ἀπόστολον διδάσκη ὁ ἀπόστολος Παῦλος· Τὸ Ἀλληλούϊὰ ψάλλει Δαυίδ εὐαγγελικῇ φωνῇ, κατέρωντε [κατέρωτα] εἰς τὰ ἄγια δῶρα· Τὸ ἄγιον εὐαγγέλιον διδάσκούσιν δ' εὐαγγελισταὶ, καὶ ὁ μὶ ἀκούόμενος ταῦτα ἐν ὅλῃ ψυχὴ, ἔστην ὁ ἐπικατάρατος· Οἱ κατοιχούμενη ἠσὶν ὁπρο [οἱ πρὸ] τοῦ βαπτήσματος. Οἱ πιστοὶ εἴπω ἠσὶν οι δικαιοι. Εὔξαστε οἱ κατοιχούμενοι. Τότε ὑπερι [οἱ περὶ] τοῦ βαπτίσματος ὁ ποιστοὶ μνημονεύοντε καθῶς ὁ Κύριος εἴπεν. ὁ δὲ μηστικὸς ὕμνος τοῦ χερουβικου ἔστιν ὕμνος ἀγγελικὸς, καὶ παρακλίσει τῶν ἐπουρανίων δυνάμεων, διὸ λέγει πᾶσαν οὖν βιοτικὴν ἀποθόμεθαν μέριμναν, ὡς τὸν βασιλέαν τῶν ὅλων ὑποδεξόμεθα.

32. Τότε ὁ ὀφθαλμός σου μήτε ὅθεν μήτε κῆνθεν ἐπάρεται, ἐκ τοῦ ἀγίου θυσιάστιρίου, διότι παράστασι ἀγγελικὴ ἐστῇ, ὃν εὐλογοῦσιν οἱ ἱερεῖς· δίο φοστίρες προσκυνοῦσιν τῶ ἄχραντο σῶμα σου, καὶ τὸ τίμιον αἷμα τοῦ κυρίου ἡμῶν Ἰησοῦ Χριστοῦ, ὃν οἱ ἄγγελοι τρέμουσιν παρι-στάμενι. 33. ὅταν δὲ εἴπομεν· Ἀγαπήσωμεν ἀλλήλους, καὶ ἢ της εὑρεθῇ ἔχων μάχην με τῶν ἀδελφὸν αὐτοῦ, καὶ τὴν ὥραν ἐκείνην οὐ

22. John said: 'Lord, tell me then *who the readers represent*, when they come as cantors to the pulpit?' 23. 'Listen, righteous John: the bishop, as ruler in the church, corresponds to the Archangel Michael across the *veil of cloud*, because he carries the holy gifts, through the veil of oblation at the altar, and makes *the Great Entrance*, while the layman is not worthy to rise from his knees.'

24. John said: 'Lord, tell me also about the liturgy, when the priest makes the offertory prayer and goes to celebrate the Eucharist.' 25. 'Listen, righteous John: then *the angel of the Lord*, who guards the holy gifts, *departs.*' 26. 'Lord, tell me also about the *antiphons* (the *introit*)—what do they represent?'

27. 'Listen, righteous John: when the *Lord descended to Hell*, he shattered the bolts and gates, and resurrected together the dead of ages past. Then *David* rejoiced and the prophets sang these antiphons.'

28. 'Tell me also about the *Great Entrance*.'

29. 'When the bishop takes *the Holy Gospel, an angel descends* into the priest's throat, as when he says, *"Go forth in peace".*'

30. John said: 'Lord, tell me also about *the Gradual*, the Alleluia, the Epistle, the Gospel, the blessing of the Catechumens, the Sanctus, the Mysteries, the Kiss of Peace, the Sanctuary Doors, the Creed—what each of these reveals.'

31. 'Listen, righteous John: *David sings* the Gradual—*"Your spirit goes before* the person who is holy." *The apostle Paul* represents the apostolic teaching. David sings the *Alleluia with a voice worthy of the Gospel*, anticipating the declaration (?) over the holy gifts. The four Evangelists teach the holy Gospel; so the person who does not *listen with full attention* is accursed. *The Catechumens* are those awaiting Baptism; *the Faithful*, who are the righteous, urge the prayer of the Catechumens; then the Faithful (those who have received Baptism) *have 'in remembrance' what the Lord said.* The mystical *hymn of the Cherubim* is the angelic hymn which invokes the heavenly powers, and so it says: "Let us lay aside therefore all the cares of life, to receive the King of the Universe." 32. Then your eye is not to be lifted up, this way or that, from the holy altar, because it is a heavenly presence which the priests are blessing. So sun and moon worship your *undefiled* body, and the precious blood of our Lord Jesus Christ, in whose presence the angels stand in awe. 33. When we say, *"Let us love one another"*, if anyone is found with a quarrel against his brother, and he will not give

δώσει τῷ ἀδελφῷ αὐτοῦ ἀγάπην, ἐπικατάρατος ἐστὶν ἕως τοῦ οὐρανοῦ. 34. Ὁ δὲ εἰς τὰς θύρας ἔξω φθασθῇ, οὗτος ἄπρακτος τῷ Θεῷ κέκραγε. 35. Τὸ δὲ ἅγιον τῆς πίστεος σύμβολον, ἐστὶν ἡ καλὴ ὁμολογία, ἣν ὁμολόγισαν οἱ καλοὶ πάτερες.

36. Ὁ δὲ Ἰωάννης εἶπεν· Κύριε, ὑπέ μει τεῖ [εἶπε μοι τί] ἐστὶν στόμεν καλὸς [στῶμεν καλῶς] στομὲν μετὰ φόβου, καὶ περὶ τοῦ μεγάλου τρισαγίου, καὶ τὰ σὰ ἐκ τῶν σῶν σοὶ πρὸσφέροντες, καὶ ἐπάρσεως τὸ πάτερ ἡμῶν, καὶ τὰ ἅγια τοῖς ἁγίοις, καὶ τῆς ἀπολύσεως τῆς ἁγίας λητουργίας, καὶ πῶ ἑκάστων διλῇ.

37. Ἄκουσον, δίκαιε Ἰωάννη. Τὸ στόμὲν καλῶς ἐστὶν ἀγαπὸν τὸν Θεόν. Τὸ στόμεν μετὰ φόβου, φόβυσθε τὸ ὄνομα τοῦ Θεοῦ. Τὸ τρισάγιον ψάλλουσιν τὰ Χερουβὶμ καὶ ἀποκρίνονται τὰ Σεραφὶμ. Ζώά ἠσὶν ὁ ἀετος, ὁ βοῦς, ὁ λέον. Ἄγγελος λογικὸς ἄνθρωπος, καὶ τὸ ὑποπόδιον τοῦ δεσπότου Θεοῦ. 38. Τὰ σὰ ἐκ τῶν σῶν ἠσιν ἦλθεν ὁ κύριος εἰς τὸν Ἅδην καὶ σηνέτριψεν τὰ πνεύματα τοῖς πονηρίας, καὶ τὰς πύλας τοῦ Ἅδου, καὶ συνύγηρεν τὸν προτόπλαστον Ἀδάμ. Τὸτε εἶπεν πρὸς τὰ πνεύματα· Τὰ σὰ ἐκ τῶν σῶν σοὶ προσφέρονταις, κατὰ πάντα καὶ διὰ πάντα. Καὶ ἀπεκρίθησαν οἱ ἄγγελοι καὶ εἶπον· Σὲ ὑμνοῦμεν.

39. Καὶ ὅταν ἀνοίξει τὰς θύρας τῆς ἐκκλησίας κρατὸν κάλαμων καὶ γράφον, καὶ τὸ δυσεμὸς [δυσήκοον?] ἐστὶν, διὅτι ἀστραπὴ οὐκ ἰδεν, καὶ βροντὴ οὐκ ἱκουσεν, ἀλλὰ καὶ ὀφθαλμος αὐτῶς ἐπ᾽ ἐμὲ θεόρῇ, καὶ διὰ τοῦτο ἄνθρωπος οὐ θέλῃ βλέπην, μάλλιστα δὲ νήψει ὁ πρεσβείτερος τὸν ἄρτον, καὶ εἴπῃ τὰ ἅγια τοῖς ἁγίοις, τότε κατέρχετε τὸ πνεῦμα τὸ ἅγιον ἐπ᾽ αὐτοὺς. 40. Καὶ ὅταν εἴπῃ· ἐν εἰρήνη προέλθωμεν, τότε ἄγγελος διδῶν τὴν εὐλογίαν ἐν πιστει καὶ φοβο παρισταμένους, καὶ ἐν ὀρθότιτι στηκόντας εἰς τὴν ἐκλησίαν, ὅταν πληρώσι ὁ πρεσβίτερος τὴν εὐχὴν τῆς ἁγίας ἐκκλησίας, καὶ τὴν δέησιν τοῖς ἐν οὐρανοῖς.

41. Ὁ δὲ Ἰωάννης εἶπεν· Ὁ τιμῶν τὸν ἱερέα τὶ μισθὸν ἔχει; 42. Ἄκουσον, δίκαιε Ἰωάννη· Ὁ τιμῶν τὸν ἱερέαν, τιμὰ αὐτὸν ὁ Κύριος ἐνόπιον τῶν ἀγγέλων καὶ ἀνθρώπων. Ὁ τιμῶν τὸν ἱερέαν μετὰ πίστέως, τὴν εὐχὴν αὐτοῦ λυτροῦτε τὰς ἁμαρτίας αὐτοῦ. Καὶ ὦ της λέγει ὅτι ἀγαπὰ τὸν Θεὸν, καὶ τὸν ἱερέαν οὐ τήμὰ, ψεύστην ἐστὴν.

43. Ὁ δὲ Ἰωάννης εἶπεν· Ὑπέ μει καὶ δια του βαπτήσματος. 44. Ἄκουσον, δίκαὲ Ἰωάννη· Τὸ βάπτησμα εἰς ἄφεσιν ἁμαρτιῶν

the kiss of peace to his brother at that time, that man is accursed as high as heaven.

34. *The person outside* the Doors *who is in a hurry* to get in, that man has called upon God in vain. 35. The *holy Creed* of the Faith is the good Confession which the good Fathers have made.'

36. John said: 'Lord, tell me what each of these signify—*"Let us stand well, let us stand with fear"*; the great *Trisagion*; the Offertory sentence, '*We offer you* what is yours from your own'; *the lifting up* of the prayer, *"Our Father"*; *"Holy things for holy people"*; and *the Dismissal* from the holy Liturgy.'

37. 'Listen, righteous John: to say "Let us stand well" means "Love God", and "Let us stand with fear" refers to being in awe of the Name of God. *The Cherubim sing the Trisagion*, and the Seraphim respond; the Living Creatures are the Eagle, the Ox and the Lion. The angel is a man endowed with reason, who is the footstool (servant) of God his master. *38.* "We offer you what is yours from your own" means that the Lord went into Hell and destroyed the spirits of wickedness and the gates of Hell, and resurrected the first-created man, Adam. Then he said to the spirits, "We offer you what is yours from your own, in all and through all". The angels answered with the words, "We praise you".

39. And when he opens the *Sanctuary Doors*, he is *holding a reed-pen* and writing; some will be *ill at ease [disobedient?]*, because they do not wish to see what lightning has not seen, and thunder has not heard, but in this way the eye can *gaze upon me* [cf.1 Cor. 2.9-10]. Above all, the presiding bishop will consecrate (purify) the bread, and say, *"Holy things for holy people"*; then the *Holy Spirit descends* upon them. 40. And when he says, *"Let us go forth in peace"*, then *an angel gives the Blessing* to those who are present in faith and fear, standing upright in Church [and in orthodoxy standing firm in the Church], while the bishop completes the prayer of the holy Church and the supplication to those in heaven.'

41. John said: 'What reward does the *person have who reveres the priest?*' 42. 'Listen, righteous John: someone who reveres the priest is revered by the Lord in the presence of angels and human beings. The one who reveres the priest in faith, is freed from his sins by his prayer. If anyone says that he loves God, and does not revere the priest, that person is a liar (cf.1 Jn 4.20).'

43. John said: 'Tell me also about *Baptism*.' 44. 'Listen, righteous John: Baptism is for the forgiveness of sins; and so it is appropriate that

ἐστὶν, καὶ διὰ τοῦ τούτο ἀρέσκεται ἡ κουρᾶ τέταρτος ἀμβὰ του ἐνιαὐτοῦ· ἰδὲ τοῦ πρεσβειτέρου ιβ'· καὶ λαϊκοῦ ἤτοι διὰ τοῦτο γρωρίζεται τὸ ἄγιον βάπτισμα, καὶ ὁ μὴ ποιῶν οὗτος ἁμαρτάννει.

45. Ὁ δὲ Ἰωάννης εἶπεν· Κύριε ὑπέ μει καὶ οἱ μεταλαμβάνοντες ἀκούρευτι τίναῖς οἰσὶν.

46. Ἄκουσον, δίκαιε Ἰωάννη, τινὸς αἱ οἱ τρίχαι διὰβοῦ τὸν ὀφθαλμῶν, αὐτοῦ ὀκ ἐστὴν ἄξιο κοινωνίας αὐτοῦ· ἐπικατάρατος ἐστὶν ὁ πρεσβίτερος μετάδιδὸν αὐτῶν.

47. Ὁ δὲ Ἰωάννης εἶπεν· Κύριε ὑπέ μει καὶ περὶ τῶν γυναικῶν.

48. Ἔως εὐλογησθῆ ἡ γηνὶ μετὰ τοῦ ἀνδρὸς αὐτῆς, καὶ ἀν διὰβοῦν αἱ τρίχες τῆς κεφαλῆς τῶν ὀφθαλμῶν αὐτῆς, καὶ οὐκ ἐστιν ἀξία μεταλαβεῖν. ὁμίος καὶ ἀπὸ τῆς ἀγιὰσθῆ ἡ καὶφαλῆ αὐτῆς μετὰ τοῦ ἄνδρὸς αὐτῆς. ἐᾶν της κόψι τρίχας ἀπὸ τῆς κεφαλῆς αὐτῆς, ἐστὶν ἐπικατάρατος.

49. Ὁ δὲ Ἰωάννης εἶπεν· Κύριε ὑπε μει καὶ περὶ τῆς ἀγάπης.

50. ἀγαπίσωμεν ἀλλοίλους, μεγάλη ἐστὶν ἡ ἀγάπη, μακροθημὴ, χριστεύεται, ἡ ἀγάπη ἐστὶν ἡ λαυρότης τοῦ ἡλήου, φεδροτέρα τῆς θαλάσσης. Ἡ ἀγάπη παντα στέγι, παντα ἐλπίζει, παντα ὑπομένει, ἡ ἀγάπι οὐδὲ ποτε ἐκπίπτη.

51. Ἰδε εἰρήνη Θεὸς ἐστὶν, καθὼς τὸ εὐαγγέλιον λέγει· Μακάριοι εἰρηνοποιοὶ ὅτι αὐτοὶ υἱοὶ Θεοῦ κληθήσονται. Καὶ παλην λέγει. Εἰρηνη ἡμὴν, ἵνα ἀγαπᾶτε ἀλλήλους.

Αὐτῷ ἡ δόξα καὶ τῶ κράτος εἰς τοὺς αἰῶνας. Ἀμὴν.

hair be cropped (tonsured) four times a year for the lay brother—and monthly for the priest—because by these means the holy Baptism is made public, and the person who does not do this commits sin.'

45. John said: 'Lord, tell me, what of those who take communion without a haircut?'

46. 'Listen, righteous John: the person whose hair comes below the eyes is not worthy of communion; the priest who gives it to him is accursed.'

47. John said: 'Lord, tell me also about women.' 48. 'Until a *woman* has been blessed together with her husband, she is not worthy to communicate, if the *hair* of her head comes below her eyes. Similarly, after her head has been sanctified with her husband (cf. 1 Cor 11.3; Eph. 5.23), the woman who cuts the hair of her head is accursed.'

49. John said: 'Lord, tell me also about *love*.' 50. '*Let us love one another* (1 Jn 4.7). Great is *love, patient and kind* (1 Cor. 13.4). Love is the brightness of the sun, reflecting more radiance than the sea. *Love bears all things...hopes all things, endures all things. Love never ends* (1 Cor. 13.7-8).

51. Look, God is the *Peace*, just as the Gospel says: *Blessed are the peacemakers, for they shall be called sons of God* (Mt. 5.9). Again the Gospel says: *Peace be with you...that you love one another* (Jn 20.19-21; 15.12).'

To God be glory and power for ever. Amen.

Explanatory Notes

For the title, relating to John Chrysostom, see the elaborate version in the Coptic text (BM Oriental MS 7024) *An Encomium on Saint John the Baptist by Saint John Chrysostom*, translated by E. Wallis Budge:

> The Encomium which our holy father Saint Apa John, Archbishop of Constantinople, who was glorious in every respect, the holy golden-mouth, pronounced to the glory and honour of Saint John the Baptist, the holy forerunner and kinsman of the Christ, than whom among those who have been born of women no greater hath ever risen up, whom God exalted in honour and glory, above all the saints, who excelled the angels in purity (or, holiness). [Apa John Chrysostom] pronounced this encomium in connexion with the passage which is written in the Gospel according to [Saint] Matthew when he explained to us the meaning of the words which are written therein, 'What went ye out into the desert to see?' [Matthew 11.7]. In the peace of God! May His holy blessing come upon us, and may we all gain salvation together. Amen.

1.

John approached our Lord: The almost casual opening is noteworthy for the lack of the usual reference to a theophany in a particular place and/or an account of transportation to heaven or the underworld. It is always possible that such a scene has been lost from the start of this text.

how many sins…: The question about the number of sins is reminiscent of the classification of 'mitzvoth' in the Jewish Law. Simeon Kayyara (a Babylonian scholar of the ninth century) classified the laws in the Pentateuch as numbering 613. There are 248 positive commandments (the number traditionally associated with the number of bones in the human body) and 365 negative commandments (as the number of days in the year). The Talmud differentiated between those ordinances that would have been deducible even if Scripture had not prescribed them, and those that could not be logically derived. Medieval scholars referred to these as 'rational' and 'revealed' respectively. The Torah itself recognizes a distinction between inadvertent and deliberate sin (cf. Lev. 4.2; Num. 15.22-30).

what kind of sin is unforgivable: This text identifies three categories of sin in response to the question: collaborating with the devil to deny the Lord; incest; and failure to work except on Sunday (by implication dishonouring the Lord's day and effectively subverting the seven-day order of Creation). There are a wealth of comparisons with this identification of the unforgivable sin, including the distinction between forgivable sins and those with fatal consequences made in 1 Jn 5.16. The nature of mortal sin is not spelled out, but would presumably be recognised by the readers (since it belonged to the sphere of death rather than life); in context it is likely to mean identifying oneself with the works of Antichrist, an observable fact which defined the person as not belonging to that Christian community (1 Jn 2.19). Similarly in the letter to the Hebrews the post-baptismal sin of apostasy is seen as unforgivable (6.4-6; cf. 12.16 with the model of Esau who 'sold his birthright'). In the Gospels it is blasphemy against the Holy Spirit which is declared unforgivable: Mk 3.28-29 and 8.38 with their parallels. Within the particular context of the *Didache* (the work of Christian prophets as wandering charismatics) it is the questioning of inspired prophecy which is unforgivable: 'And you shall not tempt or dispute with any prophet who speaks in the Spirit; for every sin shall be forgiven, but this sin shall not be forgiven' (11.7). In the Johannine situation collaboration 'with the devil and his demons' is the work of a spirit that does not confess Jesus and therefore is not from God (1 Jn 4.3). The basic attitude is a dualism between two ways, the way of life and the way of death. The presupposition is that the acceptance of baptism by the Christian convert represents an acceptance of the saving effect of Christ's death, which should have a transforming effect on life as a Christian; any outright rejection of such transformation is unforgivable.

3.

the second sin: Incestuous relations have sometimes received official favour, as with brother/sister marriage for some Egyptian Pharaohs, but were prohibited between specified degrees of kinship in Ancient Israel (cf. Lev. 18.6-18). The listing of prohibited relations in Leviticus is prefaced by a prohibition of the practices of Egypt and Canaan; it is the case that some of the proscribed relationships would have been allowable among the Patriarchs, according to earlier narratives. The Talmud later enlarged the definition of incest. For this apocalypse to give so high a profile to incest as unforgivable seems unusual and surprising, unless it points to a local issue. Modern ethical thinking recognizes it as a prevalent problem in various small-scale societies and focuses on the physical consequences of inbreeding and the psychological risk for the mother when conceiving a child as a result of incest or rape.

like the Jews, in the river of fire: cf. Ante Nicene Fathers 8.585; *2 Apoc. Jn 22* and the *Apocalypse of Paul*.

4.

until Sunday: Sunday observance is a recurrent theme in this generation of apocalypses. See also the sermon series *De die dominica*, attributed to John Chrysostom, among others. The observance of Sunday, and at least the partial rest from work for the sake of worship, is indicated as early as Tertullian, *De Oratione* 23: 'In accordance with the tradition, we must only on the day of the Lord's resurrection guard not only against kneeling, but every posture expressing anxious care, deferring even our business affairs, lest we give any place to the devil.' Sunday as a day of rest is indicated more comprehensively by Ephraem Syrus in a sermon: 'Honour is due to the Lord's day, the first-born of all days, for in it lie hidden many secrets. Pay your respect to this day, for it has taken away the right of the first-born from the sabbath... Blessed is he who honours it with spotless observance... The law ordains that rest be granted to servants and animals, in order that labourers, serving girls and employees may cease from work. While our body rests, it does indeed cease from work, but we sin on the day of rest more than on other days... The Lord's day is a holy day.'(from *S. Ephraem Syri hymni et sermones* [ed. T.J. Lamy; 1882], I, pp. 542-44)

5.

the holy day of the Lord: Rev. 1.10 uses the expression 'the Lord's day' to denote the timing of the Seer's initial vision in the context of early Christian worship. For an account of the development of ideas, consult Willy Rordorf, *Sunday: The History of the Day of Rest and Worship in the Earliest Centuries of the Christian Church* (ET A.A.K. Graham; London, SCM Press, 1968). Growing Christian observance of Sunday (as the day of Resurrection) is in contrast to, yet parallel with, Jewish observance of the Sabbath. The uneasy relationship between the two sayings attributed to Jesus in Mk 2.27 and 28 indicates the dimension of the problem: a proper critique of human institutions, and an acknowledgment of the supreme lordship of Christ.

6.

Sunday is the Lord: *Did.* 4.1, discussing the duty of the catechumen in the Church, gives the instruction 'My child, thou shalt remember both night and day him that speaketh unto thee the Word of God; thou shalt honour him as thou dost the Lord, *for where the teaching of the Lord is given, there is the Lord.*' The text here italicized expresses the presence of Christ where he is commemorated and his teaching recalled. This basic idea is intensified in such as John Chrysostom's vision of heaven on earth, realised in the liturgical forms of Church observance (see Introduction, above).

7.

at the ninth hour on Saturday: Orthodox Christianity follows the practice of Judaism and that of some Syriac Christians in that the liturgical day runs from sunset to sunset. *Did.* 9–10 indicates that the earlier idea of 'the breaking of the bread' was a complete meal, for the satisfaction of hunger (cf. 1 Cor. 11.20-22), and therefore took place in the evening. *Did.* 14.1 ('On the Lord's own day, assemble in common to break bread and offer thanks; but first confess your sins, so that your sacrifice may be pure') points to a regular preparatory act of confession of sins as part of the weekly liturgy. In this text the ninth hour is given as the time of the liturgical office and particularly of the act of confession.

The church practice of confession varied greatly, but there is a general indication of development from public to private styles of confession. Tertullian had described an extended and public process whereby the individual enlisted the help of the church in reconciliation: 'This confession is a disciplinary act of great humiliation...it teaches the penitent to cast himself at the feet of the presbyters, and to fall on his knees before the beloved of God, and to beg of all the brethren to intercede on his behalf (*De paenit.* 9). The Greek historian Sozomen describes the move towards a more private practice in the fifth century: 'Now in seeking pardon it is necessary to confess the sin, and since from the beginning the bishops decided, as is only right, that it was too much of a burden to announce one's sins as in a theatre, with the congregation of the church as witness, they appointed for this purpose a presbyter, a man of the best refinement, a man silent and prudent. To him sinners came and confessed their deeds' (*H.E.* 7.16).

God blesses like Abraham: This probably refers to God's blessing of and promise to Abraham, as in Gen. 12.2-3.

8.

If someone fasts: The normal practice of fasting for the Eastern Church was twice a week (on Wednesdays and Fridays) outside the fasting season of Lent. According to *Did.* 8, these two days were chosen to distinguish Christians from the strict Jewish practice of fasting on Mondays and Thursdays. But according to Epiphanius weekly fasting practice for Christians did not become universal until the later fourth century (*Haer*. 65.6; *Exp. fid.* 22). The impression here is of someone of extreme diligence in fasting, who yet falls short because of the non-observance of Sunday. Even Montanism, with its two weeks of partial fasting, exempted Saturday and Sunday. The extended fast as a special preparation for Easter, especially in Holy Week, became widespread in the fourth century, as a symbolic identification with the Passion of Christ. Fasting was regarded as a regular feature of monastic training (*askesis*).

10.

Whoever says...is a liar: The language is notably Johannine, in the sense that it is reminiscent of 1 John, e.g., 4.20.

12.

[Listen, righteous John] Fasting: The usual formula of reply is lacking at this point.

ascended to the heavens: One of the reasons behind the practice of fasting, apart from the virtues of self-discipline and ethical sincerity in saving food for the needy, is to intensify prayer and promote a heightened sense of spiritual awareness in the believer. Presumably this is the reference here, rather than the more drastic sense of fasting to death.

13.

the monk: This is the first indication of this work's explicit involvement with monasticism.

bread, wine or olive oil: See *Did.* 13.3-6: 'Thou shalt therefore take the first fruits of every produce of the wine-press and threshing-floor, of oxen and sheep, and shalt give it to the prophets, for they are your chief priests... In like manner when thou openest a jar of wine or of oil, take the first fruits and give it to the prophets.' These are the specified items of produce of which the prophet receives the firstfruit, because the Christian prophet has succeeded to the role of high priest of Israel. In one sense the monk might be reckoned the successor of the prophet; instead he represents the poor, and by virtue of sharing the hardship of the poor—fruitful fasting—he appreciates the charitable gift of the firstfruits which the poor receive.

14.

seculars: Literally this refers to those priests living 'in the world' contrasted with the 'monks' or members of religious orders who live according to monastic rule. Charitable 'sharing with the poor' is an individual act for clergy 'in the world' who may have property of their own to share.

16.

'anoint your face': Mt. 6.17-18.

'Go into your room': Mt. 6.6. Note that 'openly' is added to the quotation, to make the contrast explicit, as read in the text of Matthew by some authorities (L,W,Θ). Notice how the pattern of the Matthaean text is followed here, in linking together fasting and prayer.

commemorations of your saints: The saints are those separating from ordinary society and consecrated to God, in a 'transvaluation of values'. The martyr (or saint in witness and dying) would re-enter society, personifying Christ in his suffering; the martyr's kinship with Christ accorded him/her special powers. The commemoration of such witnesses and martyrs initiated a cult which involved the love feast (*agape*) and the martyr shrine (*memoria*). In this way the tomb of the dead saint provided a focus and model for the living. Devotion to the saints grew rapidly. By the fourth century the saints who are commemorated at the Eucharist, and are seen as offering prayer to God, are clearly distinguished from the 'ordinary' dead who would be beneficiaries of this liturgical sacrifice. John Chrysostom makes this distinction and exhorts his hearers to have confidence in the potency of the martyrs' intercession. In his sermons, particularly those preached at martyr celebrations, John stresses the rich fellowship which devotees on earth may enjoy with the saints in heaven. (Pragmatically, he and other fourth-century bishops made efforts to import sacred relics to Constantinople, because it did not have martyrs of its own.) The Orthodox idea of the communion of saints is vividly expressed as a golden chain by Symeon the New Theologian in the eleventh century: 'The Holy Trinity, pervading all men from first to last, from head to foot, binds them all together... The saints in each generation, joined to those who have gone before, and filled like them with light, become a golden chain, in which each saint is a separate link, united to the next by faith, works and love. So in the One God they form a single chain which cannot quickly be broken.' (*Centuries* 3.2-4).

slander: Nau commented on this reference that slander was traditionally a monastic vice. A further possibility might be to associate this reference with the contentious text of 1 Cor. 14.34 which declares that women 'are not permitted to speak' in church. John Chrysostom was one of the earliest commentators to see the simple verb λαλειν as referring to a localized problem of unauthorized gossip and chatter by women during service; in the words of Robert W.Allison the picture is of 'the Corinthian women as a bunch of chattering magpies whose hubbub contributed greatly to the disorderliness there' ('Let Women be Silent in the Churches (1 Cor. 14.33b-36): What did Paul Really Say, and What did it Mean', *JSNT* 32 [1988], pp. 27-60 [36]). In fasting too, proper control and steps to avoid disorder are required.

17.
'a little wine': See 1 Tim. 5.23.

demon's defeat: Any particular allusion, beyond the general ethical point in this reference, remains obscure.

18.
Wednesday and Friday: See *Did.* 8.1; *Didas.* 21 (see n. on 8 above)

Pentecost: In the Orthodox tradition all Wednesdays and Fridays (and in some monasteries Monday as well) are designated as fast days. The exception is for such days which fall between the feasts of Christmas and Epiphany, during Easter week, and during the week after Pentecost. In addition there are specially designated periods for fasting: the Great Fast of Lent; the Fast of the Apostles beginning on the Monday eight days after Pentecost and lasting until the Feast of St Peter and St Paul on 28 June; the Assumption Fast of the first two weeks of August; and the Christmas Fast of 40 days before the Festival.

martyr-saints: i.e. their feast days; see the note on 16 above.

burial: The allusion is presumably to funerary feasts, at which the normal Christian discipline (from as early as the fourth century Clementine Liturgy, in Book 8 of the *Apostolic Constitutions*) is to eat and drink with moderation. The Agape, or fellowship meal, was regularly associated with funerals in the Early Church; the practice continued into the fifth and sixth centuries, when the immoderate character of the gatherings led to its suppression. The meeting of friends and relatives of the deceased for hymns and prayers continued as a commemoration on the third, ninth and fortieth days after the death, and on the anniversary.

19.

Fasting is rich in divine grace: The redemptive as well as the disciplinary aspects of fasting have already been mentioned in the note on 12 above. 'Fasting and self-control are the first virtue, the mother, root, source and foundation of all good.' (Nicodemus the Hagiorite, *Philokalia* 4.232).

20.

(Chrysostom): The Greek text here includes the initial letters (Χρ) often used in manuscripts as an abbreviation of the name Chrysostom. As Nau points out ('Une deuxième Apocalypse', p. 217) this is the responsibility of the scribe who drew up the title for this work and perpetuated the confusion between John the Theologian and John Chrysostom (see also the Introduction).

symbols of the Church: Among the exterior symbols of the Church is the fact that the building has a single dome, which represents Jesus Christ as head of the Church.

From this point onwards we have effectively a liturgical commentary, in the responses given (and thereby authorized?) by Jesus, which follows the order of the Liturgy of John Chrysostom. I would like to record my thanks to a former student, Mr Kevin Jones of Canterbury for his detailed assistance with this liturgical material.

21.

chancel gates: The Royal or Holy doors in the Iconostasis (or screen of icons) represent the entrance to the kingdom of God, which is the Sanctuary

sanctuary: The altar is seen to represent both the throne of God in his heavenly kingdom, and also the tomb of Christ.

The reference to *remembrance* is strongly Eucharistic (1 Cor. 11.24-25) relating the fulfilment of the Messianic banquet of the Kingdom to the Resurrection of Christ.

The Lord's breast: in the context of Last Supper and Eucharist, recalls the posture of the beloved disciple in Jn 13.23, 25. On the other symbolism it is interesting to compare the liturgical commentary on the Byzantine liturgy by the seventh/eighth century St Germanus, Patriarch of Constantinople, for whom the *paten* corresponds to the hands of Joseph of Arimathea and of Nicodemus who wrap the body of Jesus for burial (Jn 19.40), while the ambo is the stone of the tomb on which the angel sits (Mt. 28.2).

the layman is not worthy: Explicitly it is only ordained males who are admitted to the sanctuary. Many canons of church councils corroborate such a prohibition of access to sanctuary or altar by laypeople (even to seculars as opposed to religious).

deaconess: See Rom. 16.1. The deaconesses are regarded as non-functioning at the Divine Liturgy (on the basis of the most uncompromising reading of 1 Cor. 14.34 and 1 Tim. 2.12). The instructions of *Apostolic Constitutions* 3.15 are explicit: 'Ordain also a deaconess...for the ministrations towards women'. This women's order seems to have developed in the East in the third century, to perform a ministry exclusively to women (pre-baptismal unction, reserved sacrament for sick women, and the keeping of the women's door). See J.G. Davies, 'Deacons, Deaconesses and the Minor Orders in the Patristic Period', *JEH* 14 (1963), pp. 1-15.

reading desk: This is the ambo, pulpit or raised reading desk, reached by a flight of steps, from which the Scriptures were read. The practice was probably adopted by Christians from the synagogue (cf.1 Esd. 9.42). John Chrysostom, instead of preaching from a sitting position, developed the practice of using the ambo for sermons, because his voice had been weakened by ascetic exercises.

22.
who the readers represent: Obviously the reference is to the orders of ministry, participating in the Liturgy; lay-readers are not meant. The bishop is still held as the ruler in the Church (see 23, and 1 Tim. 3.4). The priest represents the Saviour himself, or the angel of God proclaiming the resurrection. The deacon is an angel of the Lord, or the successor to John the Baptist.

23.
veil of cloud: The veil separates earth and heaven, while the earthly liturgical practice corresponds to the heavenly. For the concept of the heavenly altar see Rev. 8.3. The Greek word used for 'cloud' and 'veil' is νεφέλη which is close to the idea of ἀήρ, used for the liturgical veil to cover the oblations. But there are connections of thought with the καταπέτασμα used of the curtain in the Holy of Holies of the Temple in Jerusalem. In many Orthodox churches an actual veil is drawn across the Holy Doors at the point of the Great Entrance. The idea of the veil/

cloud is both defining and protective of sanctity; on occasion in the Old Testament tradition it is not only protective but also obstructive, as in Lam. 3.44 where God deliberately veils Jerusalem in cloud, so 'that our prayer should not pass through'.

The language describing Christ as High Priest in Hebrews speaks of the function of offering gifts (Heb. 5.1). Christ's particular gift is his own life-blood by means of which 'we have confidence to enter the sanctuary...by the new and living way which he opened for us through the curtain' (καταπέτασμα, Heb. 10.19-20).The first part of this representative and mediating work is seen as carried out by the Archangel Michael in *3 Baruch*. At 11.4 'Michael the commander of the angels comes down to receive the prayers of men'. Again at 14.2 'Michael is even now presenting the merits of men to God'.

the Great Entrance: In Orthodox rites this is the offertory procession of the Holy Gifts, that is the bringing of the bread and wine, from the altar of prothesis (where the elements are prepared) to the main altar in the sanctuary. For details see G. Dix, *The Shape of the Liturgy* (Westminster: Dacre Press, 1945), pp. 290-91.

The laity would not normally be kneeling at this point. But during the period of the Great Fast (Lent), when this Liturgy of the Presanctified is commonly used on days other than Saturdays and Sundays, then all would kneel for the Great Entrance. Such a reference to kneeling in the particular context of the Great Fast gives much clearer sense than Nau's translation ('Une deuxième apocalypse', p. 218): 'le laïque n'est pas digne de pénétrer (?) jusqu'en haut'.

25.

the angel of the Lord...departs: This would seem to contradict the view expressed by St John Chrysostom himself, who says: 'When the priest calls upon the Holy Spirit and offers the tremendous sacrifice... At this moment the very angels of God encompass the priest, and...lend their presence and take up the entire space around the altar' (*De Sacerdotis* 6.4).

At the Little Entrance—the Gospel procession—the priest prays thus: 'Grant that the Holy Angels may enter [the sanctuary] with us, that together we may serve and glorify thy goodness.'

There may be some confusion or corruption in the text here, regarding the Great and Little Entrances (see below, 28-29).

26.

antiphons: This refers specifically to the three sets of Scriptural verses, sung as responses by one choir after verses of psalms or hymns sung by a second choir, as found in the liturgies of both Basil and Chrysostom, prior to the Little Entrance.

introit: The third antiphon alone is properly called the Introit, or entrance song. 'Son of God, who rose from the dead, save us who sing to thee: alleluia'. During the Easter period this is sung in an expanded version. A variety of Psalm verses are incorporated, e.g., from Ps. 95.

27.

the Lord descended to Hell: Given the context of Resurrection, already established in the question about the third antiphon, it is natural to see this as a reference to the image of Anastasis and the Harrowing of Hell. It is more explicit in §38 below.

The key text on this subject is the Gospel of Nicodemus, found within the Acts of Pilate. The legend depends upon the Johannine tradition of Nicodemus and Joseph of Arimathea (Jn 3.1-15; 19.39). According to the apocryphal gospel, 'after the Resurrection of Christ, rumors circulated in the Jewish community that others had been resurrected too. Temple authorities delegated Nicodemus, Joseph, and other rabbis to inquire specifically about Karinus and Leucius, the twin sons of Simeon, who were said to have returned from the dead. The brothers' account of what they saw in Hades after they died, when Jesus broke down the gates of Hades and resurrected them along with other righteous men, forms the basis for the descent narrative.' (Alan E. Bernstein, *The Formation of Hell: Death and Retribution in the Ancient and Early Christian Worlds* [London: UCL Press, 1993], p.274).

The expanded form of the Old Roman Creed that we know as the Apostles' Creed is an important articulation of the growing belief in Christ's descent to Hell. This belief is based on New Testament texts such as Mt. 12.39-40; 27.52-53; Acts 2.24; Rom. 10.7; 1 Pet. 3.18-20, although these references are by no means universally accepted. The meaning attached to the belief is equally disputed. Is Christ's descent to accomplish the eschatological victory over the evil powers? Or does it represent the full enormity of sin which Christ bears on our behalf, such that the cross is the ultimate dereliction, a 'living hell'? Or is it the means of preaching the Gospel to those such as the Old Testament worthies who lived before Christ?

David: Again the convention of referring to the Psalms by the name of David the traditional author (but see the particular emphasis on David as a prophet in *2 Apoc. Jn* 8; cf. Cyril of Jerusalem, *Mystagogical Catechesis* 5.2, 6).

28.

the Great Entrance: See the note on 23 above, for the procession of the Holy Gifts from the altar of Prothesis into the Sanctuary.

29.

the Holy Gospel: This answer clearly refers to the Little Entrance, the Gospel procession, and not the Great Entrance, or Offertory Procession, which was the question asked in 28. Textual confusion might well be expected, but notice the tendency to merge (or confuse) these processions in 24-25 above.

an angel descends…: This vivid description of inspiration might be compared with the prophetic act of consuming a scroll of revelation, as in Rev. 10.10; Ezek. 2.8; 3.3.

'Go forth in peace': Originally this was the final item in the Liturgy—the Greek form of 'Ite Missa est'—(although now in Orthodox practice it is followed by the Ambo prayer and the distribution of the Antidoron, which stands in place of the consecrated 'elements'). What seems to be suggested by this text, and 25 above, is the particular involvement (and inspiration) of the angel in the procession towards, and away from, the altar.

30.

the Gradual: Psalms were sung between biblical readings at the Eucharist. Of these, the Gradual is sung between the Old Testament lesson and the epistle; it was so called because the singer did not ascend to the top step of the ambo (reserved for the gospel) but stood on a lower step (*gradus*). In the Orthodox liturgy this is properly called the Prok(e)imenon: in the seventh century this was a variable chant sung after the Old Testament lesson; by the ninth century the Old Testament lection had disappeared, leaving just the chant.

After this the sequence should be: Epistle, Alleluia, Gospel and the dismissal of the catechumens. The second part is the Liturgy of the Faithful which comprises: Kiss of Peace, the Doors, Creed, Sanctus and the Mysteries (presumably denoting the Anaphora and Epiclesis, rather than simply the Bread and Wine).

31.

David sings: See note on 27 above.

'Your spirit goes before...': The Prok(e)imenon is literally 'what is set forth' (or appointed to be read). It could be a whole Psalm text, or certain verses from a Psalm, or suitable sacred words repeated up to three times, with Psalm texts inserted between the repetitions. The song of Mary from Luke 1 is frequently used at this point before the Epistle. One possible origin for the sentence quoted here is Ps. 143.10.

The apostle Paul: Paul has a majority shareholding in the traditional authorship of the New Testament letters. The New Testament was conventionally divided between the Gospel and the Apostle, according to many early Christian writers. There was no difficulty then in referring to Paul's apostolic and authoritative teaching, as embodied in the Epistle on the majority of occasions.

Alleluia: Between the Epistle and the Gospel the Alleluia is sung three or nine times, with verses from Scripture intercalated.

with a voice worthy of the Gospel: This particular detail is also found in the *Apoc. Paul* 29. The idea seems to be that he sings with the voice of an angel of the Lord, comparable with the angelic declaration that 'guards' the holy gifts, at a later stage in the liturgy (The Epiclesis, see notes on 25 and 30, above).

listen with full attention: The reference is to the liturgical instruction given before the Gospel passage is read: 'Wisdom. Stand and attend. Let us hear from the Holy Gospel.'

The Catechumens: After the reading of the Gospel in the Orthodox liturgy comes the Insistent Ektenia or Litany, petitioning for peace, followed by the prayers for the Catechumens before they are dismissed. This marks the transition between the service for the catechumens and the Eucharistic liturgy for the *Faithful*. The Faithful proceed therefore to *have 'in remembrance' what the Lord said*, that is to participate in the Eucharist as a remembrance of the Last Supper (see the longer, non-Western text of Lk. 22.19 and 1 Cor. 11.24-25 and also the note on 21, above.)

hymn of the Cherubim: The Cherubic hymn is partly quoted here in the text:

> We who mystically represent the Cherubim, sing the Thrice-holy Hymn to the life-giving Trinity. Let us put away all worldly care, so that we may receive the King of All.

Now follows the Great Entrance (see note on 23, above).

32.

undefiled: See *2 Apoc. Jn* 1.

33.

Let us love one another': A recurrent Johannine refrain (cf. 1 Jn 4), here quoted from the Orthodox liturgy: 'Let us love one another, that we may with one mind confess' to which the response is: 'The Father, Son and Holy Spirit, Trinity, one in essence and undivided.' On the resolution of brotherly disputes, see also Mt. 5.23-24.

the kiss of peace: Originally this was the 'seal of prayer' among the faithful. Later it came to express the charity and unity that existed among the Ecclesia. 'The kiss is therefore reconciliation, and for this reason holy.' (Cyril of Jerusalem, *Myst. Cat.* 5.3; cf. Mt. 5.23; Rom. 16.16; 1 Cor. 16.20; 1 Pet. 5.14). Just as in modern church practice, there is enormous variation between traditions in the way such a kiss or 'pax' would be conveyed. For details see Dix, *The Shape of the Liturgy*, pp. 105-10.

34.

the Doors: After the Peace is given, in the liturgy a priest or deacon announces: 'The doors! The doors! In wisdom let us attend.' Then the Creed is said. Presumably the announcement, which has now become assimilated in the liturgical text, was originally an instruction to close the doors, a remnant of the early *Disciplina Arcani*. As John Chrysostom himself said (*In Matt.* 23.3): 'We too celebrate the mysteries with closed doors and keep out the uninitiated.' In a later development the exclamations came to refer only to the royal doors of the iconastasis. Since these had already been closed at the Great Entrance, the purpose of the injunction was to guard the sanctuary against unauthorized entry.

The person outside...who is in a hurry: This resembles the Jewish Chaburah, where the late-comer was excluded if he arrived after the handwashing and its accompanying berakah. See Dix, *The Shape of the Liturgy*, p. 54.

Nau ('Une deuxième apocalypse', p. 219) draws attention also to apocryphal texts which utter woes against those who leave the liturgy before the end.

35.

The holy Creed: The Creed is presumably in the form approved by the Church Councils of Nicaea and Constantinople.

36.

'Let us stand well, let us stand with fear': These are the opening words of the Holy Anaphora: 'Let us stand aright; let us stand in awe; let us attend, that we may make the Holy Offering in peace.' Again what was originally a rubric has become incorporated in the liturgical text.

Trisagion: See note on 37, below.

'We offer you...': The Liturgy is quoted at the point of the lesser elevation of paten and chalice, after the Dominical words and the Anamnesis: 'Thy gifts of what is thine we offer to Thee, in all we do, and for all Thy blessings.' Cf. 1 Chron. 29.14.

the lifting up: This refers to the traditional posture of prayer, standing with arms raised, as in the figure of the 'Orans' in early Christian art. Cf. 1 Tim. 2.8.

'Our Father': The Lord's Prayer is said together, during which the priest lifts his hands and keeps them high.

'Holy things for holy people': Again the Liturgy is quoted directly, in an ancient liturgical formula of the Eastern rite (see also 39, below; cf. Cyril of Jerusalem, *Myst. Cat.* 5.19): 'Holy things for holy persons', to which the response is made: 'One is the Holy, One is the Lord, Jesus Christ, to the glory of God, the Father, Amen.' This immediately precedes the Communion Anthem and the actual partaking of the Eucharist. It can be described as a liturgical argument taking place between the president and the congregation.

the Dismissal: The normal Greek form is 'Let us go forth in peace', corresponding to the Latin 'Ite Missa est' (see note on 29, above).

37.

The Cherubim sing the Trisagion: The hymn normally referred to as the Trisagion is part of the Synaxis, and is comparable to the 'Gloria' in the Western liturgies. Everything in §36 is, however, concerned with the Anaphora. So, in that context, the reference is more probably to the Tersanctus. And, as with the Cherubic Hymn earlier (see note on 31, above), the preface to this item of the liturgy specifically associates the Triumphal Hymn with the heavenly creatures, cherubim and seraphim. In the liturgy the Hymn is introduced by the priest in these words: 'Singing, crying, proclaiming the Triumphal Hymn and saying...' Each verb used here in its participial form is associated with one of the four *Living Creatures* in Rev. 4.7-8, in the order of eagle, ox, lion and man respectively.

The final Living Creature in human form is here singled out for further comment. Use is made of the interchange between man and angel, as found in Rev. 22.8-9, where the subservience to God is also emphasized in similar terms.

38.

This gives a fuller description of the Anastasis and Descent of Christ to Hell (see note on 27, above). The Offertory sentence from the liturgy (see note on 36, above) is taken up again and used to provide a theological meaning for the 'Harrowing of Hell'. Clearly it represents an eschatological victory, with the destruction of the evil spirits and of the strong gates of Hell itself. But more importantly in this interpretation, Christ makes the Offertory his own. The fundamental sacrifice of self-giving is Christ's own self-offering on the cross. This death leads to resurrection, not only Christ's resurrection, but also the general resurrection, of which Christ's resurrection is a pledge (cf. Paul in 1 Cor. 15.20). The promise of general resurrection is symbolized by the raising of Adam, the first man. The raising of Adam, together with the other worthies of the Old Testament, is a traditional objective of Christ's descent to the underworld. One of the *Questions of St Bartholomew* asks about the descent of Christ into Hell. Christ is asked where he really was, while on the cross at the time when darkness covered the earth (Mt. 27.45). He answers that he had been looking for Adam in the underworld.

There could be no clearer expression of the presupposition here that the Eucharistic liturgy closely parallels the events of Christ's death and resurrection.

39.

the Sanctuary doors: Following the singing of the Communion Anthem, the priest comes out from the Royal Doors of the Sanctuary, holding the chalice and saying the liturgical words: 'With fear of God, with faith and with love come forth.' The faithful who are prepared then receive Holy Communion.

holding a reed-pen: In this apocalyptic version of the liturgy the priest is transfigured in angelic form. He resembles the 'man clothed in linen, with a writing case at his side' who puts 'a mark upon the foreheads of the men who sigh and groan over all the abominations' (Ezek. 9.2, 4). In other words, he differentiates the faithful from the disobedient. The reed is not only a writing instrument, suitable for making marks; it is also a measuring rod, and so there are resemblances too with the 'man, whose appearance was like bronze, with a line of flax and a measuring reed in his hand…standing in the gateway' (Ezek. 40.3). He measures the bounds of the holy city, just as the Seer measures 'the temple of God and the altar and those who worship there' (Rev. 11.1). This measurement is again a drawing of boundaries, between the holy temple and the outer courtyard which will be trampled by the nations. It is a clear line that is drawn between the holy and the unholy.

ill at ease (disobedient): cf. *Did.* 10.6: 'If anyone is holy let him come; if anyone is not, let him repent.' The following clauses about spiritual revelation (*gaze upon me*) and the lack of physical capacity, or volition, to see, are reminiscent of 1 Cor. 2.9-10 (which quotes from/ alludes to Isa. 64 and 65). The language is yet more highly coloured in the apocalyptic tradition of thunder and lightning (cf. Rev. 10).

the Holy Spirit descends: The illapse of the Holy Spirit which follows the liturgical words 'We offer you', consecrates or makes the Body and the Blood.

'Holy things for holy people': See note on 36, above. The words of invitation to Communion precede the singing of the Anthem: 'Receive ye the Body of Christ, and taste ye Him, Who is a Fountain of Immortality.' The Holy Spirit consecrates, but the ultimate recipients of the Spirit are those who partake in the Communion.

40.

'Let us go forth in peace': See note on 36, above.

An angel gives the Blessing: The liturgy ends with a final blessing, after which, in the Orthodox tradition, the people come forward in order to kiss a Cross which the priest is holding in his hand and to receive a small piece of bread, blessed but not consecrated, which is known as the *Antidoron*. Ps. 33.11-22 is read, which unites earth and heaven in the perspective of God. See note on 25, above. Repeatedly we have noticed the role of angels within the liturgy which blends earth and heaven.

41.

the person who reveres the priest: The Orthodox Church has three 'major' orders: Bishop, Presbyter and Deacon (which can have its own identity, rather than being an apprenticeship for priesthood); and two 'minor' orders (Sub-deacon and Reader). In the second half of the fourth and in the fifth centuries the title 'priest' was normally applied to the Bishop, and only occasionally to the Presbyter.

John Chrysostom was himself the author of a treatise on priesthood (*De Sacerdotio* [ed. A.M. Malingrey; Sources chrétiennes, 272; Paris, 1980]), probably written around 390 CE. It is presented as a dialogue between himself and his boyhood comrade Basil, including autobiographical material designed to explain that his original refusal to be forced into ordination was based on his sense of unworthiness for the priestly office. The work then describes, in J.N.D. Kelly's words (*Golden Mouth: The Story of John Chrysostom. Ascetic, Preacher, Bishop* [London: Gerald Duckworth, 1995]), 'the awesome dignity and terrifying responsibilities of a priest or bishop, privileged as he is (for example) to baptize, to absolve sinners, even to make Christ present on the altar, but also liable to be held to account in the life to come for the misdeeds any of his charges may have committed' (p. 84).

43.

Baptism: John Chrysostom's work in preparing candidates for baptism is documented by two sets of his catechetical lectures, delivered between enrolment early in Lent and Easter week, continuing after the baptism on the night of Easter. The message to the newly-baptized (in Kelly's summary of the lectures, *Golden Mouth*, p. 89) 'is that, reborn as they now are in Christ, they must dazzle people by their exemplary conduct, avoiding for example excess in food and drink, keeping well clear of the distractions of horse-racing and the theatre, visiting the shrines of martyrs to obtain the healing of body and soul their relics bestow, resolutely adopting a routine which includes daily prayer in church before getting down to the day's business, and returning in the evening to implore God's forgiveness for any sins they may have committed'. These texts presuppose believers' baptism; John Chrysostom himself was not baptized until the end of his student days. Baptism in the New Testament church appears to have been an act of repentance and confession of faith (cf. Acts 2.38; 3.19; 18.8).

The Eastern rite of baptism is by threefold immersion, signifying the death of a sinner and resurrection and redemption as a new Christian. With this initiation the whole Church receives the new member. The cosmic significance of the act is illustrated by this prayer, to consecrate the water: 'Great art Thou, O Lord, and marvellous are Thy works, and there is no word which sufficeth to hymn Thy wonders. Before Thee tremble all the powers endowed with intelligence. The sun singeth with Thee, the moon glorifieth Thee, the stars meet together in Thy presence, the light obeyeth Thee, the water springs are subject unto Thee. Wherefore O King, who lovest mankind, come Thou now and sanctify this water by the indwelling of the Holy Spirit, and grant unto it the grace of redemption and the blessing of Jordan. Make it the fountain of incorruption, the gift of sanctification, the remission of sins and the remedy of infirmities.'

hair be cropped (tonsured): The public example, in conduct and practice after baptism, is demonstrated particularly in the tonsure. The shaving of part or all of the head became a general custom in fourth and fifth century monasticism, and then a form of admission to the clerical state to differentiate it from the minor orders. Eastern practice was to shave the entire head, without leaving a fringe.

48.

woman/hair: This section of the apocalypse clearly has a preoccupation with haircuts and length of hair, matters which in the secular world are culturally relative, but on which rigid stances are often adopted. In 1 Cor. 11 Paul seems to describe the assumptions of contemporary Greek culture, where women must cover their hair because otherwise they shame their heads (it is the equivalent for a woman of disgracing herself by shaving her head), and where men with long hair were often regarded as homosexual. Paul himself may be reacting to this situation in the light of his Jewish background, or because of his new-found Christian freedom.

John Chrysostom had a characteristically masculine attitude towards women. In his *Discourse 2 on Genesis*, commenting on Gen. 1.26-27. he writes: 'the man is in the 'image of God' since he had no one above him, just as God has no superior but rules over everything. The woman, however, is 'the glory of man', since she is subjected to him.' John Chrysostom provided an extensive treatment of the moral aspects of marriage in several treatises *On Marriage and Family Life* (trans. C.P. Roth and D. Anderson; Crestwood: St Vladimir's Seminary, 1986). Marriage is no obstacle to salvation, for it is divinely ordained. But the original intention (for the procreation of children) has been contaminated by the indulgence of sexual instincts, so that strong souls may rather seek virginity. Marriage, however, if capable of repressing evil desires, may like virginity promote spiritual salvation.

F. Nau, referring to the curse at the conclusion of 48, observes that the text of a *Didascalia of our Lord Jesus Christ* has a different emphasis. According to his edition and translation (*Revue de l'Orient chrétien* 12 [1907], p. 219), it reads: 'Woe to women who have adorned their hair for the holy day of Sunday.'

49.

Love: The answer to the question neatly harmonizes quotations from the Johannine and Pauline traditions on the subject of *Agape*. Among John Chrysostom's many sermon expositions are 88 homilies on the Gospel of John delivered in 391 CE (see Migne, *PG* 59), and 14 homilies (out of a total of 44 on the whole Corinthian correspondence) interpreting 1 Cor. in 392/93 CE (see Migne, *PG* 61). The prime emphasis of these sermon/commentaries in the Antiochene tradition—and John Chrysostom was one of the most highly esteemed exegetes in antiquity—rests in the understanding of the relationship between Christian faith and morals.

51.

Peace: There is a rich tradition of Biblical theology focused on the terms *shalom* and *eirene*, but it is attractive to see this reference in a more liturgical context as well. The rite of 'the Peace' or 'the kiss of Peace' is found as early as Justin Martyr's *1 Apology* 65.2: 'After the prayers have been completed, we greet each other with a kiss.' In the New Testament there is some basis for this in the 'holy kiss' of Rom. 16.16; 1 Cor. 16.20; 2 Cor. 13.12; 1 Thess. 5.26; and in 1 Pet. 5.14 ('kiss of love'). In the Eastern liturgy the Peace retained the position after the prayers in worship, while the Western tradition moved it to the Eucharistic celebration. It could also be used at baptism, ordination, marriage, veneration of martyrs and burial in the early church. As a conclusion to the prayers, and a conclusion to this theological dialogue, the emphasis would be on reconciliation. Peace and love come together to God's glory.

Chapter 5

THE THIRD APOCALYPSE OF JOHN

Introduction

The third Apocalypse does indeed retain the same interrogatory format as the other two. The significant change is that it is no longer John asking the questions (as when he speaks with the elder in the canonical apocalypse, e.g., Rev. 7.13-17), but now it is St John the Theologian who gives the authoritative answers, in response to the questions of James the brother of the Lord.

The Greek text of this Apocalypse was published in the first volume of A. Vassiliev's *Anecdota Graeco-Byzantina* (Moscow, 1893), pp. 317-22. The text was derived from the codices of St Mark in Venice, number 87, class II, fol. 255-62, dating from the fourteenth to fifteenth century. It is clear that there are several lacunae in the sense of the text, besides which this may well be a truncated version of a substantially longer original.

Such 'question and answer sessions' can include quite a mixture of traditional materials (see for example the questioning of the Cherubim in the Coptic text, The Mysteries of Saint John the Apostle and Holy Virgin). *3 Apoc. Jn* appears more concentrated and systematic, with its focus on two particular themes : the future judgment of souls, and the exhortation to penitence. Compared with the future concerns expressed in *2 Apoc. Jn*, this apocalypse is altogether more doom-laden and pessimistic in its visions of hellish torment. The separation of the sinners from the righteous is a sharp division reflected in the structure of the text itself (*3 Apoc. Jn* 3–10; 12–16). Even though the righteous also go through a refining trial by ordeal, the radical divide resembles the separation of sheep and goats (Mt. 25) or even more the gulf fixed between the rich man and Lazarus (Lk. 16.26). 'There is between the sinners and the righteous a great chasm, and in the chasm a fire which burns the sinners, but on the righteous there is a refreshing dew' (*3 Apoc. Jn* 16, cf. Ignatius, *Magn.* 14).

The idea of the unquenchable fire of Gehenna, as in Mk 9.48, has been expanded far beyond the lake of fire in Rev. 19.20, so as to become a variety of fiery tortures and punishments, as in the tradition of the Apocalypses of Peter and of Paul. In the same way the devouring worm that never dies, also from Mk 9.48, has a tormenting role: the sinner-soul is abandoned with the worm, but 'the worm has no authority to devour the soul until the Lord's Second Coming' (*3 Apoc. Jn* 6). The sinful victims—and even the righteous souls—are made to witness the torments and punishments; they witness the anticipatory terror of the place of punishment (*3 Apoc. Jn* 7, 9). We are close to the sentiments expressed by St Thomas Aquinas: 'Hell-fire is said to be eternal only on account of its endlessness. There is change in their punishments, witness Job 24: they shall go to excessive heat from the waters of the snows. Hence in hell there is not true eternity, but rather the experience of time.'

3 Apoc. Jn applies a simple 'rewards and punishment' theodicy to the judgment of each individual. It is clear that repentance is the action required above all other. As in the case that is put to Job by his 'comforters', if you acknowledge your sin and are truly sorry, God will forgive.

> I tell you this categorically, James friend of God, God does not listen to the requests of unrepentant sinners (*3 Apoc. Jn* 10).

> Woe to the priests who sin and do not repent!' (*3 Apoc. Jn* 32).

> After a man's death there is no such thing as repentance or forgiveness of the penitent. But again I tell you not to lose hope in God's loving-kindness towards us, because God himself says, 'Him who comes to me I will not cast out' (*3 Apoc. Jn* 35, cf. Jn 6.37).

As in the apocalyptic traditions going back as far as *1 Enoch*, there has been an eschatological transposition of the Old Testament theodicy (e.g. Ps. 1): the reward and the punishment, assigned in this life to the righteous and the wicked respectively, are transposed after death into the age to come. Such apocalyptic eschatology presupposes a clear and neat distinction between the righteous and the wicked. This distinction is given superhuman, cosmic dimensions. To talk in these terms may seem to the modern reader premature, presumptuous and primitive. But in apocalyptic eschatology the final judgment clearly remains with God alone. The threat of judgment is meant to induce the audience to make the right choice, and secure their future as individuals.

The colourful language and imagery of *3 Apoc. Jn* also still shows the influence of Greek thought about the afterlife. As in Plato's *Phaedo* 81b-d, 107d, 108b-c,

> in the land of Hades the soul is met by its guardian spirit, a personal supernatural guide, which leads it to the place of judgment. [cf. *3 Apoc. Jn* 2, 4]. A soul that is well disposed follows its guide properly, whereas a soul that excessively loves its body…must be forcibly removed to the next world by the appointed spirit [cf. *3 Apoc. Jn* 12–14]. When such a soul reaches the place of judgment, the other souls avoid it and refuse it counsel or guidance, so that it wanders aimlessly, until finally it is thrust into the place assigned to its kind.[1]

The cosmology of the underworld is complex; as Homer described it, Tartarus lies far below Hades, and is fed by four rivers. The third river is Pyriphlegethon, and it falls into a region burning with great fire (cf. *3 Apoc. Jn* 5). 'The dead populate the interior of this complex, riddled, spongelike earth. They are assigned to different regions at the judgment after their deaths.'[2] Whereas in *3 Apoc. Jn* (at least in its truncated text) there is a simple distinction between the reward of the righteous penitent and the punishment of the impenitent sinner, for Plato there was a wider range of options, the four fates of the holy, those of indeterminate character, the guilty but curable, and the incurably wicked.

The second major theme of *3 Apoc. Jn*, the necessity of penitence, has already been mentioned several times. In its exhortation this text offers a range of exemplars of true penitence (*3 Apoc. Jn* 23–27). It may resemble a rogues' gallery, but the greater the offence, so the more impressive is the example of penitence, and the more wonderful is God's forgiving grace. The seven examples are Simon Peter and his threefold denial; Mary (Magdalene = hairdresser/prostitute) the amalgam of the sinful woman as symbolized by the story of Lk. 7.37-50 who is said to have sinned with 1703 men; Manasseh who murdered his son, 40 elders and Isaiah; the penitent brigand at the crucifixion who had murdered 99; David the prophet/king seen as adulterer with Bathsheba and 99 others; Andrew of Crete (guilty of an incestuous relation-

---

1. Bernstein, *The Formation of Hell*, p. 54. Cf. *3 Apoc. Jn* 8, 9.
2. Bernstein, *The Formation of Hell*, p. 55.

ship with his own mother); and finally Cyprian the sorcerer who became a bishop.

There is no obvious logic in the order of these exemplars. But it is reasonable to make deductions from any clues which this selection might offer. At first sight the inclusion of the notorious king of Judah, Manasseh (2 Kgs 21) is surprising. But the penitential psalm known as the Prayer of Manasseh, to be found in the Old Testament Apocrypha, was added to the Psalter in some early Greek bibles, and its use in the Christian Church is attested by its inclusion in both the *Didascalia* (early third century) and the later *Apostolic Constitutions*. Cyprian the sorcerer is not to be confused (as the Anglican Book of Common Prayer does) with Cyprian the bishop of Carthage who was martyred some half century earlier. Cyprian of Antioch was a pagan magician and astrologer who, according to a doubtful legend, used his skills to ensnare a Christian virgin Justina, but instead was converted by her. Justina became head of a convent, and Cyprian a bishop, but both were beheaded in Diocletian's persecution early in the fourth century.

The most recent historical reference here is to Andrew of Crete, the theologian and hymn writer, who was Archbishop of Gortys, briefly became a Monothelite in 712 CE, then retracted, and who died c. 740 CE. From this it it would be a fair inference that the date of composition for the third apocalypse is around the end of the eighth century or early in the ninth.

Τοῦ Ἰακώβου τοῦ ἀδελφοῦ τοῦ Κυρίου ἐρώτησις καὶ ἀπόκρισις πρὸς
τὸν ἅγιον Ἰωάννην τὸν Θεολόγον.
Δέσποτα εὐλόγησον.

1. Εἰπὲ ἡμῖν, Ἰωάννη Θεολόγε, περὶ τῶν ἐσχάτων ἡμερῶν τῶν
ἀνθρώπων· πῶς ἀπέρχεται ἡ ψυχὴ ἐκ τοῦ σώματος καὶ ποῦ μέλλει
κατοικεῖν ἕως τῆς δευτέρας παρουσίας τοῦ Κυρίου ἡμῶν Ἰησοῦ
Χριστοῦ;
2. Ὁ δὲ Ἰωάννης λέγει πρὸς αὐτόν· ἄκουσον, Ἰάκωβε. ἐὰν ἔλθῃ
κέλευσις τοῦ ἀοράτου θεοῦ ἡμῶν τοῦ χωρίσαι ψυχὴν ἐκ τοῦ σώματος,
ἔρχεται ὁ ἄγγελος ὁ ἐξ ἀρχῆς ἦν μετὰ τὸν ἄνθρωπον καὶ ὁ πρῶτος
ἀρχάγγελος Μιχαὴλ μετὰ ξίφων πυρίνων, καὶ μετ᾽αὐτῶν τῶν δύο
ἄλλοι τέσσαρεις, καὶ ἀναλαμβάνουσιν τὴν ψυχὴν ἐκ τοῦ σώματος καὶ
ἀκολουθοῦν τοῦ σώματος ἕως τοῦ μνήματος μετὰ τῆς ψυχῆς καὶ
παραστήκουν ἐν τῷ μνήματι ἕως οὗ σφραγισθῇ τὸ μνημεῖον ἀπὸ τοῦ
ἱερέως.
3. Καὶ τότε ἡ ἁμαρτωλὴ ψυχὴ θρηνεῖ σφόδρα καὶ λέγει· οἴμοι,
οἴμοι! ὅτι ἀφῆκα φῶς δύναντα καὶ ἀπέρχομαι εἰς σκότος τὸ τόποτε
ἐκεῖ μὴ γεννώμενον. οἴμοι! ἀφῆκα τοὺς φίλους μου καὶ ἀπέρχομαι εἰς
χώραν ἣν οὐχ ἑωρακά ποτε. οἴμοι, οἴμοι! ὅτι ἀφῆκα τὸ σῶμά μου ὅλον
χνοῦς ἐστιν. ἀλλὰ χαρὰν πρόσκαιρον μετ᾽αὐτὸν εἶχα καὶ ὑπάγω ἐκεῖ
ὅπου χαρὰ καὶ δόξα τῶν ἁμαρτωλῶν οὐκ ἔστιν.
4. Καὶ μετὰ ταῦτα παραλαμβάνουσιν αὐτὴν οἱ ἄγγελοι καὶ
ἀναβαίνουσιν ἕως τοῦ ἀέρως. καὶ ἀπαντῶν αὐτῶν αἱ τάξεις τῶν
δαιμόνων ὡσεὶ νέφος καὶ ὡσεὶ κόρακες μελανίζοντες καὶ συμπλέκων
τὴν ψυχὴν τὴν ἁμαρτωλὴν καὶ λέγουσιν οὕτως· ἐν τῇ βαπτίσει αὐτῶν
ὑπὸ τοῦ ἱερέως ἀπαρνήσατε ἡμᾶς, καὶ πάλιν τὴν σφραγίδαν αὐτοῦ
ἀρνησάμενος καὶ ἐποίησεν τὰ ἡμῶν θελήματα ἕως τοῦ σώματος αὐτοῦ.
5. Καὶ τότε κραυγὴ γίνεται τοῦ ἀρχαγγέλου Μιχαὴλ καὶ συνάγον-
ται μύριαι μυριάδες ἀγγέλων μετὰ ξίφων φλογερῶν καὶ τοῦ τιμίου καὶ
ζωοποιοῦ σταυροῦ καὶ ἀπολαύνονται αἱ τάξεις τῶν δαιμόνων ἕως
χάος τοῦ ᾅδου. καὶ τότε ὑπάγουσιν τὴν ἁμαρτωλὴν εἰς τὸν πύρινον
ποταμὸν καὶ δέχεται τὴν ψυχὴν ὁ πύρινος ποταμὸς καὶ φλογίζεται ἡ

THE THIRD APOCALYPSE OF JOHN

Question and answer to Saint John the Theologian from James the
Lord's brother.
Master, give us your blessing.

1. 'Tell us, John the Theologian, about the last days of mankind. How
does the soul leave the body, and where will it reside until the *Second
Coming* of our Lord Jesus Christ?'

2. John says to him: 'Listen, James. If a command comes from our
God who is invisible, that a soul should go from its body, *then comes
the angel* who followed the person from the beginning, and Michael the
first archangel, with the fiery swords, and with these two four others;
they take up the soul from the body, and they and the soul follow the
body to the grave; they are present at the grave, until the tomb is sealed
by the priest.

3. Then the soul of the sinner laments greatly: 'Alas, woe is me! *I
left the light as it faded; I come away into the darkness, *never to be
reborn*. Oh! I left my friends, and come away to a land I have never
seen. Alas, woe is me! I left my body to be nothing but dust. By means
of my body I had a time of joy, but I go away where there is no joy or
glory for sinners.'

4. After this the angels take the soul with them and go up to the
kingdom of the air. Out of all the beings, the ranks of the demons,
making a black cloud like crows, interweave with the *sinner-soul* and
say: 'At the Christian baptism by the priest he denied us; but in contrast
he denied the baptismal sign and did our will as far as his body was
concerned.'

5. Then comes a great shout from Michael the Archangel; *thousands
upon thousands* of angels gather, with flaming swords and the priceless,
life-giving cross, and the ranks of demons are banished to the pit of
Hell. Then the angels take the sinner to the river of fire. The soul is

(* Indicates a probable lacuna in the Greek text)

ψυχὴ τὰς δυναστείας τῶν κολάσεων. καὶ ὅτε περάσει ἡ ψυχὴ τὸν ποταμὸν μελονομένη λέγει τὸ Ὑπὸ ἀμαρτωλῶν πλανηθέντα καὶ ταύτοις τοῖς βασάνοις ὑποβληθέντα, ἀλλὰ Κύριε, Κύριε, μὴ εἴδω ταύτην τὴν κόλασιν ποτε.

6. Καὶ παραμένει ἐκεῖ ἡμέρας τρεῖς καὶ θεωρεῖ τὸν βρυγμὸν τοῦ ποταμοῦ καὶ τὴν δύναμιν τῶν βασάνων καὶ τότε ἀπέρχεται ἡ ψυχὴ ὑπὸ τῶν ἀγγέλων καὶ προσκυνεῖ τὸν θρόνον τὸν τετράμορφον καὶ ἀπάγουν αὐτὸν οἱ ἄγγελοι εἰς τὸν σκώληκα τὸν ἀκοίμητον καὶ καταλείπουν τὴν ψυχὴν ὡς μὴ ἔχων [ὁ σκώληξ] ἐξουσίαν καταβιβρώσκειν αὐτὴν ἕως τῆς δευτέρας παρουσίας τοῦ Κυρίου.

7. Καὶ λέγει ἡ ἀμαρτωλὴ ψυχὴ μετὰ δακρύων· οὐαί μοι τῷ ἀμαρτωλῷ καὶ ἀμετανόητῳ ὅτι τῶν αὐτοῦ βασάνων ὑπεβλήθην! οὐαί μοι τῷ ἀμαρτωλῷ καὶ ἄφρωνι ὅτι ἤκουον τοῦ Εὐαγγελίου καὶ κατεγέλων τοὺς ἱερεῖς τοὺς ἡμῖν διαμαρτυροῦντας, ἤκουον τῶν προφητῶν καὶ ὡς μὴ ἀκούων αὐτοὺς ἐπολοτεύομην. οὐαί μοι τῷ ἀμαρτωλῷ. ἀλλὰ Κύριε, Κύριε, μὴ εἴδω τοῖς βασάνοις τούτοις πώποτε. καὶ παραμένει ἐκεῖ ἡμέρας θ´ καὶ τότε ἀπέρχεται ὑπὸ τῶν ἀγγέλων καὶ προσκυνεῖ τὸν θρόνον τὸν πυρίμορφον καὶ ἀπάγουν αὐτὸν εἰς τὰς κολάσεις πάσας. καὶ ἀπὸ πάντων καταισχύνεται καὶ βοοῦν αἱ κολάσεις πρὸς αὐτόν· δεῦρο, ἄξιε τῶν ἑτέρων κολάσεων. οὐκ ἠθέλησας τὸ φῶς, δέχου τὸ σκότος. οὐκ ἠθέλησας παραδείσου τὴν χαράν, δέχου τῶν κολάσεων.

8. Καὶ τότε θρηνεῖ ἡ ψυχὴ μετὰ δακρύων καὶ λέγουσα· οὐαί μοι τῷ ἀμαρτωλῷ τῷ πλανηθέντι ἐν ἀμαρτίαις καὶ μὴ μετανοήσαντι. καὶ παραμένει ἐκεῖ ἡ ψυχὴ ἡμέρας μ´ καὶ ἀπάγεται ὑπὸ τῶν ἀγγέλων καὶ προσκυνεῖ τὸν θρόνον τοῦ Κυρίου· τότε ὀρᾷ τὸν Υἱὸν τοῦ θεοῦ καὶ λυπηθήσονται οἱ ἄγγελοι καὶ ἀρχάγγελοι ὅτι ὑπάγῃ ἡ ψυχὴ εἰς κόλασιν αἰώνιον μετὰ πονηρῶν ἀγγέλων.

9. Καὶ γὰρ οὐκ εἰσὶν οἱ ἄγγελοι πονηροί, μὴ γένοιτο, ἀλλὰ διὰ τὰς πράξεις τῶν ἀμαρτωλῶν γενήσονται καὶ οἱ ἄγγελοι πονηροὶ καὶ ἀπάγουνται ἀπέναντι τῶν κολάσεων ὅπου μέλλουν κολάζεσθαι εἰς ὅλους τοὺς αἰῶνας, καὶ θεωρεῖ τοὺς βασάνους ὅπου μέλλουν κολάζεσθαι καὶ λέγει· Κύριε, Κύριε, ὁ ποιήσας τὸν οὐρανὸν καὶ τὴν γῆν, μὴ ἔλθῃ ἡ δευτέρα παρουσία καὶ ὑποβληθῶ τῶν αὐτοῦ βασάνων.

10. Ἀλλὰ τοῦτο λέγω, Ἰάκωβε φίλε θεοῦ, ἀμαρτωλῶν ἀμετανοήτων θεὸς οὐκ εἰσακούει.

11. Ὁ Ἰάκωβος λέγει πρὸς αὐτόν· Θεολόγε Ἰωάννη, ἀνάγγειλόν μοι καὶ περὶ τῶν δικαίων.

12. [ ] ὅταν δὲ χωρίζεται ἡ ψυχὴ ἐκ τοῦ σώματος αὐτοῦ λέγει· εὐχαριστῶ σοι, θεέ μου, καλὲ βασιλεῦ οὐράνιε, ὅτι ἀπεχωρίσθην

received by the *river of fire*, and is aflame in the power of the punishments. If the blackened soul crosses the river it says: 'Deceived by men, and subjected to these *torments*, but—Lord, Lord!—may I not know this punishment for ever.'

6. The soul stays there for three days, observing the way the river devours and how powerful are the torments, then departs with the angels and worships the fourfold throne. The angels take him to the *worm that never dies*; there they leave the soul, because the worm has no authority to devour the soul until the Lord's Second Coming.

7. The sinner-soul, in tears, says: 'Woe to me, the *unrepentant* sinner, that I am subjected to these torments! Woe to me, the stupid sinner, that I heard the Gospel and yet mocked the priests who witnessed and warned us; I heard the prophets but led my life as if I did not hear them! Woe to me, the sinner! But Lord, Lord, may I not know these torments for ever!'

The soul stays there for nine days, then goes away with the angels, and worships the throne that looks like fire. The angels take him to all the punishments. He shrinks in terrified shame from them all. The torturers shout to him: 'Come here, you deserve other punishments. You did not want the *light*; now accept the *darkness*. You did not want the joy of *Paradise*; now accept the tortures.'

8. Then the soul laments in tears: 'Woe to me, the sinner who went astray into many offences and did not repent!' The soul stays there for 40 days, then goes away with the angels and worships the throne of the Lord. Then he sees the Son of God. The angels and archangels become distressed because the soul may go away into eternal punishment in company with wicked angels.

9. Not that the angels are wicked as such, heaven forbid, but, through the actions of the sinners, the angels also will become wicked. These angels are taken away to face the tortures, where they will be punished for evermore. Each observes the torments where they are to be punished and says: 'Lord, Lord, the Creator of heaven and earth, may the *Second Coming* arrive so that I be no longer subjected to these torments.'

10. But I tell you this categorically, James, friend of God, God does not listen to the requests of unrepentant sinners.'

11. James says to him: 'John the Theologian, reveal to me also what happens to the *righteous*.'

12. * 'When a righteous soul goes from its body, it says: "I give thanks to you, my God, great king of heaven, that I am separated from a

πηλίνου σώματος καὶ ἐφάνην ἐγὼ φωτεινὸς καὶ αὐτὸς κατάκειται ἐν
γῇ διαλυθείσας ἣν ἄξια· καὶ γὰρ ἀπέρχομαι εἰς φῶς τοῦ παραδείσου
ὡς οὐκ ἐπαρέβην ἐντολὴν τῶν ἱερέων οὔτε λόγους τοῦ ἁγίου
Εὐαγγελίου.

13. Καὶ τότε ἀπάγουν αὐτὸν ἐν τῷ ἀέρι καὶ θεωροῦντες αὐτὸν οἱ
δαίμονες κατακρύπτονται ὡς οὐκ εἰσὶν ἄξιοι προσαπαντῆσαι τῷ
δικαίῳ, ἀλλὰ μᾶλλον θεωροῦντες αὐτὸν μακρόθεν θρηνοῦντες ἄμετρα
καὶ λέγουν· οὐαὶ ἡμῖν ὅτι οὐκ ἐσμὲν ἄξιοι μόνον ἵνα θεασώμεθα αὐτόν.
καὶ ὑπάγουν αὐτὸν οἱ ἄγγελοι εἰς τὸν πύρινον ποταμὸν καὶ περνᾷ ὡς
περιστερὰ πετάζουσα καὶ παραμένει ἐκεῖ ἡ ψυχὴ ἡμέρας τρεῖς καὶ
λέγει οὕτως· εὐχαριστῶ σοι, Κύριε, ὅτι ἄσπιλος καὶ ἀκόλαστος τῶν
βασάνων τούτων διεπέρασα. καὶ προσκυνεῖ τὸν θρόνον τὸν τετράμορφον, καὶ συνακολουθοῦσιν αὐτὸν οἱ ἄγγελοι καὶ ἀπάγουν αὐτὸν εἰς
τὸν σκώληκα τὸν ἀκοίμητον, καὶ τότε βοοῦν αἱ κολάσεις· ἄπαγε ἀφ'
ἡμῶν, ψυχὴ φωτεινή, μὴ ἐγγίσῃς ἡμῶν ὅτι οὐκ ἐσμὲν ἄξιοι.

14. Καὶ τότε λέγει ἡ ψυχή· εὐχαριστῶ σοι, Κύριε, ὅτι αὐτῶν τῶν
βασάνων ἀλλότριός εἰμι ἐγώ. καὶ παραμένει ἐκεῖ ἡμέρας θ΄. καὶ τότε
ἀπάγεται ὑπὸ τῶν ἀγγέλων καὶ προσκυνεῖ τὸν θρόνον τὸν
τετράμορφον καὶ ἀκολουθοῦσιν αὐτὸν οἱ ἄγγελοι χαίροντες καὶ
ἀγάλλοντες ὅτι αὐτῶν τῶν βασάνων οὐκ ἐστὶν ἄξιος ἵνα μόνον ὁρᾶν
αὐτούς· ταῦτα περιμένουν τοὺς ἀμετανοήτους καὶ ἁμαρτωλούς.

15. Καὶ παραμένει ἐκεῖ ἡ ψυχὴ ἡμέρας μ΄ καὶ τότε ἀπάγεται πάλιν
καὶ προσκυνεῖ τὸν θρόνον τὸν τετράμορφον καὶ τότε ὁρᾷ τὸν Υἱὸν τοῦ
θεοῦ καὶ τότε χαίρει ὁ Πατὴρ σὺν τῷ Υἱῷ καὶ τὸ ἅγιον Πνεῦμα καὶ
πάντες οἱ ἄγγελοι καὶ οἱ ἀρχάγγελοι μετὰ λαμπάδων καὶ δόξης
πολλῆς καὶ ἀπάγουν αὐτὸν ἐνώπιον τοῦ παραδείσου καὶ θεωρεῖ τὴν
δόξαν αὐτοῦ ἣν μέλλει λαβέσθαι καὶ λέγει· Κύριε, Κύριε, ἃς ἔλθῃ
σύντομα ἡ δευτέρα παρουσία σου ἵνα λάβω τὴν δόξαν μου.

16. Καὶ ἔστιν μέσα τῶν ἁμαρτωλῶν καὶ τῶν δικαίων χάσμα μέγα
καὶ ἐν τὸ χάσμα πῦρ φλέγων τοὺς ἁμαρτωλούς, πρὸς δὲ τοὺς δικαίους
δρόσος καὶ δροσίζει αὐτούς.

17. Καὶ λέγει αὐτῷ ὁ Ἰάκωβος· εἰπὲ ἡμῖν, εὐλογημένε δοῦλε τοῦ
θεοῦ, Ἰωάννη Θεολόγε· καὶ πῶς μέλλει σωθῆναι πᾶσα ψυχή, ὅτι
οὐδεὶς ἀναμάρτητος;

18. Καὶ λέγει αὐτῷ Ἰωάννης· ἄκουσον, ὦ Ἰάκωβε, σκληρὸς ὁ
λόγος ὃν σὺ ἐρωτᾷς με. μαρτυρεῖ μοι ἅγιον Εὐαγγέλιον ὅτι ἔχων
ἑκατὸν πρόβατα καὶ πλανηθῇ ἓν ἐξ αὐτῶν, οὐχὶ ἀφεὶς τὰ ἐνενήκοντα
ἐννέα τῷ ὄρει πορευθῇ ζητῶν τὸ ἀπολωλὸς καὶ εὑρὼν αὐτὸν βαστάξῃ
τοῦτον ἐπὶ τῶν ὤμων αὐτοῦ καὶ ἔρχεται ἐπὶ τοὺς φίλους καὶ ἀδελφοὺς

body of clay and appear *full of light*, while it lies in earth, decomposing as it deserves. For I go away to the light of Paradise, as I have not transgressed the command of the priests or the words of the holy Gospel."

13. Then they take the soul in the kingdom of the air; the demons, on seeing him, bow in shame *because they are unworthy* to meet the righteous soul, but rather watch him from a distance, as they lament uncontrollably and say: "Woe to us because we are not worthy merely to look at him!" The angels take him away to the *river of fire*; the soul passes over, fluttering like a dove, but remains near there for three days and says this: 'I thank you, Lord, that I have crossed over these torments, unspotted and free from punishment.' He worships the fourfold throne. The angels accompany him and take him to the worm that never dies. The torturers then shout: 'Get away from us, you soul so full of light; do not come near us, because *we are not worthy.*'

14. Then the soul says: 'I thank you, Lord, that I am a stranger to the tormentors themselves.' He stays there nine days; then he is taken away by the angels and worships the *fourfold throne*. The angels follow him and *rejoice delightedly* because he has not deserved these torments, not even to look at them. Such things await the unrepentant sinners.

15. The soul stays there for 40 days, then is taken again and worships the fourfold throne. Then he sees the Son of God. The Father rejoices together with the Son; the Holy Spirit and all the angels and archangels take him with torches in great glory to the gate of Paradise. He gazes at the glory which he is about to receive and says: 'Lord, Lord, *may the interval* before your Second Coming *be cut short*, in order that I may receive my glory.'

16. There is between the sinners and the righteous a great chasm (Lk. 16.26), and in the chasm a fire which burns the sinners, but on the righteous there is *a refreshing dew.*'

17. James says to him: 'Tell us, you blessed servant of God, John the theologian: how is any [every] soul to be saved, because nobody is without sin (Jn 8.7)?'

18. John says to him: 'Listen, James: it is a hard (cf. Jn 6.60) question which you ask me. The holy Gospel testifies to me: *a person with 100 sheep*, when one of them strays, does he not leave the 99 on the hillside and go to look for the lost one; when he has found it, he *carries* it on his shoulders, and comes to his friends and brothers, and says: rejoice with

αὐτοῦ λέγων ὅτι συγχάρητέ μοι ὅτι εὗρον τὸ ἀπολωλὸς πρόβατόν μου;

19. Οὕτως καὶ ἐὰν πλανηθῇ τις ἐν ἁμαρτίᾳ καὶ πάλιν μετασ-τρέφεται καὶ ἐξέρχεται ἐν τῷ ἱερεῖ ἐξομολογούμενος τὰς ἁμαρτίας αὐτοῦ πάσας, τότε ὁ διάβολος αὐτοῦ φεύγει ἐκ τὴν θύραν τῆς ἐκκλησίας ἕως ᾅδου καὶ λέγει· οὐαί μοι ὅτι ἠπώλεσαν [ἀπώλεσα] τὸν ἐμὸν φίλον.

20. Καὶ τότε παραλαμβάνει αὐτὸν ὁ Κύριος ἡμῶν ᾿Ιησοῦς Χριστὸς τῆς δεξιᾶς χειρὸς καὶ λέγει τοῖς ἀγγέλοις αὐτοῦ· συγχάρητέ μοι ὅτι πρόβατον ἀπολωλόμενον ηὗρον. καὶ μεγάλη χαρὰ γίνεται ἐν τῷ οὐρανῷ καὶ ἐν τῇ γῇ ἐπὶ ἁμαρτωλῷ μετανοοῦντι. καὶ ἐὰν μέλλῃ αὔριον ἐξομολογήσασθαι καὶ ἀφῶν τὴν ἁμαρτίαν σήμερον κατοικεῖ τὸ ἅγιον πνεῦμα ἐν αὐτῷ. ὅτι ἐὰν ἁμαρτάνῃ ἄνθρωπος ἐκφεύξεται ἐξ αὐτὸν τὸ ἅγιον πνεῦμα καὶ παραστήκει αὐτὸν ὡς σκιὰν νυκτὸς καὶ ἡμέρας καὶ ἐκδέχεται τὴν ὀδύνην ἵνα κατοικῇ ἐν αὐτὸν καὶ ὁ Κύριος ἡμῶν.

21. Οἰκτείρει ὁ προφήτης ὅτι· νεώτερος ἐγενόμην καὶ γὰρ ἐγήρασα καὶ οὐκ οἶδα δίκαιον ἐγκαταλελυμένον οὐδὲ τὸ σπέρμα αὐτοῦ ζητοῦν ἄρτους.

22. Καὶ ἐγὼ ᾿Ιωάννης λέγω ὅτι οἰκτειρήσει ὁ Κύριος ᾿Ιησοῦς Χρισ-τὸς ἐν τῇ δευτέρᾳ
ἐλεύσει αὐτοῦ, οἰκτειρεῖ καὶ σώζει τὴν ψυχήν.

23. Δείξω σοι ὑπόδειγμαν καὶ μὴ ἀφελπῇς [=ἀπελπίσῃς] ἀπὸ τῆς φιλανθρωπίας τοῦ θεοῦ. ἐάν τις καὶ μὴ ἀνωὰ ἔχῃ ὑπόδειγμα, [ἰδὲ] τὸν Πέτρον, ὅτι τρίτον ἀρνησάμενος τὸν Κύριον ἡμῶν ᾿Ιησοῦν Χριστὸν καὶ πάλιν διὰ θερμῶν δακρύων ἐσυνεχωρήθη εὐθὺς καὶ οὐράνιος κλειδοῦχος ἐγίνετον διὰ τῆς θερμῆς μετανοίας.

24. ᾿Εὰν ᾖ πόρνος, ἰδὲ τὴν Μαρίαν τὴν πόρνην ὅτι ἥμαρτεν εἰς ἄνδρας χιλίους ἑπτακοσίους τρεῖς καὶ οὐκ ἐγίνωσκεν ξένον οὔτε ἴδιον, ἀλλὰ ὀλιγοψύχῃ διὰ τῶν δακρύων ἐξήλειψεν πάσας τὰς ἁμαρτίας αὐτῆς. ἐὰν ᾖ φονεὺς καὶ μετανοῶν θερμῶς, ἰδὲ τὸν Μανασσῆν ὅτι τὸν υἱὸν αὐτοῦ εἰδώλων θυσίαν ἐποίησεν καὶ μετὰ τεσσαράκοντα πρεσ-βυτέρους ἐφόνευσε καὶ τὸν ᾿Ησαΐαν ἐνέπρισε, ἀλλὰ διὰ ἐπιστροφῆς θερμῆς στεναγμῶν καὶ δακρύων μέχρι τῶν τεσσαράκοντα ἡμερῶν ὁ βυθὸς ἐγεμίσθη καὶ συνεχωρήθη ἐκ τῶν πολλῶν ἁμαρτιῶν. ἰδὲ καὶ τὸν λῃστὴν ὅπου κλοπαὶ καὶ φόνοι καὶ αὐτὸς ἐνενήκοντα ἐννέα φόνους ἐποίησεν, ἀλλ᾿ ἐν πίστει θερμῇ καὶ βοῇ μεγάλῃ ὅτι εἶπεν ἐν τῷ σταυρῷ· μνήσθητί μου, Κύριε, ἐν τῇ βασιλείᾳ σου, τὸν παράδεισον ἔλαβεν.

me, because I have found my lost sheep? (Mt. 18.12-14 and Lk. 15.4-7 conflated; cf. Jn 10.11-12).

19. In the same way if anyone strays in sin, and has a change of heart and comes out and confesses all his sins to the priest, then his devil flees out of the church door and goes to Hell, with these words: 'Woe to me, because I have lost my friend'.

20. Then our Lord Jesus Christ receives him by his right hand and says to his angels: Rejoice with me, because I have found my lost sheep. And there is great joy in heaven and earth over a sinner that repents (Lk. 15.6-7). If a person intends on the next day to make confession and abandon the sin, tomorrow the Holy Spirit dwells in that person. For if a person sins, the Holy Spirit leaves him, but stands by like a shadow, night and day, and awaits the woes (of the last days), in order that our Lord may dwell also in that person.

21. The prophet indicates God's compassion in these words: I have been young, and now am old; yet I have not seen the righteous forsaken or his children begging bread (Ps. 37.25).

22. Also I, John, say that the Lord Jesus Christ *will have compassion* at his Second Coming: he has compassion and saves the soul [Jn 3.17; 10.9; cf. Rom. 9.15; Exod. 33.19 LXX].

23. *I will show you an example*, so that you will not lose hope in God's loving kindness towards mankind. So that one may not be foolish, take *the example of Peter*: he denied our Lord Jesus Christ a third time, and yet, in contrast, as a result of fervent tears, he was immediately forgiven and became key-holder of heaven, after his fervent repentance.

24. If the sin is prostitution, look at *Mary* [Magdalene] *the prostitute* [cf. Lk. 7.37], because she sinned with 1703 men, and did not know whether they were strangers or family, yet faint of heart she expunged all her sins *through her tears*. If the sin is murder but the repentance is fervent, look at *Manasseh*, because he offered his son as a sacrifice to idols, and after murdering 40 elders he put Isaiah to the flames; yet by a fervent conversion, with groans and tears until a deep sea of 40 days' worth was filled up, he obtained forgiveness from his many sins. Look also at the brigand, where thieving and killing are concerned—he himself committed 99 murders—yet with fervent faith and a loud cry uttered on the cross (*Remember me, Lord, in your kingdom* [Lk. 23.42]), he received the gift of paradise.

25. Ἐὰν ᾖ μοιχός, ἰδὲ τὸν Δαυὶδ τὸν προφήτην ὅπου ἔλαβεν τὴν τοῦ Οὐρίαν γυναῖκαν, τὴν Βηρσαβεέ, καὶ ἔσχεν καὶ ἄλλαις ἐνενήκοντα ἐννέα. ἀλλ᾿ ἐξωμολογήσατο ὁλοψύχως τὸν Νάθαν τὸν προφήτην καὶ τὸ πύρινον ξίφος ἀποστράφη ἀπ᾿ αὐτόν, καὶ καθέζεται θεοπάτωρ.

26. Καὶ πάλιν ἀποδείξω σοι τὸν Ἀνδρέαν Κρήτην ὅτι καὶ αὐτὸς ἐν τῇ μητρὶ αὐτοῦ ἐμοίχευσεν, ἀλλ᾿ ἐν μετανοίας καθαρᾶς ὑμνῳδὸς καὶ ῥήτωρ τῶν θείων γραφῶν ἐγίνετον καὶ τὸν θρόνον τῆς ἐπισκοπῆς ἐδέξατο.

27. Ἐὰν μάγος ᾖ καὶ φονεύς, ἰδὲ τὸν Κυπριανὸν ὅτι καὶ αὐτὸς ἐκ γένους δαιμόνων ἐγέννατον καὶ χίλια τριάκοντα βρέφη ἀνήλωσεν καὶ ἄλλα ἐστατὸν ἐπι τὸ πλάτος ἐποίησεν ἐξύσεν καὶ πολλοὺς ἐκ τὴν ὁδὸν τοῦ θεοῦ μετέστρεψεν. ἀλλὰ δι᾿ ἐπιστροφῆς ὀρθῆς καὶ ἐξομολογήσεως θερμῆς τὰς δυνάμεις τῶν δαιμόνων ἐνίκησεν καὶ σύνθρονος τοῖς ἐπισκόποις καὶ λειτουργὸς τοῦ θεοῦ ἐγένετον.

28. Τοῦτον λέγω σοι· οὐαὶ τοὺς μὴ μετανοήσαντας ὅτι ἐν ἀνομίαις ἀποθανὼν Χριστοῦ ἀνάστασιν οὐ θεωρεῖ, ἀλλὰ κολάζεται μετὰ τῶν δαιμόνων εἰς τὸν ᾅδην, ὅτι, καθώς φησι τὸ Εὐαγγέλιον, πᾶς γὰρ ὁ ποιῶν τὴν ἁμαρτίαν δοῦλος ἐστι τῆς ἁμαρτίας καὶ ἡ ἁμαρτία υἱὸς διαβόλου ἐστίν· παραλαμβάνει τοὺς ἀμετανοήτους ὁ διάβολος καὶ ἀπάγει αὐτοὺς τῷ διαβόλῳ τῷ πατρὶ αὐτοῦ.

29. Ἐὰν δὲ ποιήσῃ θυσίαν ὁ ἁμαρτωλὸς πρὶν μετανοήσῃ παροξύνει τὸν Κύριον καθώς φησιν ὁ προφήτης ὅτι· θυσία ἁμαρτωλοῦ βδέλυγμα Κυρίῳ καὶ ἡ προσευχὴ αὐτοῦ γενήσεται [ ]. ἁμαρτάνῃ πεντηκοστὸς δὲ ἀμετανόητος ἐπικατάρατος, ὅτι λευκαίνουν αἱ τρίχας τῆς κεφαλῆς αὐτοῦ. ἐὰν δὲ ἁμαρτάνῃ γέρων ἄνευ τε τῆς γυναικὸς αὐτοῦ καλεῖται οὕτως ὅτι εἰς τὴν ἰδίαν θυγατέραν ἐπόρνευσεν ὅτι πατὴρ πάντων καλεῖται. ἤ τε καὶ γυνὴ ἐὰν λευκαίνουν τρίχας τῆς κεφαλῆς αὐτῆς καὶ πορνεύῃ καλεῖται οὕτως ὅτι εἰς τὸ ἴδιον τέκνον αὐτῆς ἐμοίχευσεν.

30. Τοὺς δὲ μετανοοῦντας πάντας εἰσακούσεται Κύριος καὶ λέγει· οὐ θέλω τὸν θάνατον τοῦ ἁμαρτωλοῦ ὡς τὸ ἐπιστρέψαι [αὐτὸν] καὶ ζῆσαι. λέγει γὰρ τὸ ἅγιον Εὐαγγέλιον ὅτι· ἄφες ἐκκόψαι τὴν συκῆν ἵνα σκάψαι περιποιοῦμαι ἐπ᾿ αὐτῷ χρόνους τρεῖς καὶ ἐὰν οὐ καρποφορῇ ἔκκοψον αὐτὴν ἵνα μᾶλλον καὶ τὴν γῆν καταργῇ.

31. Τὸ δένδρον ὁ ἁμαρτωλός ἐστιν, τὸ σκάψαι ὁ λόγος τοῦ ἱερέως, ὁ ἀμπελὼν ὁ κόσμος· ἐὰν οὐ μεταστρέφῃ καὶ φέρῃ καρπὸν καλόν, ἀπάγεται εἰς τὸ πῦρ τὸ αἰώνιον.

25. If the sin is adultery, look at *David, the prophet*, where he took Bathsheba, Uriah's wife, and kept her, together with 99 other women. But he confessed wholeheartedly to Nathan the prophet, and the fiery sword was turned away from him, and he took his seat as the ancestor of Jesus.

26. Again I will show you *Andrew of Crete*, because he committed incest with his own mother; but with purifying repentance he became a singer of praise and advocate of Holy Scripture, and received a bishop's throne.

27. If sorcery and murder are the sins, look at *Cyprian*, because he was born of a race of demons and destroyed 1300 children; he did the same to another hundred [?] outside on the broad plain. He also perverted many from God's way. But by means of a complete conversion and *fervent confession* he conquered the demonic powers, and joining the bench of bishops he became a minister of God.

28. I tell you categorically: woe to the unrepentant, because they die in their lawless deeds and do not see the Resurrection of Christ. They are punished with the demons in Hell, because, just as the Gospel says, '*Every one who commits sin is a slave to sin*, and sin is the devil's son'. [Jn 8.34; cf. 8.44; 1 Jn 3.8ff]. The devil receives the unrepentant and takes them away to the Devil his father.

29. If the sinner performs a sacrifice before repenting, he provokes the Lord's anger, just as the prophet says: '*The sacrifice of the sinner is an abomination to the Lord* [Prov. 15.8; 21.27] and *his prayer will become...*' * A man of 50 who sins without repenting is accursed, because the hairs of his head are white. If an old man sins sexually other than with his wife, he is called accursed, in that he committed incest with his own daughter, for he is nominally father of all his children. And the wife, if she is white-haired, and commits adultery, she is called accursed, in that she committed incest with her own son.

30. But the Lord will hear the prayer of all who repent. He says: *I have no pleasure in the death of a sinner, but that he turn back and live* [Ezek. 33.11]. For the holy Gospel says: 'Refrain from cutting down the *fig tree*, that I may dig around and enrich it on three occasions; if it does not bear fruit, then cut it down, so as to clear the ground instead' [cf. Lk. 13.8-9].

31. *The tree represents* the sinner; the digging is the word of the priest; and the vineyard is the world. If there is no change, with good fruit produced, the 'tree' is taken away to the eternal fire.

32. Οὐαὶ τοὺς ἱερεῖς τοὺς ἁμαρτάνοντας καὶ οὐ μετανοοῦντας.

33. Λέγει αὐτῷ ὁ ᾽Ιάκωβος· εἰπὲ ἡμῖν, ᾽Ιωάννη, περὶ τῶν θησαυρι-
ζομένων ἐν ἐκκλησίαις καὶ ὄρεσι καὶ πτωχοῖς· τί ἐστιν ἀντάλλαγμα;

34. Λέγει αὐτῷ ᾽Ιωάννης ὁ ἀπόστολος· ἱλαρὸν γὰρ δότην ἀγαπᾷ
ὁ Κύριος. ἐὰν εἴ τι ἂν δώσῃ ἄνθρωπος, ἀπολαμβάνει ἑκατόν. ἐὰν ἕνι
ἀσθενής, τὰ δὲ κουφίζονται καὶ τὰ ἐνενήκοντα ἀπολάβῃ. καὶ ἐὰν
τελευτήσῃ ἄνθρωπος καὶ λέγῃ τῷ ὑπηρέτῃ αὐτοῦ· δὸς τὰ ὑπάρχοντά
μου, τὸ μὲν ἕνα ἔχει ὁ ἐπίτροπος, ἡ δὲ μία μοῖρα ἔνι τοῦ ἀποθανόντος.

35. Πληροφορήθητε, ἀδελφοὶ οἱ ἀκούοντες· μετὰ τὸ ἀποθανεῖν τὸν
ἄνθρωπον μετάνοια οὐκ ἔστιν οὐδὲ συγχώρησις τῶν μετανοούντων.
ἀλλὰ πάλιν λέγω ὑμῖν μὴ ἀπελπιστεῖν τοῦ θεοῦ ἡμῶν φιλανθρωπίαν
ὅτι αὐτὸς εἶπε· τὸν ἐρχόμενον πρός με οὐ μὴ ἐκβάλω ἔξω.
ᾧ ἡ δόξα καὶ τὸ κράτος εἰς τοὺς αἰῶνας τῶν αἰώνων, ἀμήν.

32. *Woe to the priests* who sin and do not repent!'

33. James says to him: 'Tell us, John, about those who *store up treasure*, whether in churches or desert places or poverty; what is the exchange rate in heaven?'

34. John the Apostle says to him: 'The Lord *loves a cheerful giver* [2 Cor. 9.7]. If a person gives anything whatever, he receives *a hundredfold* in return. If there is a poor person [*or* person weak in faith] among you, his load is lightened and the giver receives ninetyfold in return. If a man dies, who has told his servant: 'Distribute my goods', then the steward has one part of the reward, and the other part is the estate of the deceased.

35. Be fully assured [Rom. 14.5; *1 Clem.* 42.3], brothers who hear this: after a man's death there is no such thing as repentance or forgiveness of the penitent. But again I tell you *not to lose hope* in God's loving-kindness towards us, because God himself says: *Him who comes to me I will not cast out* [Jn 6.37]. To God be the glory and the power for ever and ever, amen.'

Figure 5: *The Angel of the Agony.*

Explanatory Notes

The original Greek title of this text in the codex had apparently reversed the order of the named participants in dialogue, but the contents of the text show this to be mistaken.

1.

Second Coming: Early Christian belief in the resurrection of Jesus developed rapidly to see this event (in the context of Jewish belief) as anticipating the general resurrection of all on the last day (see 1 Cor. 15). It is a logical consequence that the resurrected Jesus will have an essential role in eschatological events, returning from heaven at the critical moment to fulfil this role. Such a public and ultimate return was also seen as a triumphant vindication, to counterbalance the impression of suffering and humiliation within Jesus' earthly ministry. His return functions as the moment of final salvation for those who believe in him; he also acts as the agent of God himself in judging the living and the dead at the end of time (see 1 Thess. 1.10; 4.15-17). The expectations associated with the heavenly 'Son of Man' figure of Dan. 7.13-14 were assigned to the person of Jesus in early Christian interpretation. In Paul's mystical language in 1 Cor. 15, not only will the living be transformed at the coming of Christ (15.51-55) but also all negative powers will be subjugated to Christ, culminating in his own final submission to God (15.23-28). The problems inevitably associated with the obvious delay in such a Second Coming, or immediate Parousia, were solved by Christian believers in a variety of ways in the ensuing centuries. The simplest solution, as here, was to think in terms of some waiting room for the soul after death, in expectation of Christ's eventual return.

2.

then comes the angel: the role of the angels is particularly significant in this text, escorting the souls of the sinners and guarding the souls of the righteous; the idea of an individual guardian angel (a natural but later development from Michael's role as guardian of Israel) is obviously intended here. A nice comparison is with the early fourteenth-century wall-painting of the angel figure holding the soul in a napkin, discovered adjacent to one of three earlier effigies in the north aisle of the church of St Thomas in Winchelsea.

3.

never to be reborn: the text here seems to be corrupt and there may be a lacuna. Vassiliev made several corrections in transcribing the text (e.g. ἦν for ἄ, εἶχα for ἤχα).

4.

kingdom of the air: Vassiliev corrects the text reading from ἄερως to ἀέρως.

sinner-soul: The implications of the previous paragraph are that the material body was the cause of past rejoicing and hence of sin, but this hybrid expression at least retains the ambiguous possibility that the soul too is corrupted.

5.

thousands upon thousands: see Rev. 5.11.

   life-giving cross: cf. *2 Apoc. Jn* 13.

   river of fire: see also the note on *2 Apoc. Jn* 24.

In Russian cosmology (as seen in the icon tradition) the fiery river is especially significant as having its source at the point where Satan fell. At the command of God this river fell through the earth to the nethermost regions, where it is destined to flow forever. Here is the place of death.

The language of the lake of fire and place of the second death takes its inspiration primarily from the canonical apocalypse, Rev. 19.20; 20.10; 21.8. But there are other references. As early as the fourth division of the Egyptian *Book of Gates* (either eighteenth or nineteenth Dynasty, between 1580 and 1200 BCE) there is mention of four fire-filled pits. Horus instructs the lord of the pits to undertake 'the fiery incarceration of opponents of a god who aids souls through death and is himself an example of resurrection.' (Bernstein, *The Formation of Hell*, p. 15). Fiery rivers feed the pit or lake of fire. The text of Dan. 7.10, referring to the stream of fire issuing from the presence of the Ancient of Days, can only be an indirect influence, probably indicating the ultimate source of this judgmental power. But *Apoc. Pet.* 5 speaks of 'a stream of unquenchable fire which flows, flaming with fire' and *Apoc. Paul* 32 describes a river of fire cascading over deep pits containing many souls. As mentioned in the Introduction, Plato's Socratic dialogue *Phaedo* refers to Pyriphlegethon, the third of four rivers of Tartarus, which 'falls into a region burning with a great fire, where it gathers into a body of boiling, muddy water larger than the Mediterranean Sea' (Bernstein, *The Formation of Hell*, p. 55). In the course of their eternal punishment, those who have offended against parents flow through here and find themselves in Tartarus; this is part of Plato's idea of the subdivision of the underworld on moral grounds.

torments: the original manuscript read accusative βασάνους for dative βασάνοις.

6.

worm that never dies: see also the note on *2 Apoc. Jn* 24. In Russian icons the abyss of Hell is usually surrounded by a wavy motif, probably representing the worm that shall not die. The snake in Hell is the associated counterpart of the serpent in paradise.

It may be significant that 'worms' figure in the distinctive version of the Sower parable in *Gos. Thom.*, saying 9; they combine with the thorns to dispose of the third category of seed ('Others fell on thorns, and they choked the seeds and worms ate them' [trans. R. Valantasis;

London: Routledge, 1997], p. 67). The results of various kinds of sowing are affected by a combination of natural causes and agencies. It is possible to understand the text at this purely natural level; indeed, in contrast to the synoptic gospel versions, there is no explicit allegorization in the text. But even if this is the simplest and most authentic form of the natural story, the apparent addition of the worms may point to a deeper level of interpretation by gnostic readers who identify here the destruction of the material, and the high-yielding salvation of the special, grains.

In *Apoc. Paul* 36a, one of the four church officials seen in the river of fire by Paul is a deacon who is up to his knees in the river. His hands are bloody and he pleads for mercy as worms come out of his mouth and nose. In the frozen wastes of western Hell, where the gnashing of teeth is because of the cold, there is a two-headed worm 'a cubit in size' (*Apoc. Paul* 42a); here are punished those who disbelieve in the Resurrection. Augustine of Hippo discussed the application of the Scriptural texts about worm and fire (Isa. 66.24; Mk 9.42-48) to the nature of eternal punishment (*City of God* 21.9). 'Now as for this fire and this worm, there are some who want to make both of them refer to the pains of the souls, not of the body... Each one of us must choose as he thinks fit... He may ascribe the fire to the body and the worm to the mind, the former literally and the latter metaphorically, or he may attribute both, in the literal sense, to the body... The important thing is that we should never believe that those bodies are to be such as to feel no anguish in the fire' (trans. Henry Bettenson [London: Pelican Books, 1972], p. 984).

7.

unrepentant: this writer consistently emphasizes the lack of repentance as a key factor. Cf. for this emphasis Rev. 2.5. Again there are small and obviously necessary corrections to the original text (dative ἀμετανόητῳ for accusative ἀμετανόητον and ἄφρωνι for ἄφρων.

light/darkness Paradise: see also the note on *2 Apoc. Jn* 25.

9.

Second Coming: the Day of the Lord has not yet come, for then the affliction would come to an end (cf. the impression, criticized in 2 Thess. 2.1-2 as mistaken, that the Day of the Lord has already come).

11.
righteous: it is clear that some of the text is missing between sections 11 and 12.

12.
full of light: almost Manichaean in language.

13.
because they are unworthy: Vassiliev has a small but vital correction here to the original text, reading positively ὡσεί.

river of fire: see *2 Apoc. Jn* 24 and *3 Apoc. Jn* 5 above. An interesting comparison is provided by one of the Coptic texts edited and translated by Budge (1913), the Encomium on St John the Baptist attributed to St John Chrysostom (British Museum Oriental MS.7024). In the course of a guided tour of the seven heavens, it was discovered that the third heaven had been bestowed on John the Baptist. In that most glorious place John was seen with his parents Zacharias and Elizabeth, all dressed in splendid clothes set with precious stones. Of all the gifts bestowed on John the last and greatest was a golden boat. In Wallis Budge's words, 'The boat was intended for the use of the souls of those who had loved John upon earth. These souls would, after the death of their bodies, find their way to the boat of gold, and John would ferry them over the Lake of Fire, and land them in the Third Heaven, which was John's peculiar appanage. No soul, good or bad, could enter this Heaven except after baptism in the river of fire, which consumed the wicked, but to the righteous followers of John seemed only like a hot bath. There was also another boat, which was provided with oars and lamps. When the souls of the righteous had taken their places in it, the oars worked by themselves, and rowed it over the dark waters, lamps lighting it on its way' (Budge, *Coptic Apocrypha*, p. xx).

We are not worthy: the dualist distinctions are maintained in a physical manner.

14.
fourfold throne: τετράμορφος meaning 'in fourfold form' is used of the tradition of four Gospels by Irenaeus, and comparisons are made with the four living creatures of Ezekiel and the Apocalypse (*Adv. Haer.* 3.11.8 [M.7.885B, 889B]). It is a related word meaning 'square', τετράγωνος, which is used of the New Jerusalem in Rev. 21.16 ('the

city lies foursquare' or 'is laid out as a square'). Since New Jerusalem is the site of 'the throne of God and of the Lamb' (Rev. 22.3), it seems more likely that the latter idea rather than the former is influential in the present passage.

rejoice delightedly: the original text reads χαίρου καὶ ἀγάλλου. In the following clause Vassiliev has corrected plural εἰσίν to singular ἐστὶν.

15.

may the interval be cut short: cf. Rev. 6.9-10.

16.

refreshing dew: cf. Ignatius, *Magn.* 14 for a similar spiritual sense; a close comparison is found in the reference to the double effect of the river of fire ('fire and pain; dew and relief') according to St John Chrysostom (*Homilies* 4.11 on Matthew [7.69B]); cf. *Coptic Apocalypse* 8 below.

18.

a person with 100 sheep: The recurrent theme of repentance is put into the sharpest focus by this interpretation of the dominical saying about the lost sheep. The open door to penitence (even to the extent of *3 Apoc. Jn* 35) is quite unusual in apocalyptic writings, simply because of the neat dualism between righteous and wicked, separated from each other in their different worlds. For example compare the early apocalyptic text of *1 En.* 1.8-9:

> And to all the righteous he will grant peace. He will preserve the elect, and kindness shall be upon them. They shall all belong to God and they shall prosper and be blessed; and the light of God shall shine unto them.
> Behold, he will arrive with ten million of the holy ones in order to execute judgment upon all. He will destroy the wicked ones and censure all flesh on account of everything that they have done, that which the sinners and the wicked ones committed against him. (Translated by E. Isaac in *OTP*, I, pp. 13-14.)

Traditionally such apocalyptic texts are calculated to reassure the righteous (who seem to be losing) that the wicked (who seem to be winning) will not always have matters in their favour. The present text presumably has its own reasons for reflecting a greater flexibility, with the option (and indeed the message) of penitence. It is more focused on a comparison of the future existences of hell and heaven, the import of which is to preach a warning to all.

18.

carries: the manuscript of this apocalypse reads βαστάζης, corrected by Vassiliev to βαστάζῃ. The word used in Lk. 15.5 is ἐπιτίθησιν.

22.

will have compassion: corrected reading οἰκτειρήσει for the manu-script's curious οἰκτηρίτεσι.

23.

I will show you an example: The exemplars of penitence are introduced, beginning with Simon Peter. Some of the others resemble a 'rogues gallery', but the greater the offence, the more extreme the penitence, and ultimately the forgiveness is entirely a matter of divine grace. While Peter is credited with the scriptural number of three denials, there is clear evidence of what might be called rhetorical exaggeration for maxi-mum effect in the case of other sinners.

the example of Peter: his three denials of Jesus after the arrest in Gethsemane are recorded in Mk 14.66-72, with parallels in the other Gospels. Mark's version is recounted in such a way as to raise suspicion that Peter may even have cursed his Lord (14.71)—an action regarded as a cardinal offence in the early Church (1 Cor. 12.3). But Peter's story clearly did not end there, as Acts and Jn 21 among other Church tradi-tions attest. Christian iconography shows Peter denying Jesus and weep-ing bitterly, but also holding the keys of Church power, after his for-giveness and recommissioning.

24.

Mary the prostitute: as very commonly in Church tradition. Mary Mag-dalene has been identified here with the woman who is a penitent sinner in Lk. 7.37. It suits the argument in this apocalypse, but there is no warrant in Luke's Gospel for such harmonization, any more than for an identification with Mary the sister of Lazarus.

'Mary, called Magdalene' is mentioned, among other women, in Lk. 8.2-3 with the added description 'from whom seven demons had gone out'. The word *M'gadd'la*, meaning 'hairdresser', was a common euph-emism for a prostitute. Traditions from Tertullian onwards among the early Church Fathers conflated her with other women and other Marys. In 591 CE the newly composite Magdalene figure was proclaimed with papal authority by Gregory the Great in a sermon preached in the basilica of San Clemente in Rome: 'We believe that this woman whom Luke calls a female sinner, whom John calls Mary, is that Mary from whom Mark [*sic*—only in the Longer Ending at 16.9!] says seven demons were cast out' (*Homilia 33, Homiliarum in Evangelica*, Lib.2, in *PL* 76, cols. 1592-93). Hostile Jewish verdicts identified her with Jesus' mother and linked her prostitution with accusations of the Virgin Mary's adultery (*Shab.* 104b, late third century). She was also linked with the 30 years of penance in the desert performed by Mary of Egypt, but this was only a tradition from the twelfth century, localized at St Baume in Provence. Presumably in earlier traditions the Magdalene's life of debauchery was thought to be forgiven by Jesus (on analogy with Jn 8.11) and she is accordingly commissioned to tell the news of the Resurrection (e.g. Jn 20.17). She is regularly seen as an example of penitence. Since Origen she is also regarded as a symbol of erotic asceticism, and language from the Song of Songs is applied to her. In the modern novel *The Last Temptation* by Nikos Kazantzakis (London: Faber & Faber, 1995) she constitutes the final test for Christ, symbolizing erotic love as 'the sweetest the world can offer'.

Recent interest in Mary Magdalene, from Gnostic or feminist perspectives, is documented in studies such as: articles by Katherine Ludwig Jansen and Karen L. King in Beverly Mayne Kienzle and Pamela J. Walker, (eds.), *Women Preachers and Prophets through Two Millennia of Christianity* (London: University of California Press, 1998); Antti Marjanen, *The Woman Jesus Loved: Mary Magdalene in the Nag Hammadi Library and Related Documents* (Nag Hammadi and Manichaean Studies; Leiden: E.J. Brill, 1996); Mary R. Thompson, *Mary of Magdala: Apostle and Leader* (New York: Paulist Press, 1995); Carla Ricci, *Mary Magdalene and Many Others: Women who Followed Jesus* (trans. P. Burns; Minneapolis: Fortress Press, 1994). The fragmentary Nag Hammadi text *The Gospel of Mary* is an attack on second-century orthodox positions in its portrayal of Mary Magdalene: 'she is the Savior's beloved, possessed of knowledge and teaching superior to that of the public apostolic tradition. Her superiority is based on vision and private revelation [the text has some similarities with the apocalyptic genre] and is demonstrated in her capacity to strengthen the wavering disciples and turn them toward the Good.' (Karen L. King, 'Introduction', in

James M. Robinson [ed.], *The Nag Hammadi Library in English* [Leiden: E.J. Brill; San Francisco: Harper & Row, 1988], pp. 523-27).

through her tears: Vassiliev has modified the word-order slightly for improved intelligibility. The woman may well be faint because of her crying, but the point is that through her extreme act of penitence the sins can be expunged.

Manasseh: traditionally the prophet Isaiah was sawn asunder during Manasseh's reign (cf. *Mart. Isa.* 5). There may be an allusion to this in Heb. 11.37. Faced with the present alternative version, one would have to conclude that there is little sound historical basis for either tradition. Manasseh was the son of Hezekiah; he reigned for 55 years (696–42 BCE)—see 2 Kgs 21.1; 2 Chron. 33.1. His reign was marked by religious syncretism (the worship of Baal, Astarte and astrological practices and divination). His long reign was bloody and reactionary. He was notorious for 'the passing of his sons through the fire' in the valley of Hinnom; it is possible that the present text on Isaiah's fate is a confused recollection of 2 Kgs 21.6.

25.

David, the prophet: cf. *2 Apoc. Jn* 8. The story of Bathsheba, the wife of Uriah, is told in 2 Sam. 11, and Bathsheba is included (although not by name) in the genealogy at the beginning of Matthew's Gospel (1.6). Nathan publicly denounced King David's secret sins (2 Sam. 12.7, 10-14), and prophesied the early death of the child born of the adultery with Bathsheba. Solomon was their second child, who acceded to the throne of Israel. David's prompt repentance has the effect of cancelling his death sentence. David became a model of penitence and spiritual reformation, not least because of the liturgical use of the Penitential Psalms (attributed to him and claimed to be inspired by David's remorse over the death of Uriah and his own adultery with Bathsheba). See, for example, W.A. Mozart's choral work *Davide Penitente* (K.469) for which Lorenzo da Ponte wrote free paraphrases in the style of the Psalms. If David who sinned so ignobly could be forgiven and become an ideal of religious leadership, no one then should be without hope. This theme re-echoed in medieval sermons.

26.

Andrew of Crete: lived c. 660–740 CE. He was the author of a series of hymns in 'canon' format, the acrostic odes of the Eastern Church, of which he is reputed to be the inventor, or at least the one who developed them structurally from simple refrains into thematic poems. The Greek canon, or liturgical poem, consists of nine odes which in turn are composed of groups of strophes (troparia); the verses of the ode were originally interspersed between the verses of the biblical canticles, as sung after the appointed psalms at Mattins. The most famous of these is St Andrew's own Great Canon (ὁ μέγας κανών), a hymn in 250 strophes on the particular theme of penitence. The Great Canon is appointed to be read in its entirety at the morning service on Thursday in week five of the Great Lent; sections of it are read at other times particularly in the season of Lent. The first ode begins with an immediate and urgent call for repentance:

> Where shall I make my beginning to mourn the deeds of my wretched life? What first-fruits shall I lay down, o Christ, to this my present weeping? But, as thou art merciful, grant me forgiveness of sins.
>
> Come, wretched soul, with thy flesh, confess to the Maker of all: and, from now, leave thy past folly and bring tears of repentance to God.
>
> I rivalled, in transgression, Adam first-created, and I knew myself naked of God, of the everlasting kingdom, and of the delight, because of my sins.

27.

Cyprian: an early version of the dubious legend about the converted magician of Antioch (c. 300 CE) was known to St Gregory Nazianzen in the late fourth century. In the calendar Cyprian shares with St Justina the feast day of 26 September, suppressed by the Holy See in 1969. Their relics are claimed to be in the baptistery of St John Lateran in Rome, where these were brought after they were beheaded in Nicomedia. The feast of the other Cyprian, bishop of Carthage, should be celebrated earlier in the September calendar. The actual date of his martyrdom was 14 September 258 CE.

fervent confession: ἐξομολογήσεως is an appropriate correction by Vassiliev for the original ἐξομολόγησις.

29.

his prayer will become…: some of the text is clearly missing here.

30.

the fig tree: cf. Lk. 13.8-9.

31.

The tree represents: Here is a most succinct allegorical interpretation of the fig tree parable.

32.

Woe to the priests: As has already been noted, in introduction and exposition, *3 Apoc. Jn* operates a simple 'rewards and punishment' theodicy, and stresses the importance of repentance. As with the critique of the religious leaders, especially the Pharisees, in the Synoptic Gospels, the point here may be the general one that those who make religious claims are the ones most at risk. Alternatively the writer may have particular 'priests' and opponents as his target (cf. the role of the 'wicked priest' in the Qumran texts). The following question (33) may suggest that the storing up of church resources is an offence particularly to be criticized. Therefore the response (34) concerns the positive aspects of charitable giving (cf. 1 Jn 3.18-22).

33.

store up treasure: cf. Mt. 6.19.

34.

a hundredfold: The reward of a full 100 per cent is perhaps modelled on the maximum harvest in the parable of the sower (Mk 4.8) or more appropriately on the initial profit made by the first two slaves in the parable of the talents (Mt. 25.14-30). This latter parable (or perhaps the parable of the rich man and his steward in Lk. 16.1-10) may also influence the phrasing of the third example concerned (as we might say) with the executor and the estate. The second example is the most puzzling as it stands. Despite the nearby quotation from 2 Cor. 9.7, and the use of the term ἀσθενής in the Corinthian correspondence for the 'weak in faith', in the present context the possible translation of 'poor' (experiencing actual poverty) seems more appropriate. But why then is the reward apparently reduced to 90 per cent? Either the gift to relieve poverty need not be so large, and so the reward is correspondingly reduced, or more likely that the scale of the gift is enhanced with the addition of 10 per cent which would otherwise go to reward the giver. Whether this is a system of rewards, and in what historical context, is unclear. It may be that it is seen as a more appropriate use of church funds than the hoarding of ecclesiastical treasures.

35.

not to lose hope: The final word is one of encouragement to the returning penitent; he is welcomed like the Prodigal Son. But the warning is also given: after a person's death there can be no opportunity for penitence.

Chapter 6

THE COPTIC APOCALYPSE OF JOHN

Introduction

The final example in this comparison of Johannine apocalypses is a Coptic text. For practical reasons there is on this occasion no original text or new translation, but merely the reproduction of the translation made by E. Wallis Budge for his work *Coptic Apocrypha in the Dialect of Upper Egypt*. I use this with a measure of caution, simply because the modern Coptic scholar tends to distrust Budge's work; he published a large number of books, but in all his editions it has been remarked that he was patching together bits and pieces in an unreliable way. The primary incentive for me to make limited use of this apocalypse was the fact of its inclusion in the brief list of 'Apocryphal Apocalypses of John' made by Elliott.[1] But closer examination of the contents of this text more than justified its treatment as an appendix to the present opportunity for comparative study.

This Coptic Apocalypse is found in British Museum Oriental MS. 7026. According to its colophon it was written by Victor the deacon in 1006 CE ('on the third day of the month Thoth, in the fourth Indiction, in the seven hundred and twenty-second year of the Era of the Martyrs, which is the three hundred and ninety-fifth [*sic* for eighty-fourth] year of the Hijrah [or Departure of Muhammad the Prophet from Mecca in 622]'). The Coptic 'Church of the Martyrs' dates from the Great Persecution of the Emperor Diocletian at the end of the third century CE and its calendar begins from 20 August 284 CE, the beginning of Diocletian's reign.

As in the first two of the apocalypses I have examined, here too it is John the Apostle who is asking questions, to satisfy his theological and general curiosity. He makes bold to speak to the Saviour himself, but

---

1. *The Apocryphal New Testament* (Oxford: Clarendon Press, 1993).

most of John's conversation is with, and his guided tour is supplied by, a fearsome angelic figure who is consistently referred to by the plural form 'Cherubim', possibly because he is described as 'filled with eyes' (a kind of composite of the four living creatures in Rev. 4.6) and his own revelations are almost theophanic ('The words of the Father are hidden within him', 2a). The dialogue format is established between John and the angel. John is the sole recipient (or channel of communication). The Seer himself is designated both as Apostle and as Holy Virgin (in the sense of Rev. 14.4). In terms of the literary genres of apocalyptic, although the revelatory discourse is dominant, the heavenly tour also has a vital function in identifying the subject-matter for the discourse.

The opening scene, as with the story of Christ's ascension in the Acts of the Apostles, is on the Mount of Olives. A cloud, embracing the world, draws the Apostles here to the presence of the resurrected Christ. St John presumes upon his special loving relationship with Christ (as represented in the role of the 'Beloved Disciple' in the Fourth Gospel) to ask to be taken into heaven and shown everything. The Saviour encourages and legitimates such a full enquiry into the cosmic creation and the phenomena of nature. After a long prayer, the heavens are opened as far as the seventh heaven; the awe-inspiring figure of the angel is revealed and, as instructed, he takes John up into heaven.

John sees the Twelve Rulers of the worlds of light, and the fountain that is the source of all dew and rain falling upon the earth. The angel describes the principles that govern the succession of day and night, and identifies the different types of stars. In the East John is shown the Paradise garden, in its present state, with Adam walking about in it, burying in the ground the leaves which fell from the tree of the knowledge of good and evil. The angel emphasizes to John the sacredness of oaths sworn by water and by wheat; this is because water existed before the heavens and the earth were created, and wheat, as formed from parts of the 'invisible body of God', is as sacred as the elements of the body of God's Son. To swear a false oath by either of these is to commit an unforgivable sin.

The angel explains to John the solution to the Old Testament problem as to why King Hezekiah turned his face to the wall and wept. The ensuing conversation resembles other, more recent, theological/philosophical conversations concerned with predestination, and whether animals have souls, and whether there is an after-life for animals. The angel then closes the conversation with John, requiring him to return to the other apostles, waiting on the Mount of Olives.

It is clear that this text makes substantial use of biblical traditions, of which the Creation accounts in Genesis, the story of Hezekiah's illness, and the themes of the book of Revelation (especially Michael and the angels) are most prominent. There is little exact quotation, but rather allusions and recollections of themes, probably cited from memory. The method of use is quite expansive and creative, in what might be termed an imaginative midrashic approach. In comparison, one might suggest outrageously, with the treatment of Genesis in books 11–13 of St Augustine's *Confessions*, there is more symbol than doctrine here; there is doctrinal understanding, but it is more implicit or popular, less explicit and philosophical. There is little evidence of the application of such themes to any particular context, so as to suggest that these apocalyptic traditions must be assigned to specific dates any earlier than this dated manuscript. On the other hand there would be nothing in such general terms to preclude a significantly earlier date. But the 'careful investigation of whether this Coptic writing goes back to a Greek substratum' called for by Wilhelm Schneemelcher is beyond the scope of my present work.[2]

An early eleventh-century Coptic context is, however, entirely plausible for this text. A number of themes from the text immediately assume greater significance when associated with such a context. In a discussion of apocalypses the esoteric character of the text is scarcely surprising; but the 'mysteries' referred to in the title, the secret knowledge received by John from the Cherubim in the seventh heaven, might be regarded as more than usually esoteric. They do invite a general comparison with gnostic traditions which were, of course, represented strongly in Egypt (the Nag Hammadi texts preserved by Coptic monks, and the Corpus Hermeticum from Alexandria). And the fact that the text was written in Coptic, while Arabic had been used extensively since the tenth century, suggests that such material was intended to be accessible only to the learned monks and clergy. As today, Coptic was still used in the liturgy but had become increasingly a 'sacred tongue' mastered by the higher clergy rather than a common language. Copts had written original works in Arabic since the middle of the tenth century, and the patriarchs had begun to insist that Arabic translations be made of Coptic liturgical texts.

There are other likely points of connection with Coptic traditions. The Archangel (and 'governor') Michael has a central role in this text as he does in Coptic iconography. Here Michael is the ruler of the cosmic powers (the angels), the intermediary with Adam, and the intercessor for humanity before the Father. There are interesting connections between the earlier Pharaonic religion of Egypt and Coptic beliefs, so that the later figures have taken on some of the characteristics of the earlier. As Antonie Wessels says,

> the Egyptian God Horus, who harpooned the crocodile (the crocodile was one of the figures of Seth, the enemy of Osiris, the father of Horus), is not only the precursor of [the saint] who slew the dragon, but also of many other combative saints who are very popular among the Copts.[3]

One would expect an interest in life after death and the fate of the soul; these are standard features of Christian hope, and we have seen how these issues are treated in the other apocalypses. But again there are links with the earlier Pharaonic beliefs which make the Egyptian context especially appropriate for these ideas. Not only is there a preoccupation with the afterlife, but also an enthusiasm for theriomorphic images, which might help to explain the interest in the souls of animals and their function in maintaining the offices of divine worship during the night. The centrality of the themes of water and wheat in this text is also particularly appropriate to an Egyptian context, where historically the issues of controlled inundation of the Nile and the provision of a grain supply have always been politically and religiously vital. In Old Testament terms this is symbolized by the story of Joseph. In the present text water and wheat have apparently evolved in a liturgical and sacramental significance for the Coptic community.

The most conclusive and significant of these connections with a Coptic context emerges from the history of relations between the Copts and their Moslem rulers. During the Shi'ite dynasty of the Fatimids (969–1171) the Copts largely received official favour and protection. They held high positions of state under al-Mu'izz (969–75) because he was sympathetic towards them. They were similarly favoured by al-'Aziz (975–96) whose wife was herself a Christian, and social differ-

---

3. Antonie Wessels, *Arab and Christian? Christians in the Middle East* (Kampen: Kok, 1995), p. 143 n. 64.

ences between Moslems and protected (*dhimmi*) Christians were suppressed. The sole exception to this favourable situation occurred throughout the reign of al-Hakim bi 'Amr Allah (996–1021):

> Persecutions of the Jews, Christians and even fellow Moslems took place. Included in some of his regulations were provisions for destroying churches or turning them into mosques. The possessions of certain churches and monasteries were confiscated... Crosses had to be removed from churches, and even from wrists on which they had been tattooed... He gave Christians a five-pound cross and the Jews a heavy bell to wear around their necks. Al-Hakim forced Christians to renounce their religion and persecuted them. He also levelled many churches... In 1009/10, the Church of the Holy Sepulchre in Jerusalem was set ablaze at his insistence. Toward the end of his life, al-Hakim was influenced by certain Coptic monks. The position of the Copts then improved somewhat again. In 1013, he even permitted Jews and Christians who had converted to Islam to return to their original religion or to emigrate to Byzantine territory... During the regime of al-Zahir (1020–1036) permission was again given to rebuild churches and Christians who had been forced to convert were again given permission to return to their original faith.[4]

It is no coincidence that the Coptic apocalypse was written in 1006 in the middle of this extraordinary time of harsh and obsessive persecution. One must assume that al-Hakim was reacting violently to the attitude of his Coptic mother. Such circumstances provide the social and psychological context for a work written out of the apocalyptic tradition to meet the needs of an increasingly desperate Coptic community. It is noteworthy that the text is not so much concerned with judgment as with the inner escapism of an esoteric divine knowledge and a certainty concerning predestination.

---

4. Wessels, *Arab and Christian?*, pp. 132-33.

THE MYSTERIES OF SAINT JOHN THE APOSTLE AND HOLY VIRGIN

(Brit. Mus. Ms. Oriental, No. 7026)

ALPHA   OMEGA   JESUS CHRIST

Fol. 1

THESE ARE THE MYSTERIES OF JOHN THE APOSTLE,
THE HOLY VIRGIN, WHICH HE LEARNED IN HEAVEN.
IN THE PEACE OF GOD. AMEN.

And it came to pass that when the Saviour had risen from the dead, He came on to the Mount of Olives, and sat down. And He made a cloud to envelop all the countries wherein were the Apostles, and it gathered them together into the presence of the Saviour upon the Mount of Olives. And John answered and said unto the Saviour, 'My Lord, behold Thou didst say unto me: "Thou art My beloved one, and thou hast found grace before Me". Now therefore, my Lord, I wish Thee to take me into heaven, and shew me all [the mysteries] so that I may know them.' And the Saviour made answer and said unto him, 'John, enquire thou of Me fully, and I on My part will hide nothing from thee. Rise up, and let us pray to My Father, Who is blessed, and He shall hear us.'

Then the Saviour and the Apostle [John] rose up, and He prayed a long, blessed prayer. And when He had said (literally, given) the Amen, the heavens moved away upon this side and on that, and they opened out one beyond the other to the seventh heaven. And behold, a great Cherubim came out from heaven, and the whole place shone with bright light, and the whole of his body was *full of eyes*, and flashes of lightning shot out from him.

Fol. 2

Then the Apostles became like unto dead men, and they fell down upon the earth through fear; but the Saviour took hold of their hands, and raised them up, and removed the fear from them, and stablished their hearts for them. And John answered [and said], 'My Lord, explain to me the order of the Cherubim, which is exceedingly terrible.' The Saviour made answer and said unto John, 'Hearken unto Me, and I will shew you everything. Thou seest the Cherubim. The words of the Father are hidden within him, from their beginning until their fulfilment. Behold, I will make him to come to thee so that he may explain everything, O My beloved John.'

And the Saviour turned Himself towards the Cherubim, and He said unto him, 'I tell thee to take My beloved John into heaven. And thou shalt explain unto him every question which he shall ask thee.' Then straightway the Cherubim lifted up John upon his wing of light, and he bore him up unto heaven. And when he arrived at the first gate the gate-keepers opened the door to him with readiness and fear. Now I, John, saw great mysteries in the *First Heaven*. I saw twelve men seated upon twelve thrones, within the great gate, in great glory and dignity. And I said unto the Cherubim, 'Master, who are these who are seated in such majestic dignity?' The Cherubim said unto me, 'Seest thou these twelve men? These are the twelve *Rulers* of the worlds of light, and each one of them ruleth for one year at a time; but Michael is he who ordereth their opera-

Fol. 3   tions, so that the earth bringeth forth its fruit all the same.' [And I said], 'There doth come a year sometimes when there is a famine in one place or another.' The Cherubim answered and said unto me, '*Behold, I have shewn thee* that which thou didst [ask] me.'

And I answered and said unto the Cherubim, 'My Lord, there cometh a year when water is scarce, and yet there is plenty, and there cometh a year when water is exceedingly plentiful, and yet there is a famine; [how is this?]' [The Cherubim] answered and said unto me, 'Seeth thou that the water is under the feet of the Father? If the Father lifteth up His feet, the water riseth upwards; but if at the time when God is about to bring the water up, man sinneth against Him, He is wont to make the fruit of the earth to be little because of the sins of men. Now if at the time when He is about to bestow a little fullness, and men keep guard over themselves so as not to commit sin, the Father is wont to bless the earth so that it may bring forth fruit, and abundance cometh through the supplication of Michael. If only men were to know of the *supplications of Michael* at the time when the water should come upon the earth, they would never commit sin at all. However, Michael taketh with him twelve times ten thousand angels, and they go into the presence of the Father, and they cast themselves down before Him, and they do not rise up again until God sendeth the waters down upon the world.'

Then I answered and said unto the Cherubim, 'I have heard one say that "*God created* the heavens and the earth", and again, that "God created the waters from the beginning".' And the Cherubim said unto me, 'Hearken, and I will inform thee concerning everything. Before ever God created the heavens and the earth, water was in existence, and there is no one whatsoever who knoweth anything about the creation of water except God Himself. For this reason whosoever shall *take an oath* which is false, in the name of water, shall never receive forgiveness. And whosoever shall take an oath [which is false] by the wheat-plant, [shall also never receive forgiveness, for], the same ordinance applieth to both the water and the wheat-plant.'

Fol. 4

And I said to the Cherubim, 'My Lord, I wish that thou wouldst inform me concerning the matter of the wheat-plant, and tell me where, in the beginning, before the earth had been cultivated, it was found that man might live upon it.'

The Cherubim said unto me, 'Hearken, and I will inform thee concerning everything. Now it came to pass that God having created Adam placed him in the Paradise of joy, and He gave him a command saying thus: "*Of every tree which is in Paradise* thou shalt eat, with the exception of the tree of the knowledge of that which is good and of that which is evil; of that thou shalt not eat. And on the day wherein thou shalt eat thereof thou shalt certainly die." Now the Devil was jealous of Adam when he saw with what great glory he was surrounded. The sun and the Moon, the two great luminaries, used to come daily and worship Adam before they rose above the earth. And the Devil went and led astray Adam and his wife, until at length they were cast forth out from Paradise; and they were banished to the land of *Eueilat*, where Adam lived a life of care and anxiety. Now after all these things, Adam was an hungered, and he could not find food to eat similar to that which they were wont to eat daily in Paradise.

Fol. 5   And he cried out to the Lord in grief and in tribulation of heart. And the Son of graciousness (or, goodness), Who acted as sponsor for him, had compassion upon him, and He spake unto His Good Father, the Lord of the Angels and of the Spirits, saying "Behold, the man whom We have created in Our image and likeness is an hungered, and I am sorrowful on his account, O My Father. Now, if it be Thy will, do not let him die before Thy face."

And in this wise did His Father of Compassion answer and say unto His beloved Son, "If it be that Thou art moved with compassion for the man whom We have created, and who hath cast [My] commandment behind him, go Thou and *give him Thy flesh* and let him eat thereof, for it is Thou who hast undertaken to act as his advocate."

And the Son of Goodness made answer and said unto His Father, "Blessed be Thy word. That which Thou hast said I will do." Then the beloved Son came forth from the presence of His Good Father, and He took a little piece of His right side, of His divine flesh, and He rubbed it down into small pieces, and brought it to His Holy Father. His Father said unto Him, "What is this?" And He said, "This is My flesh, according to what Thou didst say unto Me." His Father answered and said unto Him, "Yea, certainly, My Son. Wait, and I will give unto Thee some of My own flesh, which is invisible."

Then His Father took out a portion of His own body, and He made it into a grain of wheat, and He brought forth the seal of light wherewith He set a seal upon the worlds of light, and He sealed the grain of wheat in the middle thereof. And He said unto His beloved Son, "Take this, and give Thou it unto

Fol. 6   Michael, the Archangel, and let him give it unto Adam, and let him tell Adam that he and his sons shall live thereon. And Michael shall teach him to sow it, and to gather it in at harvest." Then Jesus called Michael, and said unto him, "Take this [grain], and give it unto Adam so that he and all his sons may live thereon." And Michael came to Adam, and he was on the Jordan, and it was the eighth day since he had eaten anything, and he was crying out to the Lord [for food]. And Michael said unto him, "Peace be to thee! The Lord hath heard thy prayer, and He hath sent unto thee a seed of grain." And when Adam heard these words from Michael, his body recovered its strength, and he came from the water, and cast himself down at the feet of Michael. And Michael gave unto him the grain which had been sealed with the seal of light, and he taught him how to sow it and to reap it, and he went up into heaven with [great] glory. Therefore the water, and the wheat-plant, and grain, and the throne of the Father stand in one category, and they are the equals of the Son of God.' Now I John saw these things, and I rejoiced when I had heard them.

And it came to pass after these things that the Cherubim raised me up up upon his wing of light, and carried me into the Seventh Heaven, and I saw mighty miracles take place therein. I saw [there] all the ranks of the angels. The first rank [contained] the Seraphim, who were *dressed in the grain-plant*, and they had golden censers in their hands, and they said, 'Hallelujah!' The angels in the second rank had *golden phials* in their hands, and they were filled with dew, and they were emptying them out on to the fields. Now Michael was the governor who was over them, and he appointed unto each one of them his work.

Fol. 7

And I saw another great and wonderful thing. Whilst I John was looking at the angels as they were all divided into ranks, I found that the name of Michael was written upon all their garments, and that the angels were crying out his name always. And I answered and said unto the Cherubim, 'How doth it come to pass that the *name of Michael* is written upon their garments? And wherefore do they cry it out?' And the Cherubim answered and said unto me, 'No angel is allowed to come upon the earth unless the name of Michael is written upon his garments, for otherwise the Devil would lead them astray.'

After this I saw a great fountain of water, whereof the waters were as white as snow, or as I might say, its waters were like unto milk, and there was an angel standing above it, and his wings were dipped in the water. *And the place round*

about the fountain was planted with trees which were laden
with fruit, and the fruits thereof were of a very great many different kinds. And this fountain was like unto a sea, and every
tree which grew by the side of it consisted entirely of one
branch.

And I, John, saw another great and wonderful thing there. I
saw the root of a tree which emitted water into the fountain.
And I said unto the Cherubim, 'My Lord, explain to me the
matter of this fountain, the water whereof is white, and the
matter of this angel, which standeth above it.' The Cherubim
said unto me, 'This is the fountain which poureth out the *dew*
upon the earth.' I said unto him, 'How is it that this angel is
standing above it, with his wings always dipped in the waters
of the fountain?' The Cherubim said unto me, 'Seest thou this
angel? His work is this. Every time the trumpet soundeth he
riseth up, and he shaketh his wings which are full of dew, and
he smiteth the heavens therewith, and the heavens open, one
beyond the other, so that the dew may distil through them
upon the earth.' And I said unto the Cherubim, 'In what way
do these Seven Heavens open, one beyond the other, so that
the daylight may penetrate them and fall upon the world?' And
the Cherubim answered and said unto me, 'Hearken, and I will
explain everything to you. There are *seven trumpets* appointed
over the dew, and all these are wont to sound before the dew
cometh upon the earth. When the first trumpet soundeth, and
the second, and so on until the seventh, the dew followeth the
sound of the trumpets from one heaven to the other. The seventh trumpet belongeth to Michael, and when Michael bloweth
his trumpet, the dew runneth swiftly, and all the governors
withdraw, until it cometh upon the earth in order to make all
the fruits to swell (or, increase).'

Now, whilst I was marvelling [at these things], I saw
another angel coming from a distance in wrath, and he stood
up by the fountain which was filled with dew; he wept, and his
eyes dropped blood into the fountain which was full of dew.
For he was filled with wrath against all mankind, and the
whole of the place trembled and shook when he stood up there.
Then the heavens opened on this side and on that and every-
where, and I saw a great and mighty angel come forth from the

Fol. 8

Fol. 9

heavens, and they called his name Michael, and he was girt about the loins with a girdle of gold. There was a sponge in his hand, wherewith he wiped away all the tears of the angel of wrath, and he drove the Angel of Wrath afar off, saying, 'Get thee gone from this fountain, thou Angel of Wrath, for thou wishest to bring a famine upon the earth.'

And I said unto the Cherubim, 'My Lord, shew me the matter of the Angel of Wrath whose eyes drop blood into the fountain.' He said unto me, 'Seest thou the Angel of Wrath? He is the Angel of Famine. If Michael were to cease from the wiping away of his tears [of blood] which he letteth drop, and were to allow them to enter the fountain, the [water thereof] would come to an end and the dew which falleth down upon the earth, and diseases and dissensions would break out, and the land would be smitten with famine.' And moreover, he said unto me. 'There are forty legions of angels, each legion containing ten thousand angels, who sing hymns over the dew until it cometh upon the earth, without any blemish at all in it.'

After these things he brought me to the Land of *Edem*. He placed me upon his wing of light, and he brought me to the place where the sun riseth, by the side of the fountain which supplieth water to the *four rivers*, Phisôn, Tigris, Gêôn (the Nile), and the Euphrates. I saw the Paradise of joy, which was filled with all kinds of trees which bore fruits of all kinds. And I said to the Cherubim, 'My Lord, I would that thou wouldst shew me the tree [of the fruit] whereof Adam ate, and *became naked*, and God was afterwards wroth with him.' The Cherubim answered and said unto me, 'Thou askest a question which concerneth great mysteries, but I will hide nothing whatsoever from thee. Now therefore, rise up, set thyself behind me, and I will explain to thee everything, and I will shew thee the tree [of the fruit] of which Adam ate.'

Then I rose up and I followed him. I walked through the Paradise, and I looked round about, and I saw *the tree in the middle of Paradise*; now it had no fruit upon it, and thorns grew all over it, and the trunk went down into the ground a very long way. And I answered and said to the Cherubim, 'Make me to understand the matter of this tree which hath no fruit on it, and which is grown over with thorns.' And the

Fol. 10

Cherubim said unto me, 'This is the tree [of the fruit] of which Adam ate and became naked.' And I said unto him, 'There is no fruit on it; where did he find the fruit which he ate?' And the Cherubim said unto me, 'A kind of fruit did grow on it, and it was not without fruit [at that time].' And I said unto him, 'Of what kind was its fruit?' He said unto me, 'It was *a kind of apple.*' And I said unto the Cherubim, 'Shall it remain wholly without fruit, or not?' And he said unto me, 'This is the order which God laid upon it from the beginning.'

Now whilst I was marvelling at these things I saw Adam. He was coming along at a distance, and he was like unto a man who was weeping. He was spreading out his garment, and he was carrying away in his garment [the leaves] which were under the tree, and pouring them out on the ground, and burying them. And I said unto the Cherubim, 'Why is Adam spreading out his garment, and putting in it the dried leaves which have been blown off the tree, and digging a hole in the ground and burying them therein?' And the Cherubim said unto me, 'From the moment when the Devil entered into Paradise, and seduced Adam, and Eve his wife, the trees, which up to that time had possessed a sweet small, ceased to have any smell at all, and their leaves [began to] fall off. And Adam used to dress himself in the leaves, and to make them be witnesses for him in the judgement because of what he had done.' Then I said unto the Cherubim, 'My Lord, by what means did the Devil enter into Paradise, and seduce Adam and Eve? Unless this matter had been permitted by God he could not have entered in, for nothing can take place without [the consent of] God.'

Then the Cherubim said unto me, 'Four and twenty angels are appointed to Paradise daily, and twelve go in there daily to worship God. Now at the moment when the Devil went into Paradise, and seduced Adam, there was no angel at all in Paradise, but an agreement took place [that they should remain outside it] until Adam had eaten of the tree.' And I said to the Cherubim, 'If they agreed to this, with the consent of God, then *no sin rests upon Adam.*' And the Cherubim said unto me, 'By no means. If Adam had been patient for a short time, God would have said to him, 'Eat thou of the tree.' God removed

Fol. 11

the righteousness wherewith he was arrayed, and He cast him
Fol. 12 forth from Paradise, in order that the things which He spake
might be fulfilled [when] He should send His Son into the
world.'

And I said unto the Cherubim, 'My Lord, of what kind was
this righteousness wherein Adam was arrayed, and which he
received from His hand?' And the Cherubim said unto me,
'*On the day wherein God created Adam*, Adam was twelve
cubits in height, and six cubits in width, and his neck was three
cubits long. And he was like unto an alabaster stone wherein
there is no blemish whatsoever. But when he had eaten [of the
fruit] of the tree, his body diminished in size, and he became
small, and the righteousness wherein he was arrayed departed
and left him naked, even to the tips of his fingers, that is to
say, to his very nails. If he was not cold in the winter, he was
not hot in the summer.'

And I answered and said unto the Cherubim, 'My Lord, at
the time when God created Adam, He also created Eve with
him from the heavens (?). But, on the other hand, I have heard
that God created Adam and Eve from the beginning, and,
again, I have heard that God brought a deep sleep upon Adam,
and that when he was unconscious, He took one of the ribs
from his side, and made it into a woman, and that He filled
up the place where the rib was in his side with flesh. The
Almighty did not then create two bodies, there being [only]
one body.' And the Cherubim answered and said unto me,
'Hearken, and I will explain unto you everything. At the time
when God created Adam, He created Eve also with him, in one
body, for at the time when the Master was working at Adam,
Fol. 13 the thought concerning Eve was with Him. For this reason two
bodies came from one body, but He did not separate them
from each other immediately. At the time when He brought
slumber upon Adam, and Adam fell asleep, and slept heavily,
He brought Eve forth from him, and she became his wife. She
was, of a surety, hidden in the rib of the left side [of Adam]
from the day wherein God created him. Consider, then, with
great attention the sign which is in the sons of Adam.'

And I said unto the Cherubim, 'O my Lord, what is the
sign which is in the sons of Adam?' And the Cherubim said

unto me, 'At the moment when the ice (or, cold) was about to come upon the earth, the first things which went cold in the body of the man were his finger nails. Because at the time when God deprived Adam of the righteousness wherein he was arrayed, the first things which grew cold were his finger nails. And he wept, and cried out to the Lord, saying, "Woe is me, O my Lord. At the time when I kept the commandments of God, and before I did eat of the [fruit of] the tree, my whole body was white like my nails." For this reason every time Adam looked upon his nails, he used to cry out and weep, even as *Hezekiah, when he was sick, used to turn towards the wall, and weep.*'

[And I answered and said unto the Cherubim, 'When Hezekiah] was weeping, why did he not look at a man [instead of a wall]?' And the Cherubim said unto me, '[Hearken], and I will make everything manifest to you, O faithful virgin. Now it came to pass in the time of Solomon that the king compelled all the demons to describe to him all the various kinds [of sicknesses], and the remedies which were to be employed in healing them all, and the various kinds of herbs which must be used in relieving the pains of sicknesses, and Solomon wrote them all down upon the wall in the House of God. And any man who was attacked by a sickness [or, disease], no matter of what kind, used to go into the temple, and look upon the wall, until he found there written the remedy which was suitable for his sickness; then he would take that remedy, and would go into his house, ascribing glory to God. And it came to pass that, after Solomon the king was dead, Hezekiah plastered over the walls of the temple with lime, and the prescriptions for the relief of sickness could no longer be found. Now when Hezekiah the king had fallen sick, and was sick unto death, he could not find the prescription whereby to heal his sickness, because it was he himself who had plastered over the walls of the temple with lime. And when the prescriptions which had been written upon them could not be found again, he went into the house of the Lord, and lay down there, and he looked upon the wall, and he wept, saying, "My Lord, let not that which I have done in the matter of plastering over with lime the walls, whereon were inscribed the prescriptions for healing, be held

Fol. 14

to be a sin [by Thee], for I said, Let men make supplication to God with hope, and they shall find healing. Never shall I find a prescription for healing whereby I may be made whole." And the Lord heard [him], and had compassion upon him, and sent unto him Isaiah the Prophet, and he spake unto him, saying, "Take the fruit (?) of the wild fig-tree, and plaster it over the body, and *thou shalt find relief*." Now therefore, O John, God will never forsake the man who performeth [His commandments].'

Fol. 15 And again I said unto the Cherubim, 'My Lord, I would that thou didst make me to understand the matter of the Cherubim, whose voices cry so loudly in heaven that mankind tremble upon earth [at the sounds thereof].'

And the Cherubim said unto me, 'Dost thou see these great winds which are shut up inside their storehouses, over which the angels are set? When the trumpet soundeth inside the *covering* (or, *veil*), the gentle winds come forth, and they breathe upon the wings of the angel who is over the fountain of the dew; then the angel moveth his wings, and the dew cometh upon the earth, and the seed (or, grain) groweth in the earth, and the trees, and the crops, and the fruit. If the trumpet doth not sound, a harsh, strong noise cometh forth from heaven, and thereupon the waters of rain come upon the earth in great quantities, which make the fruits grow, and rain-storms, and thunders of which men are afraid. For it is the sound of the rustling of the wings of the Seraphim which governs the waters of rain, until they come down into the firmament; and they fall on the earth gently, for if they were to descend upon the earth in their [full] violence they would lay waste the earth just as did the water of Noah and the lightnings which came with them. [This would happen] if the Seraphim did not come down to govern the waters of the rain, for all the waters are in the sky and the heavens. Behold, I have made clear to you all mysteries.'

Fol. 16 And I answered and said unto the Cherubim, 'My Lord, I would that thou didst make me to know what it is which supporteth the sky and maketh it to be suspended thus.' And the Cherubim said unto me, 'It is suspended by faith, and by the ordinance of God.' And I said unto the Cherubim, 'What is it that supporteth the earth?' And the Cherubim said unto me, 'It is *four pillars* which support the earth, and they are *sealed with seven seals*.'

And I said unto him, 'My Lord, be not wroth with me when I ask thee this matter also; shew me, what is it that beareth up the four pillars?' And the Cherubim said unto me, 'He Who created them knoweth what appertaineth to them.' And I said unto the Cherubim, 'My Lord, what is the ordinance concerning the hours of the night and day?' He said unto me, 'Hearken, I will shew thee. God appointed *twelve Cherubim* to stand outside the curtain (or, inner veil), and they were not to toil in any way, but were to sing twelve hymns daily. When the first Cherubim had finished [singing] his hymn, the first hour came to an end. When the second Cherubim had finished [singing] his hymn, the second hour came to an end, and so on until the twelfth Cherubim. When the twelfth [Cherubim had finished singing his hymn], the twelve hours were ended.'

Then I said to the Cherubim, 'As concerning the twelve hours of the night: are there Seraphim appointed over them, or not?' And the Cherubim said unto me, 'Assuredly not, but when the *beasts*, and the *birds, and the reptiles* pray, the first hour is ended. When the second hour is ended, the beasts pray [again], and so on until the twelfth hour of the night; it is the animals of God which set limits to them.' And I said unto the Cherubim, 'Doth the sun know when the twelve hours have come to an end, so that he may depart to the place where he setteth or riseth?' And the Cherubim said unto me, 'When the angels who blow the trumpets have finished, Michael knoweth that the twelfth hymn is finished, and he speaketh to the Angel of the Sun, who goeth and bringeth to an end his course.'

And I answered and said unto the Cherubim, 'My Lord, is it God Who ordaineth the life of a man from the time when he was in his mother's womb, or not?' And the Cherubim said unto me, 'Know thou that [one] man is wont to perform very many superfluous works, [and another] very many acts of goodness, from the time when he is born to the end of his life. God, however, setteth *a sign* on the righteous man before He fashioneth him, for it is impossible to cause anything to happen without God. But sin is an alien thing (or, stranger) to

Fol. 17

God; for He Who created man was without sin. It is man who himself committeth sin, according to his wish, and according to the desire of the Devil.'

And I said unto the Cherubim, '*Man hath been born to suffering*, according to what Job said, 'My mother brought me forth for suffering'.' And the Cherubim said unto me, 'God is a compassionate Being, and He doth not forsake man utterly

Fol. 18 but He sheweth mercy upon him, for he is His own form and His own image, and is the work of His own hands. And now, O John, He will not forsake him that doeth the will of God, and he who doeth good things shall receive them doubled many times over in the House of God.'

And I said unto the Cherubim, 'My Lord, at the moment when God is about to create man, doth He give him the name *"righteous" or "sinner"*, or not?' And the Cherubim said unto me, 'Hearken, and I will shew thee. At the moment when God is about to create a man, before He placeth him in the womb of his mother, He calleth all the angels, and they come and stand round about. If the Father blesseth the soul, the angels make answer "Amen". If there come from His mouth the words, "This soul shall give Me rest", the angels make answer "Amen". If the Father saith, "This soul shall commit iniquity", the angels make answer "Amen". Whatsoever cometh forth from the mouth of the Father, that cometh to pass.' And I said unto the Cherubim, 'Is the matter of which man is fashioned more excellent than that of the beasts?' The Cherubim said unto me, 'Yes. Now when men die, each one of them is taken to the place of which he is worthy, but *so far as beasts are concerned*, whether they die, or whether they live, *their place is the earth.*'

And I said unto the Cherubim, 'Are there souls in them?' He said unto me, 'Every created thing hath a soul in it. Now therefore, the soul of every created thing is its blood.' And I

Fol. 19 said unto the Cherubim, 'Will they then be punished, or will rest be given unto them?' He said unto me, 'Let it not be that rest be not given unto them, and let them suffer not; but man is a being who can suffer, and can enjoy rest.'

And it came to pass that when I had heard all these things. I marvelled at the works which God performeth in connexion with man. And I said unto the Cherubim, '[My Lord], be not wroth with me if I ask this matter also. I would that thou didst inform me concerning the stars which we see in the firmament, and tell me why it is that we cease to see them when the sun hath risen. I would that thou didst inform me where it is they go until it is time for them to perform their service again.' And the Cherubim said unto me, 'The stars are of different orders. There are some stars which remain in the heavens until noon, but they cannot be seen because of the light of the sun. There are *seven stars* which come in the north of the world, and they remain there *in the heavens* always. And there are seven stars in the heavens which are called ⲛⲉⲉⲛⲧⲏⲣ [*the gods*]; those which are there are not permitted to emerge from their place of storehouse, except *when death cometh upon the earth.*'

And I said unto the Cherubim, 'Why is it that one star differeth from another? And why is it that a star is wont to transfer itself from the place which it had originally [to another]?' And the Cherubim said unto me, 'Hearken, and I will make known unto you everything. There are very many orders of stars which move from the place wherein they were placed originally, but the decree of God which directeth them abideth for ever. Behold now, I have made manifest unto thee all things, O beloved one of God. *Arise, get thee down* into the world, and tell therein everything which thou hast seen.'

Fol. 20   Then straightaway the Cherubim brought me down on the *Mount of Olives*, where I found the Apostles gathered together. And I told them of the things which I had seen, and when we had saluted (or, kissed) each other, each departed to his country, ascribing glory to God. And they preached in the Name of the Christ, through Whom be glory to Him, and His Good Father, and the Holy Spirit for ever. Amen.

Explanatory Notes

The accuracy—or more precisely the manner—of Budge's translation of the title to the work is disputed. His intention was presumably to ensure that John is described both as apostle and as virgin saint (bearing in mind the reference by the Seer of Revelation to παρθένος meaning 'chaste and celibate male' in Rev. 14.4). John the Apostle was traditionally referred to as 'the Holy Virgin' (see Epiphanius, *Panarion* 28.7). Holy ascetic men were often called holy virgins. The title should not be taken to suggest that there was more than one subject (or recipient) of these 'mysteries' or visions. In his zeal to prevent this misunderstanding for the 'modern' reader, Budge says rather cavalierly in the footnote to his translation: 'In the title of the Coptic text of this section strike out the word "and".' (*Coptic Apocrypha*, p. 241).

1.
Full of eyes: cf. Ezek. 1.18; 10.12.

2.
First Heaven: the heavenly journey is now widely recognized as a common motif in ancient apocalyptic literature (see the formal classification by Adela Yarbro Collins, discussed earlier). It can also be found, to the surprise of some exegetes, within New Testament texts at 2 Cor. 12.1-10. St Paul's claimed visionary experience, as an ascent through three heavens, corresponds to the original version of *T. Levi* 2.7-10; 3.1-4. The number of heavens was augmented later to seven. As in *Asc. Isa.* 7–9, the chosen prophetic figure is only able to reach the highest point of heaven because it is specifically permitted by God. The purpose is that he may receive the fullest extent of the prophetic revelation. It was clear from 2 Corinthians that the vision is held to be a source of revelation (12.1, 7) and that it was in Christ's power that the vision took place (12.2). The content of the experience was described by Paul in con-ventional apocalyptic terms as 'things which man may not utter'. The point is that these experiences are apocalyptic, but not directly revelatory, as in the most immediate kind of Hebrew or early Christian prophecy.

See Alan Segal 'Heavenly Ascent in Hellenistic Judaism, Early Christianity and their Environment', in *ANRW*, pp. 1333-94; Richard Bauckham 'The Worship of Jesus', in *The Climax of Prophecy: Studies*

Figure 6. *St Michael* © Ranworth Church, Norfolk. Photograph by Jarrolds of Norwich

on the Book of Revelation (Edinburgh: T. & T. Clark, 1993), pp. 118-49.

Rulers: the twelve figures, each reigning for a year at a time, are cosmic powers. They are angelic governors, themselves under the control of Michael (see below). Within the Coptic context we should probably identify monastic rulers and patriarchs of previous generations with such angelic rulers. The Coptic philosophy viewed monastic life as similar to the life of the angels. The monks at prayer were defenders and protectors of the peace of the world, continually standing watch at the boundaries for the sake of humanity. 'It is clear to all that dwell there [in the desert monasteries] that through them the world is kept in being, and that through them too human life is preserved and honored by God.' (B. Ward [trans.], *The Sayings of the Desert Fathers* [London: Mowbrays, 1975], p. 12).

3.

Behold I have shewn thee: a response which rather resembles that of the strict schoolmaster—'One question at a time'!

Supplication of Michael: the particular emphasis on the archangel Michael's role in maintaining the supply of water at first seems strange. But when it is remembered that the religion of ancient Egypt laid considerable stress on the annual inundation of flood-waters from the Nile, to ensure fertility by good irrigation, and regarded this as a symbol of stability and of the political power of the Pharaohs, then it is much less surprising that the Egyptian Christians in the Coptic Church should retain and 'baptise' such ideas as vital for their theology. Wallis Budge cites an Encomium of Eustathius on St Michael as supporting evidence, showing the part played by St Michael in making the waters of the Nile to rise. 'An honourable lady called Euphemia is greatly tormented by the Devil, who attacks her on every possible occasion, and is always foiled by the eikon which Euphemia carries about with her. One day the Devil said to her, "Thou art saying at this moment that I shall not overcome thee so long as thou trustest in this little wooden tablet which is in thy hands, and if this be so, know that I will come to thee another time, on a day which thou shalt not know, that is to say, on the twelfth day of the month Paoni, for on that day Michael will be in conclave with the angels, and will be bowing down and praying with all the angel host outside the veil of the Father, for the waters of the River of Egypt, and for dew, and for rain. And I know that it will happen that he will

continue in prayer ceaselessly for three days and three nights, and in
prostrations, and in bowings down, and not standing upright until God
shall hear him and grant his requests"' (*Three Encomiums on St. Michael* [ed. W.A. Budge; London: 1894], p. 90).
    'God created': Gen. 1.1-2.

4.

'Take an oath': this is an interesting variation on the idea of the unforgivable sin, and is a clear indication of the importance of water and
grain both physically for life and sacramentally for the spiritual life.
    'Of every tree which is in Paradise': Gen. 2.16-17.
    It is significant to note the effect of a Coptic context upon the use of
the biblical language of paradise. For the Copts the land of Egypt pos-
sesses equal and opposite valencies. It is the 'house of bondage', recal-
ling once more the stories of Joseph and Moses and the entry and
exodus of Israel in relation to Egypt. But for part of the story Egypt is a
place of asylum, and a refuge in times of famine. It can even be compared to Paradise itself ('like the garden of the Lord, like the land of
Egypt', Gen. 13.10) and certainly a blessing (as in Isaiah's oracle concerning Egypt—'On that day Israel will be the third with Egypt and
Assyria, a blessing in the midst of the earth, whom the Lord of hosts has
blessed, saying, "Blessed be Egypt my people, and Assyria the work of
my hands, and Israel my heritage."'—19.24-25).
    Eueilat = Havilah (Gen. 2.11; 10.7, 29; 25.18; 1 Sam. 15.7)

5.

Give him Thy flesh: the reference to the flesh or body of Christ is essentially sacramental. Christ (the second Adam in Christian theology since
St Paul) is seen as having compassion on the first Adam, regarded as
the symbol of the created order of humankind, in the creation of which
the Son collaborated with the Father. So that humanity should not die of
physical hunger, the Son is prepared to give (or sacrifice again) some
element of himself. But the sacrament will assuage spiritual rather than
physical hunger. So in addition the Father produces something of his
own 'invisible' flesh, and creates from it a grain of wheat. This will
assuage the physical hunger and accordingly be reverenced as having
inestimable value. However the effect against the famine cannot be
instantaneous! Although presented with the wheat grain when he has
not eaten for eight days, Adam is not to eat it, but is instead taught to

sow the seed and harvest the crop. The key point here is of course the value of wheat as the grain harvest of Egypt. This was recognized in the story of the Old Testament patriarch Joseph, and assumed political importance in the maintenance of the granaries of Egypt by the Emperors of Rome.

Given the Egyptian context of this Coptic apocalypse, we should perhaps take account of a broadly parallel (but explicitly gnostic) idea to be found in the *Gospel of Thomas* (Nag Hammadi Codex II, Tractate 2, Saying 108): 'Jesus said, "Whoever drinks from my mouth will become like me; I myself shall become that person, and the hidden things will be revealed to him."' The thrust of this saying is towards the gnostic revelation in the last clause; but there is also the clear sense of an established relationship and identification, as a result of drinking from the well of Christ's mouth (or eating his flesh). The identity of the religious community is thereby reinforced, building on the basic idea of Adam created 'in the image of God' (Gen. 1.26-27). This broadly gnostic understanding may also find a parallel in the distinctive version of the Sower Parable in the *Gospel of Thomas*, Saying 9 (see the reference in the explanatory notes on *3 Apoc. Jn* 6). The wheat seed produces a rich harvest when the select strains are able to escape the natural/material hazards of this world; perhaps this is why Adam in the present text has to sow the seed, not eat it.

Dressed in the grain-plant: the importance of the angels as cosmic rulers, and the importance of the wheat (grain-plant) come together in this rather curious description of the angels wearing wheaten (coloured?) clothes. Presumably it has more to do with the spiritual realities than with a literal description of angels dressed in straw.

7.

Golden phials: angels with censers (6) or here with phials or bowls are reminiscent of the original angelic figures of Revelation. In Rev. 15.17 the contents of the bowls have a destructive rather than a beneficial effect.

The name of Michael: repeatedly the importance of the archangel Michael is emphasized, most appropriately because of the special importance of Michael (with Gabriel) in Coptic belief and iconography. The very fact of his name upon the angelic garments is a guarantee of protection against the angels' being molested by the Devil when their tasks take them down to Earth. Presumably this reflects the past victory

of Michael and his angels over the Devil in Rev. 12.7-9. But there may
be an additional irony in the present circumstances of Coptic persecution, where the once 'protected' (*dhimmi*) Christians are no longer safe
in the hands of the Moslem ruler.

The place round about the fountain was planted with trees: the land-
scape here is very reminiscent of the 'river of the water of life' and 'the
tree of life' on either side, as depicted in Rev. 22.1-2.

8.
dew: cf. *3 Apoc. Jn* 16.
    seven trumpets: cf. Rev. 8.2.

9.
Edem: (Hebrew *qedem*) = the lands of the East.

the four rivers: these are in a slightly modified order compared with
Gen. 2.10-14 (Pishon, Gihon, Chiddeqel and Perath in Hebrew). There
were four rivers in the garden of God, according to ancient Persian
mythology, and Claus Westermann argued that the intention of the Genesis passage was 'to link the "information" about paradise with geogra-
phy. The purpose is to state that the rivers which bring fertility (= blessing) to the world have their origin in the river which brings fertility
(= blessing) to the garden of God.' In the Genesis version the third and
fourth rivers are readily identifiable with the Tigris and the Euphrates
respectively; but the names of the first two occur rarely elsewhere, and
it is often said that they are descriptive terms derived from two verbal
roots, meaning 'spring up' and 'burst forth' respectively. Gihon was
later identified in Jewish and Christian tradition with reasonable probability as the Nile (chiefly on the grounds that classical writers called
Ethiopia or Nubia 'the land of Cush'; but see also Sir. 24.27 and the
Septuagint reading at Jer. 2.18), and several scholars think that Pishon
is the Indus. Such an identification and ordering would provide an approximately clockwise circulation (east, south, west, north). From the
Egyptian perspective of our Coptic text the Nile (Geon or Gihon) would
be the most significant. The new ordering is not immediately explicable,
but the compass points now appear in the sequence east, west, south
and north.

10.
Became naked: strictly 'knew that they were naked' in Gen. 3.7.
    The tree in the middle of Paradise: this is the tree 'that is in the

middle of the garden'. According to the serpent, the effect of eating its fruit is to 'be like God, knowing good and evil' (Gen. 3.3-4). It is controversial whether two different trees (of life and of knowledge) are described in Gen. 2.9, or only a single one; there would of course be a dramatic irony in the woman's fear that they will die, if they eat of the tree of life. Of course the human quest for the tree (or plant) of life is at least as old as the *Epic of Gilgamesh* 11.266-95. The present state of the tree, without fruit and smothered with thorns, is presumably a dramatic expression of the aftermath of God's judgment at the fall of human kind (cf. Gen. 3.18)

A *kind of apple*: the fruit, in the story of Eve and the serpent in Gen. 3.1-7, is not identified. At some point, at least by the Middle Ages, this fruit was identified as an apple. The likely route towards such an identification was by the (possibly punning) association of two Latin words: *mālum* (apple) and *mălum* (evil thing / wrongdoing), or alternatively *mālus* (apple tree) and *mălus* (bad, evil—masculine adjective). Originally the Latin word *mālum* denoted any tree-fruit that was fleshy on the outside and had a hard kernel within, in contrast to the *nux* (or nut) which was fleshy inside a hard outer shell. So the fruit could be a peach, apricot or quince, just as much as an apple. Indeed in the context of Genesis an apricot is more likely. *Prunus armeniaca*, the apricot, is abundant in Palestine and has probably been so since biblical times. Apparently in Cyprus apricots are still sometimes referred to as 'golden apples' (cf. Prov. 25.11). Modern translations sometimes render the Hebrew *tappuaḥ* as 'apricot' in Song of Songs 2.3, 5; 7.8; 8.5. Another possible identification is with the quince (*Cydonia oblonga*) which is also indigenous to the area.

The theological link between the apple and wrongdoing or guilty action would have been possible for Latin-speaking theologians, from the Vulgate use of *mālum* (apple). Such an idea might well have appealed to St Augustine, although particular evidence is lacking. In classical mythology there is an interesting precedent for the idea of widespread repercussions from the use of an apple. This is the result of the judgment of Paris, when he awards to Venus the 'apple of discord' (the phrase occurs in Justinus 12.15.11), inscribed 'to the fairest', an event which led to the abduction of Helen and the sequel of the Trojan War. It is possible that the association of the *tappuaḥ* in the Song of Songs with love and love-sickness led to the identification of the apple with sexual temptation, widely regarded in many religious traditions as 'the forbidden fruit'. A further influence may be the reference in Wis. Sol. 10.7 (and Josephus, *War* 4.8.4) to the deceptive fruit said to grow near the Dead Sea as the 'apples of Sodom'. Once it had become established in Latin, the original pun could well be translated, for example into Coptic. After all the original root of the Latin *mălus* is the Greek adjective μελας (= black).

The theological significance of the apple, thus developed, can be illustrated by this quotation from the Old English, in a homily by Aelfric (c. 955–c. 1022 CE) on Christ's Passion: 'Through a tree death came to us, when Adam ate the forbidden apple, and through a tree life came again to us and redemption, when Christ hung on the rood for our redemption.' [*Homilies of Aelfric*, 2.240-41]

11.

No sin rests upon Adam. This retelling of the Genesis story seems to place the main active responsibility upon the Devil. How did the Devil come to be in Paradise, unless he had been permitted by God to enter? It appears that the Devil's presence and his seductive influence were only possible because the worshipping angels on their daily roster were not on duty (presumably to watch over the trees in the garden) at this particular time. Such a rest period for them, and window of opportunity for the Devil, would only have been possible by deliberate arrangement. John, considering this situation, draws the plausible and reasonable conclusion that as a result Adam should not be regarded as guilty of the original sin. But the angel does not agree with John's conclusion. It is not a question of Adam being blameless because of God's arrangement with the guardian angels. The real fault lies in Adam's sheer impatience; he was so greedy to respond to the Devil's encouragement that he did not wait to be invited by God. This was a rash presumption, because if Adam had only waited, it is suggested that God would have allowed it (in contradiction to Gen. 2.17). The impression is of a more liberal deity who responds to changing situations.

As the real sin is apparently greed and impatience, so the punishment is summary and immediate. Adam loses his clothing of righteousness and is expelled from Paradise. At the same time the sweet-smelling leaves of the trees lose their smell and wither. As they fall off the trees, Adam could use them as replacement clothing. He therefore carries around with him the symbol of his offence, which witnesses to God's judgment against him. It is not clear whether Adam's action in gath-

ering and attempting to bury the leaves is simply a penitential act
(witness his weeping) or perhaps an attempt to hide some of the evidence.

12.

On the day wherein God created Adam: the text provides us with a
highly-dramatized account of Adam's state before the Fall. Not only
was he a gigantic figure (more than six metres tall and three metres
wide), with a long neck, he also resembled a block of unblemished
alabaster. Afterwards he had shrunk to a puny figure, physically impov-
erished, particularly down to his finger nails which are the first to feel
the cold (ironically they are the only vestiges of the alabaster effect).
Whether any corresponding changes took place in the body of Eve is
not stated. It appears that the author has attempted some harmonizing of
the inconsistencies between the two accounts of the creation of human
kind, essentially preferring Gen. 1.27 to Gen. 2.21-23. The status of
woman is thereby enhanced, both by what is said about her origins, and
by what is not said about her weakness when faced by the serpent. It
seems doubtful that such changes are motivated by anything like modern political correctness or feminist thinking. Instead the aim is probably to make a universal statement about human nature and greed.

13.

Hezekiah, when he was sick, used to turn towards the wall, and weep.
This episode is the other substantial piece of Old Testament tradition
elaborated in the present text. It is the act of weeping which links Hezekiah with Adam. The story of Hezekiah's illness is to be found in 2 Kgs
20.2 and in Isa. 38.2. According to John Gray's translation of 2 Kings:

> In those days Hezekiah was mortally ill, and Isaiah the son of Amos the
> prophet came to him and said to him, Thus saith Yahweh, Give last
> injunctions to thy family for thou shalt die and not recover. Then he
> turned his face to the wall and prayed to Yahweh saying, Ah! Yahweh,
> remember how I have walked before thee in truth and with a whole heart
> and have done that which was good in thine eyes. And Hezekiah wept
> sorely.

It is clear that the act of turning the face to the wall is conditioned
according to different cultural circumstances. This could be a desire for
privacy. Or, as Gray suggests, it 'was perhaps a symbolic act of renun-
ciation of the world and turning to God alone' (*I & II Kings: A Com-*

mentary [London: SCM Press, 1964], pp. 633-34). The piety expressed in the king's prayer corresponds to the theological ideals of the Deuteronomistic historians (see 2 Kgs 18.3, 5-7); it might otherwise seem strange that God's mind should be changed by telling him what he knew anyway. More recently it might be regarded as the action of a deeply depressed person. In fact that may be closer to the attitude of Hezekiah, shared with that of Adam, in the present apocalyptic text.

It is possible that the present elaborated explanation arose because of the theological problems posed by the Old Testament story. But it seems more likely that a solution would be sought in the role of the prophet Isaiah as a miracle worker. If instead we look to the creative imagination of this apocalyptic tradition, then the most telling feature seems to be the irony inherent in the story. It is this which links the picture of Adam living with, and brooding upon, his changed fortunes, to the image of Hezekiah as the victim of his own zealous purges. According to the angel's version of events, the wall in the temple/palace complex had been covered with a tabulation of wisdom on diseases and remedies, diagnoses and prescriptions, which king Solomon had acquired as a result of his power over devils who knew all about such ailments. When Hezekiah became king, he had obliterated all this wisdom (perhaps because of the associated superstitions), by having this wall whitewashed or replastered. Such action could have been part of the religious reform mentioned in 2 Kgs 18.4 and described in the graphic detail of cultic cleansing of the temple buildings in 2 Chron. 29.3-19. Tragically (and ironically) the king, in his time of real need, perceives in his anguish that he has deprived himself of the direct help he needs, and that the consequences could well be fatal. Notice that it could just as accurately be said, from this perspective, that Adam recognises in his anguish that he has by his rashness deprived himself of that direct help from God, and the consequences of his impatience could well be fatal.

14.

Thou shalt find relief: cf. 2 Kgs 20.7; Isa. 38.21. The irony persists, as the ailment is cured by a poultice made from wild figs that is 'plastered' over the king's body. This is presumably just one of those popular, herbal remedies that could have been read from the wall, but for Hezekiah's action. In fact John Gray cites Pliny's *Natural History* 22.7 for the use of figs as a remedy to draw ulcers, and two veterinary texts from Ras Shamra (*UH* 55.28; 56.33) where a matured fig-cake, made with raisins and bean-flour, is prescribed to be injected into the nose of a horse. But in the story it is not the basic nature of the cure, but the miraculous intervention of the prophet, and ultimately the compassion of God in response to penitent prayer which matters.

15.

covering/veil (see also section 16)

Within the Coptic tradition, the 'veil' refers to the curtain which screens off the altar in the sanctuary of the church. This corresponds to the 'gate' or holy doors in the iconostasis, within the Greek Orthodox tradition, the symbolic importance of which is emphasised in the Apocalypse of John Chrysostom (see especially 23, 34). Again the descriptions of heaven are built out of a profound and symbolic understanding of the context and practice of worship on earth.

16.

Four pillars...sealed with seven seals: cf. Rev. 6 (perhaps underlining the cosmological interpretation of that text?) and Rev. 7.1. The assumption that the world has four corners and can be supported as a table by a leg or a pillar at each corner was widespread in Classical cosmology. Irenaeus had no problem in making a case for four gospels simply on the basis that the earth has four corners (see *3 Apoc. Jn* 14 above).

Compare biblical statements on creation, e.g., Ps. 102.25, 104.5.

While the Old Testament tradition thought in terms of only three continents, inhabited by the descendants of Noah's three sons, the secular *mappae mundi* of imperial Rome (such as that by Vipsanius Agrippa, the Emperor Augustus's son-in-law, for the portico of the Via Flaminia in Rome) seem to have divided the world into four continents, and this influenced Christian writers and cartographers from the fourth century onward. If there are four continents, it is logical to have four pillars to support them.

twelve cherubim: the 12 hours of the day are measured by the 12 Cherubim, each of whom sings a hymn, the singing of which lasts exactly an hour. The end of the day is marked by a kind of heavenly curfew sounded on the trumpets.

17.

Beasts, birds and reptiles: the 12 hours of the night are regulated in a parallel but distinctive way by the nocturnal prayers of the animals and birds. Their prayers mark the ending of each of the 12 hours. This particular idea may be influenced by the positive understanding of animals (which could be traced back to the theriomorphic traditions of Pharaonic religion); it is in sharp contrast to the hostile and negative view of the 'beasts' in Rev. 13 etc.

A sign: it is conceivable that here is an allusion to the Coptic practice of tattooing a cross on a believer's wrist. This custom prevails to the present day in the Coptic church.

Man hath been born to suffering: see Job 5.7; 14.1 as the texts quoted and alluded to here. Obviously there is special significance and poignancy in using such a quotation in the context of the current persecution of the Coptic Christians by the Shi'ite ruler al-Hakim bi 'Amr Allah (996–1021).

18.

'Righteous' or 'sinner': one of the key issues for discussion was clearly the question of predestination from the moment of creation by the Father's word. According to the angel's answer, it appears fairly clear that whatever was decreed by God concerning a human being before birth would happen. Previously in 17, it was suggested that although human beings were able to sin, by their own will or the Devil's, God was merciful and compassionate and would protect those who were designated 'righteous'.

So far as beasts are concerned, their place is the earth: another controversial topic, still at issue today in popular theology, is the question as to whether animals have souls. Is human kind essentially superior to the animals? The angel's answer in the text as it stands is somewhat elliptical and therefore not quite conclusive. After death each human being is taken to the place that is deserved; as for animals, whether living or dead, their place was the earth. In response to further questioning, John is told that animals do possess souls, which are in their blood. This statement appears to be the equivalent of Gen. 9.4 ('Only you shall not eat flesh with its life, that is, its blood'). After their deaths they are at rest, neither experiencing enjoyment nor suffering pain, as human beings can and do.

19.

Seven stars in the heavens: cf. Rev. 1.16

The particular Coptic term (*ne enter*) is preserved within Budge's translation at this point. Dr Jan Helderman, who teaches Coptic Language and Studies in Amsterdam, translates it simply as 'the gods' (meaning 'the demons' and referring to the stars), as frequently found in Coptic magical formulae. He does not have a high view of Budge's scholarship and suggests that Budge did not recognize the Coptic word and so for that reason retained it in the original. An alternative explanation is that he sought to preserve an esoteric sense of mystery in the text, although why uniquely at this point is unclear.

when death cometh upon the earth: presumably this refers to the dissolution of creation only at the end of time.

Arise, get thee down: the sequence of questioning is terminated, with an explicit command to communicate what has been seen.

20.

Mount of Olives: John encounters the apostles, still gathered on the mountain. After John has made his report, the apostles make a formal farewell and leave for their respective mission fields.

Chapter 7

CONCLUSIONS

The primary justification for this comparative study has been the opportunity of these texts' availability, some sense of a broad relationship in
genre and content, and the surprising fact that no such full comparison
appears to have been attempted previously. I believe that the wealth of
detail which has emerged from these texts, and the clarification of such
historic perspectives in visions of heaven and hell, has more than justified the endeavour by its results. By entering into the different historical
and geographical contexts of each apocalypse, it is possible to understand the thought processes, and to empathize (at least to some extent)
with those who speculated in this way.

A further conclusion, and arguably the more significant in terms of
text-research, is that which one might be able to observe in terms of
these apocalypses and their place in the history of tradition. There are
several dimensions to this traditional relationship, and it is important to
clarify these, especially if we wish to argue for a realistic continuum in
Johannine apocalyptic ideas.

First it is vital to chart the relationship between these texts and what
might be called the original inspiration in Christian Scripture. Frequent
reference has been made, in studying each of the texts, to the application of biblical themes and topics. It would be most useful to sym-
bolise this biblical relationship, in the most concrete way possible, by
tabulating comparatively the use of biblical quotations from the Old
Testament, and from the New Testament Gospels and Epistles. The following three figures provide this data. Naturally one could add to such a
listing, in more speculative terms, with reference to biblical allusions
rather than direct quotations.

Table 1. *Distribution of quotations from the Old Testament*

	2 Apoc. Jn	Jn Chrys. Apoc.	3 Apoc. Jn
Deut. 32.8 (LXX)	26	–	–
Exodus 33.19 (LXX)	–	–	22
Isaiah 6.3	17	–	–
40.4-5	15	–	–
66.24	24	–	–
Ezekiel 33.11	–	–	30
Psalm 9.17	21	–	–
9.18	24	–	–
18.11	20	–	–
18.41	22	–	–
37.25	–	–	21
37.29	25	–	–
49.14	21	–	–
51.7	15	–	–
51.19	8	–	–
89.44-45	8	–	–
98.6 (LXX)	9	–	–
102.25-26	19	–	–
103.14-16 (LXX)	12	–	–
106.3	28	–	–
125.3	23	–	–
146.4 (LXX)	12	–	–
Proverbs 15.8	–	–	29
21.27	–	–	29
Ecclesiastes 12.4	9	–	–

Table 2. *Distribution of quotations from the New Testament Gospels.*

	2 Apoc. Jn	Jn Chrys. Apoc.	3 Apoc. Jn
Matthew 5.9	–	51	–
6.6, 17-18	–	16	–
7.6	28	–	–
13.43	23	–	–
18.12-14	–	–	18
22.30	11	–	–
24.30	16	–	–
25.33	23	–	–
Mark 9.48	24	–	–
Luke 13.8-9	–	–	30
15.4-7	–	–	18
15.6-7	–	–	20
15.26	–	–	16
22.19 (longer)	–	31	–
23.42	–	–	24
John 3.17	–	–	22
6.37	–	–	35
8.7	–	–	17
8.34, 44	–	–	28
10.9	–	–	22
10.11-12	–	–	18
10.16	27	–	–
14.23	28	–	–
15.12	–	51	–
20.19-21	–	51	–

Table 3. *Quotations from the New Testament Epistles and Revelation*

	2 Apoc. Jn	Jn Chrys. Apoc.	3 Apoc. Jn
Romans 2.12	22	–	–
9.15	–	–	22
14.5	–	–	35
1 Corinthians 2.9-10	–	39	–
11.3	–	48	–
11.24-25	–	31	–
13.4, 7-8	–	50	–
15.41	23	–	–
2 Corinthians 9.7		–	34
Philippians 2.10	17	–	–
Ephesians 5.23	–	48	–
1 Thessalonians 4.17	13	–	–
1 Timothy 5.23	–	17	–
Hebrews [1.10-11]	19	–	–
4.13	17	–	–
1 John 3.8-10	–	–	28
4.7	–	33, 50	–
4.20	–	42	–
Revelation [4.8]	17	–	–
5.2, 6	18	–	–
21.4, 25	27	–	–

The other important relationships that it is necessary to consider are those between the actual texts I have been studying. It would be vital to define these quite precisely, and to sustain the connections, if any case is to be made for a continuity in Johannine tradition. The lack of the most precise historical data for most of the texts, and the recognition that they may represent later versions of earlier texts, increase the need for scholarly caution in these respects.

I feel that the most helpful contribution to be made at this stage would be in the form of some observations about the kind of linkage I have noticed between these texts. There are three main themes, concerning the nature of these apocalyptic communications (the interrogative genre), their relatedness to patterns of Christian worship (the liturgical context and structure), and finally the theological concepts of the future Church and individual salvation.

Scholars have debated, even with reference to the canonical book of Revelation, whether this is a work of prophecy or of apocalyptic. The most satisfactory answer is probably in terms of synthesis rather than alternative polarization. The phenomenon of Christian prophecy, represented elsewhere in the New Testament documents, is an on-going mode of Christian preaching and teaching in the early centuries. John the seer is a respected figure, charged with the duty of communicating Christian truth, which he frequently does in oracular manner in response to questioning. To achieve the substance of his communications, he too must ask questions and receive inspiration. The dialogue format which is a consistent feature of all these texts (even allowing for the variations in personnel) is itself a natural working out of the logic of the situation. Apocalyptic teaching provokes not only intellectual curiosity, but also the desire to apply such ideas to the immediate context of the believer. The pressure is on for yet more and more revelations, and the tutorial format seems ideal to provide training in new revelation.

Another important area of research in the canonical book of Revelation is its relationship to the Christian practice of Sunday worship and the evolution of liturgical patterns. There is no denying the relationship of the text to a visionary experience 'on the Lord's day' (Rev. 1.10), or the function of passages resembling Christian 'hymns' to provide exhortation and reassurance in the times of crisis. But it is far too early to find actual liturgical texts from the early Christian churches, and the texts of Revelation may be the inspiration of liturgy rather than being inspired by it. The circumstances of the Apocalypse attributed to St John Chrysostom are very different, and reflect a sustained liturgical practice and symbolism which we know from Eastern Orthodoxy. But such a liturgical evolution of apocalyptic ideas, indeed a communication of the message through the medium of worship, is a very natural development within the continuity of tradition.

So far I have observed continuity both in the prophetic role of the seer in dialogue, and in the intensification of ideas in the medium of liturgy. Where we might most expect to find a discontinuity is between the ecclesiological dimension of the book of Revelation and the dominant concern for individual destiny in the later apocalyptic texts. It is true that Revelation's vision of the future of the Church properly stands comparison with the Church history of Acts, the concepts of the Church in Ephesians, and the motif of God's pilgrim people in Hebrews, in the context of New Testament ecclesiology. But this does not exclude a concern for the individual, the witnessing role of the believer, and the protected status of God's servant, over against the fate of (and the ultimate judgment upon) the disobedient unbeliever. The later apocalyptic texts have an understandable proccupation with the destiny of the individual, spelled out in terms of the fates of heaven and hell. But it is important to notice that here too the collective identity of the Christian Church is recognized (not least at worship), as the nature of Christian existence is projected into the future. Here too is continuity, rather than discontinuity, in what may be fairly characterized as a Johannine apocalyptic tradition.

SELECT BIBLIOGRAPHY

General

Alison, J., *Living in the End Times: The Last Things Re-imagined* (London: SPCK, 1997).

Almond, Philip C., *Heaven and Hell in Enlightenment England* (Cambridge: Cambridge University Press, 1994).

Baxter, Mary K., and Mark K. Baxter, *A Divine Revelation of Hell* (New Kensington, PA: Whitaker House, 1997).

Bernstein, Alan E., *The Formation of Hell: Death and Retribution in the Ancient and Early Christian Worlds* (London: UCL Press, 1993).

Bremmer, Jan M. (ed.) *Studies on the Apocryphal Acts of the Apostles*. I. *Acts of John*; II. *Acts of Paul and Thecla* (Kampen: Kok, 1995, 1996); III. *The Apocryphal Acts of Peter: Magic, Miracles and Gnosticism* (Leuven: Peeters, 1998).

Camporesi, Piero, *The Fear of Hell: Images of Damnation and Salvation in Early Modern Europe* (Cambridge: Polity Press, 1991).

Collins, John J. (Guest ed.), *Apocalypse: The Morphology of a Genre* (Semeia, 14; Society of Biblical Literature, 1979).

Delumeau, Jean, *History of Paradise: The Garden of Eden in Myth and Tradition* (trans. Matthew O'Connell; New York: Continuum, 1995).

Farmer, Ronald L., *Beyond the Impasse: The Promise of A Process Hermeneutic* (Studies in American Biblical Hermeneutics, 13; Macon GA: Mercer University Press, 1997).

Horne, Brian, *Imagining Evil* (London: Darton, Longman and Todd, 1996).

Hunsinger, George, 'Hellfire and Damnation: Four Ancient and Modern Views', *Scottish Journal of Theology* 51.4 (1998), pp. 406-34.

Janssens, Y., 'Apocalypses de Nag Hammadi', in J. Lambrecht (ed.), *L'Apocalypse johannique et l'Apocalyptique dans le Nouveau Testament* (Bibliotheca Ephemeridum Theologicarum Lovaniensium, 51; Gembloux: Duculot; Leuven: Leuven University Press, 1980), pp. 69-75.

Lalleman, P.J., *The Acts of John: A Two-Stage Initiation into Johannine Gnosticism* (Studies on the Apocryphal Acts of the Apostles, 4; Leuven: Peeters, 1998).

Layton, Bentley, *The Gnostic Scriptures: A New Translation with Annotations and Introductions* (Garden City: Doubleday; London: SCM Press, 1987).

McDannell, Colleen, and Bernhard Lang, *Heaven: A History* Yale (New Haven: Yale University Press, 1988).

Paley, Morton D., *The Apocalyptic Sublime* (New Haven: Yale University Press, 1986).

Pauls, Michael, and Dana Facaros, *The Traveller's Guide to Hell* (London: Cadogan, 1998).

Pike, David L., *Passage Through Hell: Modernist Descents, Medieval Underworlds* (Ithaca, NY: Cornell University Press, 1997).

Schneemelcher, Wilhelm, *New Testament Apocrypha*. II. *Writings Relating to the Apostles; Apocalypses and Related Subjects* (trans. R.McL. Wilson; Cambridge: James Clarke, 1992).

Schüssler Fiorenza, Elisabeth, 'The Phenomenon of Early Christian Apocalyptic', in D. Hellholm (ed.), *Apocalypticism in the Mediterranean World and the Near East* (Tübingen: J.C.B. Mohr, 1983), pp. 295-316.

Silverstein, Theodore, and Anthony Hilhorst, *Apocalypse of Paul: A New Critical Edition of Three Long Latin Versions* (Cahiers d'Orientalisme, 21; Geneva: Patrick Cramer, 1997).

Turner, Alice K., *The History of Hell* (London: Robert Hale, 1995).

Thompson, Damian, *The End of Time: Faith and Fear in the Shadow of the Millennium* (London: Sinclair-Stevenson, 1996).

Walker, D.P., *The Decline of Hell: Seventeenth Century Discussions of Eternal Torment* (London: RKP, 1964).

Weinel, H., 'Die spätere christliche Apokalyptik', in H. Schmidt (ed.), *ΕΥΧΑΡΙΣΤΗΡΙΟΝ (Gunkel Festschrift)* (Göttingen: Vandenhoeck & Ruprecht, 1923), pp. 141-73.

2nd Apocalypse of John

Borgehammar, Stephan, *How the Holy Cross Was Found: From Event to Medieval Legend, with an Appendix of Texts* (Bibliotheca theologiae practicae, 47; Stockholm: Almqvist and Wiksell, 1991).

Brock, Sebastian, *The Luminous Eye: The Spiritual World Vision of St. Ephrem* (CIIS; Rome, 1985).

Drijvers, H.J.W., and J.W. Drijvers, *The Finding of the True Cross: The Judas Kyriakos Legend in Syriac (Introduction, Text and Translation)* (Corpus Scriptorum Christianorum Orientalium, 565; Leuven: Peeters, 1997).

Drijvers, Jan Willem, *Helena Augusta: The Mother of Constantine and the Legend of her Finding of the True Cross* (Studies in Intellectual History, 27; Leiden: E.J. Brill, repr. 1995).

Koonammakkal, Thomas, 'St Ephrem and "Greek Wisdom"', in R. Lawrence (ed.), *VI Symposium Syriacum 1992 Cambridge* (Orientalia Christiana Analecta, 247; Rome: Pontificio Istituto Orientale, 1994), pp. 169-76.

Matthews, E.G., Jr, and Joseph P. Amar (trans.), *St Ephrem the Syrian: Prose Works—Commentary on Genesis, Letters to Publius, Homily on Our Lord* (The Fathers of the Church, Patristic Series, 91; Catholic University of America Press, 1995).

Frend, William H.C., *The Archaeology of Early Christianity: A History* (London: Geoffrey Chapman, 1996).

Murray, Robert, SJ, *Symbols of Church and Kingdom: A Study in Early Syriac Tradition* (Cambridge: Cambridge University Press, 1975).

Palmer, Andrew, 'The Merchant of Nisibis: Saint Ephrem and his Faithful Quest for Union in Numbers', in J. den Boeft and A. Hilhorst (eds.), *Early Christian Poetry: A Collection of Essays* (Supplement to *Vigiliae Christianae*, 22; Leiden: E.J. Brill, 1993), pp. 167-233.

Romeny, Ter Haar, R.B., *A Syrian in Greek Dress: The Use of Greek, Hebrew and Syriac Biblical Texts in Eusebius of Emesa's Commentary on Genesis* (Traditio Exegetica Graeca, 6; Leuven: Peeters, 1997).

Waldstein, Michael, 'The Providence Monologue in the *Apocryphon of John* and the Johannine Prologue', *Journal of Early Christian Studies* 3.4 (1995), pp. 369-402.

Apocalypse of John Chrysostom

Kelly, J.N.D., *Golden Mouth: The Story of John Chrysostom—Ascetic, Preacher, Bishop* (London: Gerald Duckworth, 1995).
Lukken, Gerard, *Per Visibilia ad Invisibilia: Anthropological, Theological and Semiotic Studies on the Liturgy and the Sacraments* (Kampen: Kok, 1994).
Mitchell, Margaret M., '"A Variable and Many-sorted Man": John Chrysostom's Treatment of Pauline Inconsistency', *Journal of Early Christian Studies* 6.1 (1998), pp. 93-111.
Swanston, H.F.G., 'Liturgy as Paradise and Parousia', *Scottish Journal of Theology* 36 (1983), pp. 505-19

3rd Apocalypse of John

Vassiliev, A., *Anecdota Graeca-Byzantina*, I (Moscow, 1893).

Coptic Apocalypse of John

Budge, E.A. Wallis, *Coptic Apocrypha in the Dialect of Upper Egypt* (Oxford: Oxford University Press, 1913).
Gardner, Iain, *Coptic Theological Papyri*. II. *Edition, Commentary, Translation, with an appendix on the Docetic Jesus* (Oesterreichische Nationalbibliothek; Vienna: Verlag Brueder Hollinek, 1988).
Wessels, Antonie, *Arab and Christian? Christians in the Middle East* (Kampen: Kok, 1995).

INDEXES

INDEX OF REFERENCES

78.2   52
89   52
89.44-45   35, 165
95   94
98.6   35, 165
102.25-26   43, 58, 165
102.25   161
103.14-16   37, 165
104.5   161
106.3   47, 65, 165
125.3   61, 165
143.10   96
146.4   37, 165

Proverbs
15.8   117, 165
21.27   117, 165
25.11   157

Ecclesiastes
12.4   37, 165

Song of Songs
2.3   157
2.5   157
7.8   157
8.5   157

Isaiah
6.3   25, 57,
            165
19.24-25   154
27.13   53
29.14   52
38.2   159
38.21   160
40.4-5   39
41.4-5   165
44.24   165
45.23   57
51.3   63
64   100
65   100
66.24   45, 63, 123

Jeremiah
2.18   156

Lamentations
3.44   93

Ezekiel
1.18   151
2.8   95
3.3   95
9.2   99
9.4   99
10.12   151
33.11   117, 165
36.35   63

40.3   100

Daniel
7   56
7.9-10   49
7.10   63, 122
7.13-14   121
8.16   53
9.21   53
10.13   53, 64
10.20-21   64
10.21   53
12.1   53, 64

Jonah
10.16   47

Malachi
4.5   52

Apocrypha
1 Esdras
9.42   92

Wisdom of Solomon
10.7   158

Ecclesiasticus
7.17   63
24.27   156

NEW TESTAMENT

Matthew
1.6   128
5.5   63
5.9   83, 166
5.23-24   97
5.23   97
6.6   89, 166
6.17-18   77, 89, 166
6.19   130
7.6   47, 64, 166
7.69   125
8.12   56
11.7   84
11.23   59
12.39-40   94
12.40   59
13.35   52
13.42   56
13.43   45, 61, 166
13.50   56
17.1-8   48
18.12-14   115, 166
19.28   49
22.13   56
22.30   37, 166
24.22   51
24.29   58
24.30   41, 56, 166
24.31   55
24.51   56
25   104
25.14-30   130
25.30   56
25.33   45, 61, 166
27.45   99
27.52-53   94
28.2   91

INDEX OF AUTHORS

JOURNAL FOR THE STUDY OF THE NEW TESTAMENT
SUPPLEMENT SERIES